Gay Men, Identity and Social Media

"Cassidy has answered the call a number of us have been making for a solid empirical study of social media habits in the LGBTQ communities. The specific social media venues may change with time but what his work has to teach us about identity formation and performance, the formation of social capital, and the building of social networks will influence our agendas and thinking for years to come."

—*Bruce E. Drushel, Miami University, USA*

"An elegant book that makes significant contributions to our understandings of gay male internet use, but more generally to how social media, place, and subcultures come together to shape identity."

—*Nancy Baym, Massachusetts Institute of Technology, USA*

"This work offers important and compelling insights into how gay men utilize social networking sites. Given that the online experiences of sexual minorities are woefully understudied, Elija Cassidy's study is a welcome work indeed."

—*John Edward Campbell, Temple University, USA*

This book explores how the social and technical integration of mainstream social media into gay men's digital cultures since the mid-2000s has played out in the lives of young gay men, looking at how these convergences have influenced more recent iterations of gay men's digital culture. Focusing on platforms such as Gaydar, Facebook, Grindr and Instagram, Cassidy highlights the ways that identity and privacy management issues experienced in this context have helped to generate a culture of participatory reluctance within gay men's digital environments.

Elija Cassidy is a Lecturer in Journalism, Media and Communication at Queensland University of Technology, Australia.

Routledge Studies in New Media and Cyberculture

33 **Feminism, Labour and Digital Media**
The Digital Housewife
Kylie Jarrett

34 **The Politics of Ephemeral Digital Media**
Permanence and Obsolescence in Paratexts
Edited by Sara Pesce and Paolo Noto

35 **Studying Digital Media Audiences**
Perspectives from Australasia
Edited by Craig Hight and Ramaswami Harindranath

36 **Between the Public and Private in Mobile Communication**
Edited by Ana Serrano Tellería

37 **Performing Digital Activism**
New Aesthetics and Discourses of Resistance
Fidèle A. Vlavo

38 **Online Activism in Latin America**
Edited by Hilda Chacón

39 **Becoming-Social in a Networked Age**
Neal Thomas

40 **Free Software, the Internet, and Global Communities of Resistance**
Sara Schoonmaker

41 **Gay Men, Identity and Social Media**
A Culture of Participatory Reluctance
Elija Cassidy

For a full list of titles in this series, please visit www.routledge.com.

Gay Men, Identity and Social Media

A Culture of Participatory Reluctance

Elija Cassidy

Routledge
Taylor & Francis Group
NEW YORK AND LONDON

First published 2018
by Routledge
711 Third Avenue, New York, NY 10017

and by Routledge
2 Park Square, Milton Park, Abingdon, Oxon OX14 4RN

Routledge is an imprint of the Taylor & Francis Group, an informa business

Library of Congress Cataloging-in-Publication Data
CIP data has been applied for.

ISBN: 978-1-138-83085-1 (hbk)
ISBN: 978-1-315-73702-7 (ebk)

Typeset in Sabon
by codeMantra

Contents

List of Figures and Tables

Figures

Tables

1 Gay Men's Digital Culture and Participatory Reluctance

An Introduction

On the name and shame website, Douchebags of Grindr,[1] a steady stream of screen-captured profiles representing the worst of gay men's social dating application Grindr have been appearing daily since 2011 – with added commentary from the site owner for entertainment value. From day to day and year to year, there is almost infinite repetition of the same profile types submitted, with usernames and profile text boxes exclaiming, "don't be gay", "not interested", "no olds, asians, fats or fems", "99.9% of you are disgusting", "don't message me", "too good for this app", "this app sukz" and "30+ fossils will be blocked". Beyond the intrinsic ageism, racism, femmephobia, hypocrisy, arrogance and general 'douchebaggery' constantly highlighted here, a clear overarching picture also emerges of the deep-seated antipathy many Grindr users feel towards the application and its core audience.

On the spin-off site, Poking Fun at Grindr,[2] which in addition to Grindr also covers similar applications such as Jack'd, Hornet, Hunters BBS "and all the rest", a mirror image of the attitudes on display at Douchebags of Grindr can be found in streams of screen-captured user conversations posted to the site, albeit sans comedic commentary. While the racism, ageism and other forms of discrimination and antagonism seen on these sites were part of gay male communities well before the arrival of social dating and hook-up applications (see Ayers, 2000), the recent success of Douchebags of Grindr and Poking Fun at Grindr demonstrates the extent to which ill will towards social applications designed for gay male audiences, and their users, has now become central to the culture of such spaces.

Where does this culture of hostility come from? Why would so many people employ social media profiles to condemn the very same services – and their user bases – that they themselves are members of? Is this an issue of internalised homophobia? Simply a case of social media (or dating app) fatigue? How do these patterns of use play into broader incarnations of gay men's digital culture beyond niche services, like Grindr? And why should any of this matter to more than just app designers trying to leverage gay male markets?

I first began thinking about these kinds of questions and the nature of gay men's digital cultures back in 2007. During a night out with some friends in March of that year at a small gay club in Brisbane, Australia, the man who would later become my partner approached me while I was alone at the bar. New to the city and recognising me only from a profile on a social networking site (SNS) specifically for gay men, he said simply, "Excuse me, are you Brista?" As this was before the rise of geolocative mobile phone applications, like Grindr, somewhat surprised and amused that a stranger with whom I had had no previous interaction would not only recognise me from an online profile, but also approach me to say so, I laughed – both at the novelty of the situation and in confirmation of the question – and we began chatting. Hence, with a simple reference to a profile name ('Brista')[3] I had maintained on three separate gay-oriented networking sites since the beginning of my adult life, 'Tobulus' had begun the conversation that would lead to our relationship and, eventually, his proposal.

In this way, and numerous others, social networking sites for gay men have been a central element in both my most pivotal life events and the more banal experiences of my everyday existence. Equal parts consciously and subconsciously, I have used them, among other things, to test the waters of the gay world and my own identity within it; to assist with navigating various physical spaces and real-world events across Australia designed to cater for the gay, lesbian, bisexual and transgender (GLBT) community; as an information repository and source of social capital and as a tool for simply bonding with my peers. While numerous GLBT-oriented movies, popular television programmes, newspapers and magazines attest that I am certainly not alone in this regard – that these sites are simply part of the cultural milieu of being gay in the 21st century[4] – it was only through that moment at the bar, at age 22, that I first began to fully understand this point. Or, at least, the extent to which it was true. It encouraged me to really think about and try to make sense of gay men's digital culture and to consider how my own personal experiences with it compared to those of other men my age. Being recognised from an online profile also ensured I would become more self-reflexive in my use of the three gay-specific social networking sites I was then signed up to, by making me much more conscious of the intense relationship that exists between gay men's digital culture and other spheres of gay male life.

The event that would really translate the curiosity this moment piqued into the desire to conduct formal research concerning gay men's digital culture, however, would come almost six months later, as 2007 was drawing to a close. In the interim, the range of technologies and services designed to facilitate social networking was expanding almost daily, and the ways that people engaged in this practice were rapidly changing. At the forefront of this change were mainstream social networking sites, namely, Facebook. Though it was launched in 2004 and has since become one of the most visited websites on the internet and a cultural icon at the centre of books (Kirkpatrick, 2010), documentaries (Weitzner, 2010) and Hollywood feature films (Fincher, 2010), it was the 12 months between the beginning of 2007 and 2008 that saw Facebook, in particular, and mainstream social networking sites, more generally, firmly establish themselves in Australia's public consciousness, as large numbers of internet users flocked to the service and its (then) competitor MySpace (Moses, 2008). In fact, with journalists and other social commentators scrambling to make sense of the rapidity and extensiveness of the public's uptake of SNSs, between January 2007 and January 2008, there were well over 2000 articles in Australian newspapers on Facebook alone.

It was during this time, in June 2007, that my own profile on Facebook was first established. I set it up utilising a headshot of myself from an existing account I maintained on Gaydar, a web-based social networking site designed specifically for gay men. It was the same photo from which my partner had first recognised me as 'Brista' in the bar months earlier. I reused the image because I had signed up to Facebook on the recommendation of a friend who not only spoke enthusiastically about the functionalities of the site, but also labelled it 'a new version of Gaydar'.

Designed specifically for same-sex-attracted men, Gaydar has members registered in almost 150 countries around the world. As one of the first and largest social networking sites of its kind, Gaydar was at the very centre of gay men's digital culture from the moment it was launched in London in 1999, until the arrival of geolocative mobile phone applications, like Grindr, a decade later. Although no longer owned by its original developers at QSoft Consulting, the site – which is still in operation today – offers two levels of membership (free and fee paying) and incorporates functions for profile creation, personal network displays, messaging, chat rooms, photo and video upload, participation in online group activities (e.g., competitions), mobile accessibility and much more.

Despite some of these core technological similarities, time, of course, would prove that Facebook was in fact not the same as Gaydar, as my friend had suggested, or, for that matter, any other gay-oriented networking site we had ever seen. However, from the moment it began gaining widespread popularity in Australia, Facebook became part of a culture that I, and many of my gay peers, had previously associated only with networking sites specifically for the gay male community. Fast-forward six months from March 2007, when I had first met my partner, for instance, and another 'Brista'/'Tobulus'-style scenario was playing out before me – only this time it was Facebook, rather than Gaydar, that facilitated the exchange.

On a night of celebrations for a friend's birthday, the group of people I was out with were standing together near the dance floor of the same Brisbane club where I had met 'Tobulus' earlier in the year. Midway through our conversation, we were approached by a fellow patron, who, without so much as a nod hello, handed a business card to his chosen target amongst the group (let's call him 'Sam'), then said, 'Find me on Facebook', and promptly walked away. 'Sam' and the business-card-wielding stranger (let's call him 'Matt') went on to meet via Facebook a few days later and, eventually, to have an eight-month-long relationship. This event came on the back of a number of weeks immediately following my signing up to the site in which friend requests from gay men unknown to me from all across Australia (and beyond) had flooded my inbox, where 'pokes' from brands that would typically advertise on Gaydar and other gay male SNSs began to rival those from people I knew, and where faces I recognised from local gay venues and events were frequently popping up in my 'people you might know' column – all despite my sexuality not being specified on the profile anywhere. Hence, both for me and a number of others who witnessed 'Matt' and 'Sam's' initial meeting by the dance floor that night, it was an experience that cemented mainstream social networking sites into parts of our lives we thought, however naively, that they would not touch, and in ways we had not expected. In the space of just six months, we had seen a shift from 'Excuse me, are you Brista?' to 'Find me on Facebook'. For some of the group present that night, who had had similar experiences with 'pokes' and unsolicited friend requests from gay men around the world appearing in their recently opened Facebook accounts, it was living proof, as my friend had excitedly put it when encouraging me to sign up, that 'Facebook is the new Gaydar'.

With the benefit of hindsight, of course, it is now clear that what we had witnessed that night, in September 2007, was not the arrival of a new niche SNS specifically for gay men. Any user of Facebook can attest to the fact that its remit is far too broad for the service to be classified as a networking tool for one particular community. What we had actually experienced, both on that night itself, and in the weeks prior with the array of friend requests sent our way from gay men around the globe, was simply evidence of a growing convergence between mainstream social networking services and gay men's digital culture. This convergence could also be seen at that time in the rapidly expanding number of Facebook pages being run by GLBT-oriented venues, community groups and organisations, and in the simultaneous decision of smaller-scale social networking platforms for gay men, like UK-based service, Jake, to shift all networking functionalities from their own site over to Facebook. While larger services, such as Gaydar, continued to operate independently, by 2008, Gaydar too had established its own Facebook page, and Gaydar users were beginning to include links to Facebook accounts in their Gaydar profiles.

Today, of course, this convergence continues apace. Go to YouTube and type in 'Grindr'. Search Instagram for the hashtag #instagay. Or head over to Tumblr and find the scores of accounts dedicated to gay Snapchatters. The results might not be safe for work, but they're unequivocal. Gay men's digital culture is now deeply converged with mainstream social media. While Facebook may not have become 'the new Gaydar', as my friend had exclaimed it would be in 2007, practices once confined to the realms of niche sites designed specifically for same-sex-attracted men are now very much part of mainstream social networking platforms used by the general population for posting food and travel snaps, workout shots and updates on the vast minutiae of everyday life. What these developments signal about the kinds of relationships that gay men have with SNSs, both niche and mainstream, and the roles that these services play in gay male culture more broadly have interested me since Facebook first emerged on Brisbane's gay scene in 2007. Hence, it is these issues of sociotechnical convergence within gay men's digital culture – and their associated drivers and repercussions – that are at the very centre of this book.

Set against the backdrop of the growing global push for recognition of marriage equality, and the increasing prominence of social media as premier settings for the very real developmental task of identity formation amongst the present generation of youth (James et al., 2008, p. 15), *Gay Men, Identity and Social Media: A Culture of Participatory Reluctance* is an account of how the sociotechnical integration of mainstream social media into gay men's digital cultures occurring since the mid-2000s has played out in the lives of young gay men who have experienced it and how these convergences have impacted upon more recent iterations of gay men's digital culture, helping to intensify the kind of paradoxical hostility seen on sites like Douchebags of Grindr, where users of niche SNSs designed for gay male audiences denigrate the very same sites and user communities that they themselves are members of. Providing detailed examination of Facebook's early integration into Gaydar cultures as it occurred in Brisbane, Australia, as well as discussion of recent developments across services such as Grindr, Instagram and Snapchat, it demonstrates how, through the emergence and subsequent enmeshment of mainstream social media into gay men's digital cultures, niche social networking services designed for gay male audiences have come to be experienced by users as comparatively difficult environments in which to manage identity, and thus, environments where large numbers of users would actually prefer not to be present at all. As such, I ultimately argue here that key shifts in gay men's digital culture both within and beyond community-specific social media over the past decade have increasingly been shaped in western environments by what might best be described as a culture of *participatory reluctance*.

What's Participatory Reluctance?

In the mid-2000s, social media technologies began impacting intensely upon the traditional operation of media industries by enabling publics to function as content co-creators, rather than just viewers and listeners (Flew, 2014, p. 87). As such, media scholars heralded the arrival of a new 'age of participation'. While the internet had already been written about as a highly communal and potentially democratising technology in the 1990s by likes of Rheingold (1993) and Turkle (1995), Henry Jenkins' (2006) *Convergence Culture: When Old and New Media Collide* was a tipping point of sorts in bringing issues of participation to the fore. Through this work, Jenkins (2006) popularised the term 'participatory culture', to describe the possibilities afforded by what were then known as Web 2.0 technologies for people to become contributors and producers – as well as users – of media content, or what Bruns (2008) refers to as 'produsers'. In the years since, scholars from diverse disciplinary backgrounds have sought to map and make sense of the implications of these possibilities for individuals, industries and society at large (see Benkler, 2006; Schäfer, 2011; Tapscott & Williams, 2006). Attention has been placed on the possibilities for civic engagement and connection; creative expression and collaborative culture; and the democratisation of news, ideas and creativity and also upon challenges associated with the blurred lines between producers and users fostered by the rise of participatory culture – participation gaps and digital divides – and the increasing complexity of the ethical and legal issues around privacy and intellectual property, to name just a few.

Among these discussions, and amidst the arrival of mainstream social networking services like Facebook, Jenkins' (2006) notion of 'participatory culture' and Bruns' (2008) idea of 'produsage' have been extended upon to consider issues around 'explicit' and 'implicit' (Schäfer, 2011) participation in these contexts and the role of technology in co-shaping user interactions and content development. In *Bastard Culture! How User Participation Transforms Cultural Production*, for example, Schäfer (2011) described how early discussions of participatory culture understood participation as a 'conscious practice of competent consumers', such as those who create content by engaging in online fan culture, cooperative software development or Wikipedia contribution (p. 52). Alongside this category of purposeful 'explicit' participation enabled by Web 2.0 technologies, however, Schäfer (2011) argued there is also a more subtle 'implicit' (p. 52) form of participation, where users contribute to applications, often unknowingly, simply through using them – for example, when uploading content to platforms like Flickr or watching and rating YouTube videos.

With interface design increasingly determining the forms of acceptable collaboration, connection and content contribution available to users of social media, scholarly discussions of SNSs are now beginning to consider not only forms of participation in these contexts, and their implications, but also forms of disconnection, resistance and non-use (see Karppi, 2014; Light, 2014). Ben Light's (2014) recent *Disconnecting with Social Networking Sites*, for example, puts forth a theory of 'disconnective practice' through which he argues that accessing the many social possibilities afforded by SNSs in fact requires users to engage in some element of disconnection. Light's (2014) work is not interested in the complete non-use of SNSs or in practices such as 'social media suicide' (where SNS users remove accounts entirely) but in the everyday tactics or 'disconnective practices' people enrol in order to connect with SNSs and other SNS users as far as possible on their own terms. More work needs to be done, however, with regard to how participatory cultures and disconnection might intertwine in these spaces – and with what impact. Indeed, while investigations around practices such as 'lurking' enhanced understandings of various modes of participation and (dis)engagement in virtual communities in the late 1990s and early 2000s (see, e.g., Nonnecke & Preece, 1999), when it comes to examining participation in contemporary SNSs, as Light (2014) has argued, 'it is notable how little research has been undertaken with a nuancing beyond a binary of use/non-use' (p. 3).

The term 'participatory reluctance' intersects with burgeoning discussions of this nature by describing a particular orientation to social media, and its assemblage of affordances and associated cultures, that further problematises binarised notions of connection and disconnection. It captures participation in a state of discontent, neither fully active or absent – a digital presenteeism of sorts. Of course, outside the realms of social media we have all engaged in such practices. We have all put ourselves in situations where we would prefer to be elsewhere or to do otherwise. Indeed, much of our lives take place under various forms of social duress, where, for a whole range of reasons, we voluntarily participate in life's everyday routines when we would actually prefer not to, or would rather do so under altered circumstances. Feeling like this about digital media technologies geared to encourage participation, such as social networking sites, is to experience 'participatory reluctance'.

As social media use has become integral to modern life to a degree that it in many ways compels people to participate, participatory reluctance is no doubt present at some level in a wide range of digital environments. Here, however, I theorise participatory reluctance as one of the driving forces behind contemporary gay men's digital culture and work to illustrate the key social, technical and material contexts through which this situation has emerged; what kinds of impacts it is having on young gay men and their digital lives; and what it might mean for the niche spaces of gay men's digital culture, now and into the future.

Why Does This Matter?

When I first began studying gay men's digital cultures, close to a decade ago, at times when people outside of the academy would ask, as they invariably do, what my research was about, should any mention of Gaydar (and later Grindr), or gay men's digital cultures in general, be made, people would typically come away from the discussion thinking that I spent my time online studying gay sex, gay pornography or some variation thereof. This was regardless of whether they were part of the GLBT community or not. Usually, before I had any chance to reply in these situations, people's questions were also accompanied by a snide comment of some kind suggesting I was wasting valuable resources (both my own and my university's) on the tacky and the trivial. But rather than being about gay porn, gay sex or even services like Gaydar, per se, my research has always been about understanding how the cultures and practices surrounding identity management within gay men's digital spaces are evolving alongside newer, more mainstream SNSs.

This is because while sites in the genre of Gaydar and Grindr are routinely used by men seeking sexual encounters with other men, as the work of scholars such as John Campbell (2004) and Sharif Mowlabocus (2010) has shown, gay men's digital spaces are also immensely important to their users, and to the gay community more generally, for a whole host of other reasons – many of which centre around the provision of information and support. In fact, it has been well documented in academic arenas since the very beginnings of the public internet, that online spaces designed for the GLBT community have been highly significant in the lives of young gay men. Prior to the arrival of the current generation of social media technologies, for example, Hillier, Kurdas and Horsely (2001) were investigating the internet of chatrooms, web pages and email and its role as a 'safety-Net' in the lives of same-sex-attracted youth. The vast majority of young people surveyed in their study reported that the internet played an important role in:

- putting them in touch with like-minded others;
- reducing their sense of isolation;
- offering them a sense of community and support;
- providing access to sexual health information; and
- facilitating real-life friendship and contact with other same-sex-attracted youth.

(Hillier et al., 2001)

In contrast to popular discourse, which often constructs online spaces as potentially dangerous environments for young people, in this study, chatrooms, web pages and email were all discussed as safe spaces that offered participants the anonymity to privately explore and express their identities away from the potential dangers of 'real life' that many same-sex-attracted youth have faced (Hillier et al., 2001). In his now seminal *Getting It on Online* (2004), John Campbell similarly documented the important role of online spaces in gay men's culture: focusing on gay Internet Relay Chat (IRC) channels, he chronicled the importance of online spaces for gay community formation as well as for identity management and construction. In the same year, Murphy, Rawstorne, Holt and Ryan (2004) published *Cruising and Connecting Online*. Whilst studying what they called 'gay men's chat sites' for the purpose of planning HIV prevention initiatives, Murphy et al. (2004) noted that sites such as Gaydar and Gay.com supported a broad range of relationships, making them much more than spaces in which gay men arrange sexual encounters with each other. Approximately, 60 per cent of men in their project, for instance, noted that they had established friendships through these services (Murphy et al., 2004, p. 8), indicating the much more general role these sites play as important social spaces for gay men. McKenna and Bargh (1998), Brown, Maycock and Burns (2005), Hillier and Harrison (2007) and Gray (2009) have all made similar arguments regarding the empowering affordances of online spaces for gay youth. McKenna and Bargh's (1998) work, for example, referred to the important role of digital spaces for GLBT communities in providing 'identity demarginalisation' for such groups.

In the years since many of the above studies were published, however, digital technologies have advanced significantly, and SNSs have become a familiar and ubiquitous part of the internet. Owing to Facebook's prominence and its founder Mark Zuckerberg's insistence on transparency (Kirkpatrick, 2010, pp. 278–301)[5] in online spaces, in this same period, real-name profiles and the cross-integration of social networking applications (which is sometimes entirely automated) have also become much more commonplace.[6] When I began studying gay men's digital cultures, how the erasure of nuanced relationship categories, or 'context collapse' (Hogan, 2010; Marwick & boyd, 2011), and other circumstances surrounding the rise of real-name profiles and platform integration may have been altering the role of networking sites in gay men's digital culture, and in the gay community more broadly, however, was not yet clear. It was unknown, for example, whether the extension of gay men's networks into mainstream SNSs had altered in any way the freedom that Brown et al. (2005, p. 63) argued the niche spaces of gay men's digital culture gave young users to 'experience control over their privacy and how much they [choose] to present'. The initial research project this book emerges from therefore began the process of addressing these kinds of questions by mapping the ways that young Gaydar users in Brisbane, Australia, had experienced the cultural entanglement of Gaydar and Facebook, and the ways that users managed their identities in this context.

In my own case, the collision of a pseudonymous identity created within the specific context of Gaydar with the material realities of Facebook, and its more general audience of users, had created tensions and privacy concerns that radically impacted upon my experiences with both SNSs – and, by extension, my work, social and family life through the various networks made visible in these spaces. Alongside many of my peers, I had come of age as a young gay man using niche networking sites such as Gaydar to help navigate and negotiate the physical spaces of my local GLBT community and to test the waters of my own place and identity within that community. With the expansion of gay men's social networks into mainstream services such as Facebook, however, a myriad of additional ways and spaces in which to engage with other gay men (and the various communities surrounding them) emerged. At the same time, it became necessary to consider the range of very different audiences to whom these interactions might now become visible.

This situation was further complicated by the fact that Facebook is vastly different from Gaydar in the sense that it is part of what Hogan (2012) calls the 'real-name web'. Despite the fact that it can be relatively easily manoeuvred around, Facebook institutes a 'real-name' policy as part of its user agreement (Facebook, 2015), meaning users are bound in principle by the site's terms of use to employ their real name as the title of their profile. Gaydar, by contrast, which first launched in 1999, arrived at a time when the internet was a far more pseudonymous environment, when screen names, nicks and handles were the primary mode of operation for people online (see Kirkpatrick, 2010, pp. 66–85) – and it continues to operate in this fashion today. Hence, for me personally at least, while the events of late 2007 recounted earlier in this chapter, which highlighted the cultural change embedded in the shift from 'excuse me are you Brista?' to 'find me on Facebook', were certainly of great interest, as it was clear that Facebook had begun facilitating a cultural shift of sorts in the gay community immediately surrounding my peers and I, my own feelings about these developments were significantly less upbeat than my friend who had proclaimed that Facebook was 'the new Gaydar'.

My primary concerns in this regard stemmed from the fact that by late 2007, Facebook was also very clearly facilitating great cultural change outside of the immediate context of the gay male community in innumerable aspects of broader society. To take just one aspect as an example, for instance, in work environments, organisations eager to embrace social media were increasingly asking employees to perform an abundance of different tasks in online spaces in order to ensure that they stayed in touch with 'digital native' 'Generation Y'. Use of social media for personal branding had also become a must, touted as a pillar of career protection in uncertain economic times (Levit, 2009). My experiences working as a lecturer reflected completely the findings of Gregg (2011) in this respect, who notes that universities have been particularly enthusiastic in their embrace of social media to capitalise on young people's assumed preference for online contact (pp. 114–115). Coinciding with Facebook's popular uptake in Australia, for example, began my superiors' consistent encouragement to use the site to communicate with my students, as well as to join and become an administrator of my department's Facebook page, to track the progress of our programme's alumni and to connect with my colleagues and other academics in our field both on campus and around the globe. Like teachers in classrooms at multiple levels of the education system all around the world (see Hewitt & Forte, 2006), I was also faced very early on with the question of whether staff should 'friend' students on Facebook as student friend requests began rolling in.

By mid-2008, the effects of 'context collapse' (Hogan, 2010; Marwick & boyd, 2011) had taken their toll. Having witnessed the events recounted earlier in this chapter, as well as an increasing number of other aspects of the culture of Gaydar (and the city's gay culture more generally) making their way into my experiences with Facebook, I came to the decision to cease using real-name social media, deeply dissatisfied with the trend towards compulsory publicness in these spaces. So while my Gaydar profile and the handful of other pseudonymous profiles I had maintained on SNSs targeted specifically at GLBT users remained active (at least for a while), without removing my account, or even addressing any of the multitudes of friend requests waiting for me from students, colleagues, old school friends and all manner of other acquaintances from what I see as incompatible aspects of my life, I simply stopped using Facebook. This withdrawal was in direct response to endless frustration over the lack of useable selective sharing functions on the site at that time and the sense that my capacity for informational self-determination was being increasingly eroded. Despite consistently being pressured in both social and professional settings to develop and maintain an online presence in the realm of the 'real-name web', on Facebook in particular, the cost of doing so for me personally, in the immediate context of my life as a young GLBT person, was still not worth for me the social, cultural and network capital that much research (see, e.g., Ellison, Steinfeld & Lampe 2007; Erickson, 1996; Granovetter, 1973) indicated I was missing out on.

Of course, not every young gay man witnessing the arrival of Facebook into gay men's digital cultures felt the same way. Not everybody uses SNSs at the same level of frequency and intensity, or for the same purpose (Hargittai & Hsieh, 2011). Not everybody needs to utilise social media in the course of their employment or feels the need to maintain entirely separate private and professional identities. Indeed, the extension of gay men's social networks into Facebook was a reason for excitement for many of the young gay men in my peer group. For others, such as myself, however, the growing importance of Facebook in gay men's digital culture was a cause of great distress. Whether one falls into either of these two categories, or somewhere much more in the middle, closer to ambivalence or uncertainty (as in the case of 'E' – an anonymous gay blogger in Egypt who also wrote at the time about the potential for Facebook to be 'the new Gaydar'),[7] it was immediately clear that mainstream SNSs were creating new social contexts around gay men's networks in which privacy and identity issues would have to be renegotiated. Being recognised by an online nickname from a site such as Gaydar in a commercial gay venue by another gay man is very different, for example, to being tagged by one's real name in a photograph at that same venue on a mainstream social networking site, such as Facebook. In 2007, what factors might be prompting the convergence of these two cultures and what implications it might have for users of these sites had yet to be investigated, however. Given the important place of SNSs in gay men's digital culture, and in gay male subculture more generally (Mowlabocus, 2010), my work therefore proceeded from the perspective that such investigation was essential – not only to further diversify the body of existing SNS research available at the time,[8] but also to generate knowledge that would be of use to the GLBT community and the many support services found within it.

Today, with the Australian government committing public money to fund a national debate about the merits of same-sex marriage (ahead of a non-binding plebiscite on the issue), examining questions about the ways GLBT people manage their identities across niche and mainstream social media remains as relevant as ever.

While most Western nations have come a long way in terms of the legal and social acceptability of homosexuality, GLBT people in Australia still suffer from anxiety and depression at rates much higher than the rest of the population (Leonard et al., 2012). A significant percentage of young people in the recent *Private Lives 2* (Leonard et al., 2012) project noted, for example, that they 'usually' or 'occasionally' feel the need to hide their sexuality in a range of situations for fear of abuse or discrimination (p. 8). While the centrality of YouTube to the 'It Gets Better' and 'Trailblazer' campaigns[9] aimed at raising awareness of GLBT issues demonstrates that social media are often at the forefront of efforts to prevent depression and anxiety among young GLBT people, SNSs have also been utilised as tools with which to broadcast homophobia and bully GLBT youth. The death of Rutgers University student Tyler Clementi in September 2010, for instance, was one of the most talked about cases in a recent spate of suicides among young GLBT people for the role that Twitter had played in enabling Clementi's roommate to publicly out and humiliate him.[10] In this respect, we cannot take for granted that social networking tools provide the same kind of identity demarginalisation in the same ways that McKenna and Bargh (1998) found online spaces of earlier kinds have provided for GLBT youth. Some commentators have even gone so far as to suggest that the popularisation of social networking sites such as Facebook has heralded a new era of gay teen suicide (see, e.g., Cohen, 2011).

In the wake of a number of tragic events of this kind in recent years, during the period that this research was conducted, there has been a clear and growing emphasis placed on the prevention of anti-GLBT bullying and on reducing the disparity in levels of depression and anxiety felt amongst GLBT people in comparison with the rest of the population. In Australia, national health organisations such as Beyondblue and the National GLBT Health Alliance have launched a range of campaigns and projects aimed at highlighting GLBT bullying and mental health issues, such as Beyondblue's award-winning 'Left Hand' campaign[11] – which was aimed at encouraging school-aged youth to be more accepting of homosexuality amongst their peers – and the Commonwealth Government funded 'Mindout' project[12] – which was established to work with mental health organisations (both GLBT focused and more mainstream) "to improve mental health and suicide prevention outcomes for GLBT people and populations". A similar pattern of response has also occurred elsewhere. In the UK, GLBT charity Stonewall launched new research into homophobic bullying faced by young people in schools and made challenging homophobia in educational institutions a key priority,[13] while in the United States the Gay and Lesbian Alliance Against Defamation (GLAAD) and a raft of other high-profile GLBT support groups successfully encouraged Facebook to work alongside them to adapt the SNS in ways that make it more GLBT friendly.[14]

While cause-and-effects style arguments, such as Cohen's (2011), in relation to the role of media technologies in social phenomena are rarely capable of explaining all the factors involved in such a deeply complex issue as youth suicide, in the social context described above, where mental health and online bullying have become an increasing priority for GLBT charities and health organisations alike, an enhanced understanding of how and why young GLBT people use SNSs, and how they perceive of and experience these services, both niche and mainstream, can only be a positive step towards being able to better provide the kind of online environment and support that best caters to the needs of this group. Indeed, if the potential for the kinds of social, cultural and economic benefits that can arise in the wider new media environment (see Ito et al., 2008) is to be harnessed in the specific context of services such as Facebook and other mainstream SNSs by a broad cross section of people – that is, if we are to achieve greater levels of digital equality via SNSs – public interest in these sites needs to be balanced by greater understanding of the uses to which they are being put and the ways in which they factor into the everyday lives of various socially and culturally diverse user groups.

One of the key motivations for undertaking this work has therefore been a desire to see more academic writing that deals with gay men's culture and its complex relationships to information and communications technologies (ICTs), in general, and to social networking sites in particular. When I first began thinking about gay men's digital cultures close to a decade ago, academic research on SNSs was burgeoning at pace, yet there was very little material available that engaged with the kinds of experiences that my friends and I, as young gay men, had had using these services – either niche, mainstream or both together. While much has changed in the field of social media research in the time since and the rise of geolocative mobile app-based services, such as Grindr, has helped renew and intensify efforts to understand gay men's digital cultures (see, e.g., MacKee, 2016; Race, 2014; Roth, 2015) there remains much to be done, particularly where multi-sited and cross-genre studies of gay men's social media use are concerned.

Book Structure

In the following chapters, I put forth the argument that the interplay between digital infrastructures and identity management practices within an increasingly diverse ecology of social media technologies, both niche and mainstream, has helped to fuel the emergence of participatory reluctance as a driving force in gay men's digital culture. That is, I show here how the deep-seated antipathy towards niche social networking services for gay men, which drives the success of sites like Douchebags of Grindr, appears to be increasing in conjunction with the development of more general/mainstream social media channels, which (despite their own particular limitations) tend to allow users greater freedoms in terms of self-presentation.

In support of this argument, I provide an account of young gay men's experiences of the sociotechnical integration of mainstream social media into the niche spaces of gay men's networking technologies (and vice versa), focusing on how privacy and identity management practices employed by this cohort map onto shifting notions of gay male identity and the digital infrastructures of services such as Gaydar, Facebook, Instagram and Grindr.

Chapter 2 offers a contextual framework through which to read this argument, and the findings presented later in the book to support it, by providing a brief parallel history of gay men's mediated networking practices and GLBT politics in recent decades that pays particular attention to the place of social media in helping to diversify public representations of gay male identity. Subsequent to this overview, the middle section of the book focuses on the early period of sociotechnical convergence between niche and mainstream SNSs in the context of gay men's digital culture during the mid- to late 2000s. In particular, this section examines the cultures and practices surrounding the integration of the social networking sites Gaydar and Facebook, as it played out amongst young gay men in Brisbane, Australia. Chapter 3 focuses specifically on Gaydar and the dominant cultures and practices surrounding identity management amongst 18–28-year-old users of the site. Here, I argue that an overarching culture of participatory reluctance exists on Gaydar, and that it manifests most prominently amongst the demographic studied in this project as a set of identity management practices used by these men to distance themselves as far as possible from the site and all other users of the service. How Gaydar's digital infrastructure functions to help elicit these kinds of identity management practices by contributing to the construction of an imagined audience of users that does not mesh with the self-perceptions of the gay men for whom the site was created is also discussed.

Chapter 4 sees a similar process carried out in relation to Facebook. It commences with an examination of Facebook's affordances with regards to identity management options as they stood during the late 2000s and a discussion of how these helped to establish a supplementary-style relationship between the site and Gaydar within the gay male community studied here. Demonstrating how users employed Facebook to extend, verify, connect with and navigate gay men's social networks, the chapter illustrates how Facebook's digital infrastructure functions to open up Gaydar to further criticisms by exacerbating those features of the SNS that encourage the culture of participatory reluctance discussed in Chapter 3. It is argued that this situation results from Facebook's provision of a digital framework in which a much wider range of GLBT identities than is visible on Gaydar can be expressed in a fashion that makes homosexuality, ostensibly, banal.

Throughout these chapters, we see how the digital infrastructure of Gaydar creates an environment where stereotypical ideas of gay men's identities persist at odds with the self-images and self-perceptions of many of its younger users, prompting feelings of isolation and despair. We witness how contempt for Gaydar's hypersexualised focus boils over into profile content and user engagement practices; and how hostile behaviour towards others is justified – and becomes cyclical – in this context. With the affordances of Facebook shown, by comparison, to offer individuals greater capacity to publicly present gay male identities that the demographic studied here more closely identifies with, we also see in these chapters how Facebook has been enrolled in gay men's digital cultures as a way of resisting stereotypes circulated in the context of gay-specific SNSs, and as a tool for gay male network mapping and authenticity checking.

Chapters 5 and 6 then examine what implications this supplementary-style relationship, between Gaydar and Facebook, generated for the privacy and personal safety of both users and non-users of these sites amongst the gay male community studied here – and farther beyond it. Chapter 5 examines the affordances with regards to the provisions made for privacy protection in each SNS and why the potential for breaches of privacy and safety were increased in the specific context of the relationship between Gaydar and Facebook. It does this by discussing various examples of privacy breaches brought up during focus groups conducted with research participants and also witnessed directly during site analysis work. Here, we see participants' attempts at daily Facebook cleanses, careful content curation and outright self-censorship – as well as the stories of the men for whom such efforts were ultimately ineffective, leaving them vulnerable to the implications of a growing privacy divide (Papacharissi, 2010a). Chapter 6 then rounds out the book by highlighting how the experiences of the group at the centre of this project, with regards to increased privacy concerns stemming from the technocultural entanglement of Gaydar and Facebook, also provide an insight into more recent developments in gay men's digital culture. Focusing on the period between the emergence of Grindr in 2009 and its 2016 sale to the Beijing Kunlun Tech company, this final section of the book examines how recent developments within gay men's digital culture across platforms like Instagram and Snapchat are underpinned by the continued presence of participatory reluctance within niche networking spaces for gay men, such as Grindr.

Concluding Notes

Before beginning to address particular platforms or issues around sociotechnical convergence, identity, privacy or participation in any real depth, there are a few basic features of this work that it is important to reiterate and/or expand upon prior to concluding this chapter – in particular, with regard to the scope of this study, the specificity of the data provided, the terminology used and the nature of the technologies being studied here.

Scope

It is worth noting here with regards to scope that the analysis conducted for this research was entirely qualitative. As a general methodological overview, work in the early chapters on the sociotechnical integration of Gaydar and Facebook was derived from a twin ethnography where participant observation was carried out on both Gaydar and Facebook in the Brisbane-based areas of these services and supplemented by four focus group interviews with 30 young users of the sites, mainly during the period 2010–2012. These men were not intended in any way to be representative of the entire gay male community in Brisbane, however, were nonetheless from a broad range of social, economic, religious and ethnic backgrounds, of differing education levels, and from every age in the 18–28-year-old bracket, which was used to stand in as a concrete approximation of the age span which might adequately refer to 'young' users for the purposes of this work.[15] Participants also represented a diverse range of positions in terms of the degree to which they were 'out' in all aspects of their lives, from openly identifying as homosexual in all life contexts (approx. 70 per cent) to having not told their families (or parts thereof) and/or work colleagues. Without prompting to do so, these men spoke at length about the arrival of then relatively new geolocative application, Grindr, and it is from these focus groups that users' views on that application are included here. The later work on Instagram is based on data captured through monitoring a range of Instagram hashtags central to gay men's digital culture – again with a particular geographical focus on Brisbane. More detail on data collection techniques is provided in the relevant chapters ahead. However, in none of these settings were the sites themselves or phenomena occurring on them quantitatively monitored. In the vein of textual analysis, dominant themes and patterns, particularly with regard to identity management issues, were simply sought out. The provision of numeric data is therefore limited here to those basic percentages that were capable of being generated via analysis of the focus group transcripts from this study, or via using the inbuilt search functions of the studied platforms to provide basic analytics.

Hence, while I draw on materials from well beyond the scope of a single city, the primary data on which this book is based is the result of research conducted in Brisbane, Australia. Given significant evidence suggests that, at least in urban areas, there exists a global gay culture of sorts (Sinfield, 1998), findings from this collection of localised work are articulated to broader occurrences happening in the international fight for marriage equality and across effectively global spaces, such as Facebook, Grindr and others, to make an argument about the role of participatory reluctance in gay men's digital culture that moves between the local and global.

Specificity, Terminology, Technology and Change

Referred to as either 'social network sites' or 'social networking sites' (and sometimes both interchangeably), the term SNS came to prominence in Internet Studies in the mid-2000s as a way to describe internet-enabled communication technologies that filled "a middle ground between homepages and blogs in which the individual is primary, and online communities in which the group is primary" (Baym, 2011, p. 385). In their special issue of the *Journal of Computer-Mediated Communication* on SNSs, danah boyd and Nicole Ellison (2007, p. 2) defined social networking sites as

> web-based services that allow individuals to (1) construct a public or semi-public profile within a bounded system, (2) articulate a list of other users with whom they share a connection, and (3) view and traverse their list of connections and those made by others within the system.

Many definitions of SNSs circulating in academic arenas at the time also incorporated a list of features that typify these services (see, e.g., Albrechtslund, 2008, p. 2; Goad & Mooney, 2007, p. 1; Livingstone, 2008, p. 394; Ybarra & Mitchell, 2008, p. 351). Livingstone's (2008) description of an SNS, for example, stated that social networking sites "enable communication among ever-widening circles of contacts, inviting convergence among the hitherto separate activities of email, messaging, website creation, diaries, photo albums and music or video uploading and downloading" (p. 394). Albrechtslund (2008, p. 2) noted that in addition to key facilities for constructing profiles, linking with friends and posting comments, many SNSs include "blogging, file sharing and other tools". The range of 'other tools' and features routinely included in these kinds of lists as well as the breadth of sites to which they can be attributed is a clear indication that while they have many technological similarities, SNSs are in fact highly diverse.

As Nancy Baym (2011, p. 389) has noted, SNSs "vary in their foci, technological affordances, regions in which they are most used, uses to which they are put, and social contexts that emerge through them". While many of these services are similar, no two are ever the same on all of the above measures. One clear point of variation among many SNSs that is central to this work, for example, is the intended audience or user population of the service. BlackPlanet (for African Americans), Ravelry (for knitting enthusiasts), Eons (for baby boomers) and Last.fm (for music fans) are all examples of social networking sites that have been aimed at different niche audiences. Gaydar (for gay men) also falls into this category. Simultaneously claiming itself to be one of the world's biggest dating sites as well one of the first ever successful SNSs (QSoft Consulting, 2010) – and thereby highlighting the historical tie between social networking sites and online dating services (see, e.g., Kirkpatrick, 2010, p. 72) – Gaydar resembles the social networking sites described by boyd and Ellison (2007), but, in its relatively narrow area of focus, is vastly different from sites such as Facebook. For this reason, Gaydar and other services designed for use by gay male populations are referred to here as 'niche' social networking sites.

Although the reality of human culture resembles much more of a large collection of overlapping subcultures than an essentialist or reductive mainstream/subcultural binary implies (McKee, 2005), Facebook and other sites with similar scope are referred to in this work as 'mainstream' social networking sites. Here I am simply denoting social networking sites that are not directed at any one particular cultural group and where the core focus of the site is to make visible users' content and/or connections with others. Facebook, which advertises itself as a site that "helps you connect and share with the people in your life",[16] epitomises this kind of general purpose or 'mainstream' SNS, deliberately making itself open and accessible to as many user groups as possible.

In addition to references to 'social networking sites' (both niche and mainstream), in the chapters that follow, readers will also see the much broader term 'social media' employed. As available technologies and their popular uses evolve over time, so too does the language used to define and describe them. In the same way that the term 'Web 2.0' gave way to 'social networking site' (SNS) in the mid-2000s, with the recent explosion of mobile application-based technologies, 'social media' now tends to enjoy prominence over 'social networking sites'. As Highfield (2016, p. 6) has noted this is because 'social media' functions as a "catch-all" term to acknowledge the growing importance of "mobile devices, apps and ubiquitous media", and can cover a wide range of technology including "blogs and blogging platforms, social networking sites such as Facebook, content sharing sites and apps, such as YouTube and Instagram, and forums and communities like reddit and 4chan", as well as messenger applications, such as WhatsApp and Line, and dating or hookup focused tools, such as Grindr and Tinder. Indeed, the most critical factor underpinning this linguistic shift is the capacity of the term 'social media' to account for widely diverse forms of internet-enabled communication, including those that aren't solely website based, such as many mobile apps. This work was completed during a period in which use of the terms 'social networking sites' (SNS) and 'social media' overlapped and jostled for prominence. As a result, both are used here to varying degrees reflective of the dominant terminology at the time of writing particular sections/chapters and the nature of the services being discussed.

As is the case with the language used to describe and define technology, which ebbs and flows with the tide of progress, it is also critical to remember that when speaking of public cultures we are not speaking about individual histories or people, but the "publicly affirmed and circulated descriptions" (McKee, 2005) of particular groups with which many members of those groups might not identify. Thus, in employing the term 'gay' throughout this book to refer, at times, to the various cultures and groups of participants studied here – as 'gay men', as being part of a 'gay community', as taking part in 'gay men's digital culture' and so on – I am in no way intending to imply that the term 'gay' is an unproblematic one, or that these men's identities and experiences represent all those that might identify as homosexual. Nor am I suggesting that any of the social media platforms discussed here represent all of what might be described as gay men's digital cultures. What I am interested in this project is exploring broad patterns of use amongst a particular group of people who use prominent social networking sites such as Gaydar, Facebook and others to engage with this community.

Of course, in focusing on such sites, this book also takes as its subject of inquiry a form of technology that is constantly in flux. While the services examined here were very much live at the time of writing, it is inevitable that this will not be the case at some point in the future. Many of the services discussed here were incrementally altered during the course of this work and will likely be redesigned or reorganised again in some way before the first reader of this book reaches its end. This is something all scholars of social media must contend with and acknowledge. Rather than diminishing the value of such scholarship, though, this simply adds to it another layer of significance, in that writing about social media necessarily contributes to the documentation of highly ephemeral digital spaces and practices: in this case, helping to produce not only specific platform histories, but also a record of sorts of various aspects of gay men's digital culture through time. Nevertheless, readers might take into consideration whilst engaging with this project that, while it can take some time for gaps in our body of knowledge around various technologies and how they might be used in particular cultural contexts or environments to be appropriately filled by academic work, the time it takes for technology itself to progress is much shorter, meaning that – even when dealing with the most recent of services – this work will always already be an historical document.

Finally, I should reiterate my own positioned subjectivity. As would already be apparent, of course, is my own involvement in the community and the culture being considered here. As I noted earlier in this chapter, I have used and been surrounded by the culture of GLBT social networking sites, such as Gaydar, since the very beginning of my adult life. Along with many of my friends and peers, I have engaged with these sites throughout this period on an almost daily basis. As a notional member of 'Gen Y', there does not exist for me a time when gay men's digital culture was not one and the same with gay men's culture in general; as it is for many men my age, the 'digital' in this context has always been ex-nominated. For this same period of time, I have lived in an inner-city village at the heart of the gay community in Brisbane that is home to a number of GLBT charities and organisations and in close proximity to the gay venues mentioned in the early pages of this book. I have also habitually read the local gay press, socialised at the city's commercial gay venues, and attended many of the city's public GLBT events and charity days. Hence, while I may not have experienced first-hand a time when technology was not at the very centre of Brisbane's gay male culture, I am certainly as well placed as any other member of this group to observe its present functions in the community and to try to make sense of recent changes that have occurred in this respect. Moreover, to try to remove myself from this research would not only have limited my ability to reach some of the conclusions that I have drawn about gay men's use of SNSs in this book, but it would also have diminished my level of access to the study's participants. As a corollary, the word 'I' therefore also runs through this document to an extent that it might not do in other academic works.

It is worth pointing out at this juncture, though, that, while I consider anecdotal evidence and non-traditional forms of knowledge to be significant, valid sources of information, these are not the methodological mainstay of this project. This research is based on much more than a collection of anecdotes and personal reflections. It is not 'me-search', as I once heard an older academic refer unsavourily to projects on communities to which the researcher also belongs. Indeed, one of the key motivations for undertaking this study has been a desire to see more rigorous academic work that deals with gay men's culture and its complex relationships to ICTs, in general, and social networking sites in particular. When I first began thinking about these topics in 2007, academic research on SNSs was burgeoning at pace, yet there was very little material available which engaged with the kinds of experiences my friends and I, as young gay men, had had using these services – either niche, mainstream or both together. Nor was there much in the way of scholarship on social networking sites and cultures of resistant or reluctant participation. In beginning to look critically at the place of participatory reluctance within gay men's digital culture, the following chapter provides a brief historical overview of some of the key social and technological shifts that have laid the foundation for its emergence in the contemporary social media environment and how these relate to shifting notions of gay male identity.

Notes

1 www.douchebagsofgrindr.com.
2 www.pokingfunatgrindrtumblr.com.
3 It should be noted here that all names and usernames listed in this book – be they in ordinary text or direct quotes from platform profiles or participant interviews – have been changed to protect the privacy of those concerned.
4 See, for example, *Sex and the City* (Anders, 1999, 'La Douleur Exquise!', Season 2, Episode 12), *Another Gay Movie* (Stephens, 2006), *QNews* (e.g., Issue 271), *Pride* (e.g., Issue 282), *Sydney Star Observer* (e.g., Anon, 2008, 'Goodbye 80s Homo'), *DNA* (e.g., Issue 57; Issue 66).
5 This point is also made clear in the level of attention that the concept of transparency receives on Facebook's public list of principles on the site. These can be found at www.facebook.com/principles.php.
6 Tinder profiles, for example, are automatically linked with users' Facebook profiles and many services offer the possibility of posting content across several social platforms simultaneously.
7 See 'Is Facebook the new Gaydar' on *Awkward Sex in the City* (E, 2007). The author notes in this entry that Facebook is a more positive experience for him than Gaydar, but that Facebook has also caused him serious 'ideological trauma'.
8 Early research on SNSs was very much focused on singular mainstream sites like Facebook and had been conducted using data gathered primarily from American college students, leading to a lack of information about the use of such platforms by particular niche communities or in more diverse contexts. For further information on this point, see Baym (2011).

9 Full details on the It Gets Better Project, which started in 2010, can be found here: www.itgetsbetter.org. Full details on the The Trailblazer Campaign of 2011 can be found here: www.youtube.com/watch?v=0mD8L94mgco.
10 Tyler Clementi's suicide following his forced outing via Twitter and the widespread news coverage that followed is detailed here: https://tylerclementi.org/tylers-story/.
11 Full details of beyondblue's 'Stop. Think. Respect: Left Hand' campaign can be found here: www.beyondblue.org.au.
12 Full details regarding the 'Mindout' project can be found here: http://lgbtihealth.org.au/mindout/.
13 For further details see www.stonewall.org.uk/about_us/2534.asp.
14 For further details on Facebook's 'Network of Support' see www.facebook.com/note.php?note_id=161164070571050.
15 This age bracket was determined based on the 18-year-minimum user age for Gaydar and the notional upper limit of 'Generation Y' at the time of the data collection.
16 This slogan has been present on the sign-in page of Facebook for many years. See www.facebook.com.

2 From the Hankie Code to the Hanky App

Historical Change, Technological Development and Shifting GLBT Identities

In the 1960s, amid a climate of deep social and legislative discrimination, gay men employed the 'hankie code' (Reilly & Saethre, 2014) to find their peers, using the colour and placement of handkerchiefs on the body to signal sexual preferences to each other in public space in ways that would not be recognised by the broader heterosexual population. Today, Hanky is a geolocative mobile phone application that facilitates gay male networking via the sending of self-portrait-style personal photographs, or 'selfies'. As the semantics at play here suggests, despite their many individual differences and the decades between their first uses, there is a clear continuity between these practices that goes to their very core. Each of them is entirely dependent upon mediated performances of identity – one via crude analogue codes assigned to real handkerchiefs, and the other, via a deeply layered genre of contemporary digital photography. In this way, the Hankie Code and the Hanky App are like all forms of mediated social networking that have been employed by gay male populations. They are dependent upon performances of identity, which in turn are shaped by the nature of the wider sociocultural environment in which gay, lesbian, bisexual and transgender (GLBT) people exist and the state of technology available at the time. Understanding participatory reluctance and its place in contemporary gay men's digital cultures is therefore an act of untangling complex intersections between GLBT history, gay male identity and the affordances of particular social networking platforms. Indeed, as Mowlabocus (2010) has argued, understanding the ways gay men are representing themselves online and the reasons behind their manifold digital interactions is impossible without first stepping outside of digital culture and engaging with the wider contexts, discourses and structures that frame gay male subculture more generally (2010, p. 21). Therefore, to lay the groundwork for what is to follow in the remainder of this book, in terms of contexts and frameworks for understanding the data collected and the conclusions that have been drawn from it, this chapter presents a brief overview of the evolution of GLBT politics in recent decades, paying particular attention to the place of social media in this history and its role in shaping modern conceptions of gay male identity.

Recent GLBT History and the Importance of 2004

While there is a long and fascinating history of GLBT cultures and politics that goes back centuries (see, e.g., Boswell, 1994; Foster, 2007), for most people today GLBT history begins more recently with the Stonewall riots of 1969. Although homosexuality had already been decriminalised in Canada, England and Wales two years earlier in 1967, this event is widely recognised to have signalled the beginning of the international gay liberation movement (see, e.g., Carter, 2004; Chauncey, 2005, 2009; Duberman, 1994, Ridinger, 1996). In the decades prior to this event, homosexuals were

> systematically denied their civil rights: their right to free assembly, to patronize public accommodations, to free speech, to a free press, [and] to a form of intimacy of their own choosing….they confronted a degree of policing and harassment that is almost unimaginable to us today.
>
> (Chauncey, 2009, p. 11)

It was not uncommon, for instance, to be fired from one's workplace, arrested and indefinitely imprisoned on mere suspicion of being homosexual (see Chauncey, 2009, p. 11). Hence, following the example of resistance set during the Stonewall riots, for the period of at least a decade well into the 1980s, numerous organizations and campaigns sprang up aiming to secure basic rights for members of the GLBT community who had long been disenfranchised by the deeply anti-homosexual climate of the 1950s and 1960s. British group, the Gay Liberation Front (GLF) and the Australian-based Campaign Against Moral Persecution (CAMP) formed, respectively, in 1970 and 1971, were typical of such organisations. Same-sex marriage, at this time, was not only far from entering the public sphere as a matter of concern for the wider community, but it was also not an issue that was paid any significant attention amongst even the most committed GLBT activists; their efforts were focused on campaigning for the repeal of sodomy laws and other pieces of legislation expressly classifying same-sex attracted individuals as 'perverts' and 'sexual deviants' (see Carter, 2004).

Beyond their endeavours oriented towards legislative change, such groups also worked to support the well-being of GLBT folk via the production of information leaflets and other small publications, and by operating telephone help lines. These activities made them natural focal points for early forms of GLBT community engagement and organisation. In a 2006 interview regarding her involvement in the establishment of CAMP in Brisbane and the activities undertaken by the group in the early 1970s, Cynthia McBride noted, for example, that CAMP also became a popular social space (Smaal & McKay, 2007). After discussing the various media she had helped to produce – including information leaflets on "how to behave if harassed by the police" – she recalled that:

> Our social side boomed, and every Friday and Saturday night saw large crowds dancing and enjoying the freedom to be themselves at the old clubrooms on George Street in the city. The proprietor gave us the use of these rooms as his public response to the discrimination we suffered, as he was a Jew from Lebanon and knew only too well what it felt like to be an outcast in society.
>
> (Smaal & McKay, 2007, p. 55)

As the level of organised activism (and thus, the number of avenues for support, socialization and community development) ballooned during the 1970s and early 1980s, encouraging people to come out and stand up for their rights, gay and lesbian men and women were becoming increasingly liberated (Chauncey, 2009, p. 5; Ridinger, 1996, p. 67). Legalization of homosexuality became a reality in places such as Austria (1971); Finland (1971); Norway (1972); Malta (1973); Spain (1979); the US states of Colorado (1971), California (1975), Ohio (1974) and Hawaii (1972); the Australian state of South Australia (1975) and numerous other jurisdictions (see Hogan & Hudson, 1998). It was also during this period that the American Psychological Association removed homosexuality from its *Diagnostic and Statistical Manual of Mental Disorders* (1973); Harvey Milk became the first openly gay man to be elected to public office in California (1977); and the first Gay and Lesbian Mardi Gras was held in Sydney. This kind of progress and the consistent attention it generated around GLBT issues, both at the local and international levels, created a climate in which it was possible for a newly visible gay and lesbian subculture to take shape. Linked to an expression of homosexuality centred around youthful, white, middle-class masculinity and consumption-based lifestyles connected with cities and urban localities, Alan Sinfield (1998) refers to the dominant expression of gay male identity embedded in this subculture as the 'metropolitan' model of homosexuality.

In his book, *Gay and After* (1998), Sinfield reminds us that while homosexuality has existed for millennia, the term 'gay' is a Western construction that has come to prominence only in the years since the Stonewall riots, in particular, during the same period of the 1970s and early 1980s that Weston (1995) identifies as the peak moment of the 'Great Gay Migration' from rural areas to more urban ones. Those years, Sinfield (1998) explains, allowed for the development of "significant institutions and the beginnings of a climate", where we were able to "express ourselves without too many restraints", a climate that "afforded good opportunity to those who…wanted to be what we have come to recognise as gay or lesbian" (p. 6). Initially, these opportunities arose in the context of gay villages that sprung up in cities around the Western world, colloquially referred to as 'gayborhoods', which brought together high concentrations of GLBT residents, services and symbolic displays (e.g., rainbow flags) of GLBT cultures (Ghaziani, 2014). These villages provided safe spaces where GLBT people could express themselves and find community while being able to access support, resources and businesses targeted to their needs. However, the history of these spaces also indicates that their geographical segregation, their disproportionate focus on gay men and their commercial orientation have caused problems for these areas and their residents associated with exclusion and homogenisation (Brown, 2014; Nash, 2006).

Indeed, writing at the end of the 20th century, in 1998, Sinfield argued that the dominant expression of homosexual identity – the 'metropolitan model' – that first flourished in gay villages inscribed in our culture a model of gay male identity that is not open to all – and which, while a logical response to the repression of earlier times, did not acknowledge the dispersed subjectivities of the growing openly gay population of the late 1990s. Arguing that metropolitan gay and lesbian identities were products of a particular "place and time", Sinfield (1998) postulated that the next millennium would therefore bring with it a new 'post-gay' period, where gay male subculture – and the identities connected to it – would be far more diverse. Thanks largely to the roles played by print media, television, film and, more recently, social media in this history, Sinfield's (1998) vision is now becoming increasingly possible.

Despite the arrival in the 1980s and continuation into the 1990s of the HIV/AIDS epidemic, which renewed much of the broader society's fear and distrust of the gay community, and the emergence during this time of a radical queer culture that, in many ways, bifurcated the gay population of this period, the metropolitan model nonetheless persisted during this era as the dominant expression of homosexual identity in Western societies. Epitomised by the camp, body-obsessed, club culture found in gay villages of cities all around the world, it was reproduced and reinforced in GLBT publications that, while reporting on the nature and severity of the AIDS crisis and providing the community with information on the latest drugs and therapies available, filled the remainder of their pages with material that effectively promoted these kinds of scene-centric lifestyles and identities, in order to sell advertising space to GLBT businesses (Chasin, 2000). By the end of the 1990s, when the HIV/AIDS epidemic began to show signs of receding – as the number of deaths from AIDS started to decrease rather than rise for the first time since the early 1980s (Avert, 2010a, 2010b) – this focus on lifestyle issues only further intensified. As the commercial potential of the GLBT, and, particularly, the gay male, market became clearer, "the gay men's press began to win more advertising from straight, and increasingly corporate, sponsors" (Chasin, 2000, p. 77). In the process, Chasin (2000) argues, the gay men's press significantly contributed to the consolidation of a gay niche market which – while doing little to challenge the existing metropolitan model of homosexuality – changed the relationship of the gay community to broader society, and "the relation of the press and the social movement to the economic and political mainstream" (p. 7). The placing of significant levels of attention on gay entertainment, lifestyles and identities that had made the GLBT press commercially successful in the late 1990s therefore began to carry over into television programming as well, with the arrival, around this time, of shows like *Will and Grace* (1998) and *Queer as Folk* (1999/2000). It was also around this time, in February 2000, that *DNA* magazine was launched and Gaydar (launched in 1999), and then the only social networking site (SNS) to serve a gay male user base, was developed.

While the period of the 'post-gay' envisioned by Sinfield (1998) to arrive with the new millennium was certainly imminent at this point, it might be argued that the journey towards the kind of mainstream normalization of homosexuality (defined by more diverse and non-'metropolitan' representations of homosexual identity) that largely now exists in Western culture did not begin in earnest until 2004. This was the year that Mark Zuckerberg was launching Facebook and the American people were preparing to vote in a November presidential election that would secure a second term in office for George W. Bush. That year was also, as Chauncey (2009) points out, an important moment for the GLBT rights movement in the United States. Following the overturning of the nation's last remaining sodomy laws in the landmark ruling *Lawrence v. Texas* in the previous year, in May 2004 Massachusetts became the first US state to issue marriage licences to same-sex couples. The contentious debate that erupted around these developments, driven by conservatives fearful of losing the long-running battle over the appropriate place of gay people in society, reverberated through the election. It was during this period that the issue of same-sex marriage became a legitimate matter of broad public interest/concern and effectively opened up a whole new chapter of GLBT history in the United States, and thus, in many other parts of the Western world, including Australia. This new chapter of GLBT history, which appears to be reaching its peak at present, has focused on marriage equality and the normalisation of gay identities and relationships.

Perhaps due to the line of reasoning used by pro-marriage-equality activists that emphasises the lack of any significant difference between gay people and straight people, gay love and straight love,[1] in the years since 2004, as debates over the merits of legalizing same-sex marriage have raged, there has been a marked parallel increase in the visibility – and acceptability – of a range of GLBT subjectivities in mainstream media more diverse than was commonly seen in years prior. After her career appeared effectively ruined following her coming out as a lesbian in the late 1990s, comedian Ellen Degeneres, for example, has gone on to become one of the most powerful television celebrities of the past decade, regularly winning awards for her role as the (hugely popular) host of the daytime talk show *Ellen*. Representations of gay males on television and the acceptability of such identities in the public sphere have also skyrocketed; this has occurred most notably via programmes such as *Queer Eye for the Straight Guy* (2003–2007), *Ugly Betty* (2006–2010), *Glee* (2009–2015), *Modern Family* (2009) and *The New Normal* (2012–2013), all of which, while not specifically designed to be 'gay programming', have placed homosexual characters at their very heart. The normalisation of the various gay male identities presented in these series, like the depiction of a significant number of gay male contestants – each with their own idiosyncrasies and life histories – in highly successful reality television shows (Sender, 2006), has expanded the range of possible identities associated with the term homosexual that are now visible in the public sphere. The movie industry has also played a part in this process: *Brokeback Mountain* (2005), *Milk* (2008), *A Single Man* (2009) and *Beginners* (2010), for example, are just a few of the films produced since 2004 based around a central gay character (or characters) that have told stories about gay male life, which do not reflect the dominant discourses about same-sex-attracted men encapsulated in the metropolitan model of homosexuality. Quite removed from the urban youngster who drinks spirits, wears designer clothes, goes to new clubs and has lots of sex, that Sinfield (1998, p. 16) described as embodying the 'metropolitan' model of homosexuality, rural- and suburban-based older men oriented more towards love, family and connection than they are towards sex were at the heart of these films.

Since 2004, alongside these scripted visions of more diverse homosexual subjectivities, non-metropolitan gay male identities have also been increasingly normalised via the coming out – and in some cases, 'outing' – of a number of well-known sportsmen (e.g., Tom Daley, Gareth Thomas, Orlando Cruz), entertainers (e.g., Ricky Martin, Zachary Quinto, Frank Ocean) and other public figures (e.g., Tim Cook, Nate Silver, Anderson Cooper) – and by the increasing normalisation of gay male relationships and families in media coverage given to the child-rearing endeavours of same-sex celebrity couples, such as Elton John and David Furnish, Neil Patrick Harris and David Burtka and Matt Bomer and his partner, Simon Hall. As Schiappa, Gregg and Hewes (2006) have argued in relation to the cultural importance of *Will and Grace* using the Parasocial Contact Hypothesis (a combination of the theory of Parasocial Interaction and the Contact Hypothesis), this kind of media coverage of same-sex relationships and family units can function to reduce prejudice around homosexuality, by increasing the broader community's level of exposure to homosexual people and lifestyles. The arrival of Facebook in 2004 and the explosion of social media, more generally, since that time has increased the potential for this kind of contact immeasurably. Raun (2014), Wuest (2014) and Duguay's (2016) respective work demonstrates this point in chronicling the role of platforms such as YouTube,

Instagram and Vine in increasing the visibility of non-normative genders and sexualities by aiding the production and circulation of media objects focusing on people's gender transitions, coming out stories and queer women's/lesbian identities. In short, not only does social media allow the voices of everyday GLBT people – and their families, friends and other allies – to be heard, it also works to amplify those voices beyond their own immediate networks, through the process of sharing and re-sharing. It is for this reason that mainstream social media has been the focal point of numerous campaigns for marriage equality in recent years and a supremely successful platform for rapidly spreading information and ideas that work to diversify typical understandings of homosexuality and the place of homosexual people in society.[2] The 'It Gets Better' project, which was launched in 2010, following the death of a number of young students who took their own lives after being bullied about their sexuality at school, for example, began as a single video on YouTube aimed at letting GLBT youth know that there is a place for them in society; that it does get better. The project has now grown into a worldwide movement, spread across Facebook, Twitter, Tumblr, YouTube and Google+, with (at the time of writing) over 50,000 user-created videos that have been shared and viewed more than 50 million times.[3] Nowhere is the mainstreaming of the gay liberation movement that has increasingly occurred since 2004 more evident than in these videos. Alongside the thousands of GLBT individuals who have contributed to this movement, there is an easily equal number of contributors who, while not GLBT themselves, simply wanted to voice their support for tolerance and equality. Signalling the accuracy of Sinfield's (1998) 'millennial vision' for a post-'metropolitan' model of homosexuality, those who have contributed to the 'It Gets Better' project, both from within and beyond the GLBT community, come from all walks of life: they are young and old, rich and poor, globally famous and effectively unknown, and from virtually all occupations, faiths and ethnic backgrounds imaginable.

With the likes of Barack Obama, David Cameron, Hillary Clinton and other leading politicians participating in projects such as the 'It Gets Better' campaign, and pledging their support for GLBT equality, it is not surprising that there is now an abundance of statistics indicating that public sentiment regarding homosexuality and same-sex marriage has changed drastically in the past decade. When exit polls were taken across the United States on the issue of same-sex marriage during the Presidential election of 2004, for example, it was revealed that "60 per cent of voters nationwide supported either civil unions (35 per cent) or marriage (25 per cent) for gay couples, a 50 per cent increase in support since the 2000 election" (Chauncey, 2009, p. xviii). Following a jump in support for gay marriage to 40 per cent in 2008 (Pew Research Centre for The People and The Press, 2010), by the time the Presidential election occurred in 2012, support for gay marriage had increased again – this time to a 51 per cent majority.[4] A similar situation has played out in both the UK and Australia. Public support for same-sex marriage increased amongst Britons from 52 per cent in 2004 (Mazzuca, 2004) to 71 per cent in 2012 (Stonewall, 2012) and in Australia, from 38 per cent in 2004 to 64 per cent in 2012 (Australian Marriage Equality, 2012). While Australia continued, until 2017, to debate the merits of allowing same-sex marriage, as well as the mechanism through which any shift might occur, such unions became legal across the United States and most of Britain (Northern Ireland being the one exception). Beating these jurisdictions to the achievement of full marriage equality were countries such as Canada (2005), Spain (2005), South Africa (2006), Norway (2008), Sweden (2009), Argentina (2010), Iceland (2010), Portugal (2010) and Denmark (2012) – all of which followed the lead set by The Netherlands and Belgium, where same-sex marriage was legalised in 2001 and 2003, respectively.[5]

It seems safe to say, then, in the context of this history, that representations of gay men have largely shifted in recent years from those associated primarily with the 'metropolitan' model of homosexuality (Sinfield, 1998) to become much more connected with matters of love, marriage, monogamy and family. As the research of Brown (2014) and Ghaziani (2014) shows, this shift also sits alongside the decline of neighbourhoods with a specific GLBT cultural presence and the increased visibility of sexual minority groups in more rural and suburban areas. While the expansion of legal freedoms afforded to GLBT people in Western nations has reduced the structural necessity for such villages, Ghazianai (2014) notes that this migration – a reverse of sorts of the one that occurred in the 1970s *towards* gay villages – is also part of a growing wave of intention amongst gay men and women to exhibit a 'post-gay' identity. Central to this identification is the desire to be defined by more than one's sexuality; to disentangle gayness with militancy and struggle and to live (work, socialise, reside and so on) amongst sexually mixed company (Ghaziani, 2011, p. 102). In this sense, the increased dispersal of GLBT people into neighbourhoods with more sexually diverse populations can be read as a rejection of sorts of the stereotypical, and highly exclusionary, identities created and reinforced by the commercialisation of GLBT spaces in past decades.

The Shared History of GLBT Villages and Digital Spaces

Although Wilken (2013) cautions against the use of metaphors conceiving of technology in spatial and geographical terms – for example, as a settlement, a frontier, or even just 'cyberspace' – there are similarities to be drawn between the trajectory of gay villages and the recent course of gay men's digital culture, particularly with regards to issues of GLBT identity development. Indeed, key spaces of GLBT culture, both physical and digital, have each been imbued with expectations about GLBT liberation and the free expression of identity that neither has been able to fully live up to. During the 1970s and 1980s, for example, the GLBT community's hopes for emancipation from the shackles of social isolation and legal disenfranchisement they had experienced in decades earlier were pinned on urban gay villages and a belief in their capacity to provide sheltered environments in which GLBT people could find community support and freely express their sexual and social identities. As Castells' (1983) work on the spatial configuration of San Francisco's gay community indicates, the emergence of gay villages during the 1970s and 1980s did provide significant positive outcomes for GLBT people in terms of community building, health service provision, collective identity and the generation of cultural and political power through visibility and cohesion (p. 183). However, the history of these spaces also indicates that their geographical segregation; their disproportionate focus on young, white, middle-class gay men and their commercial orientation has caused problems of exclusion and homogenisation, leading to a recent move away from these centres driven by those who do not fit within or do not support this stereotype (Brown, 2014; Nash, 2006).

Similarly, predicated on the idea that the internet offered complete anonymity (e.g., 'in cyberspace nobody knows you're a dog')[6] and a virtual space in which people could be freed from their material selves (thereby overcoming social stigmas associated with race, gender, age, size, beauty and so on), early cyberculture studies presented the internet's arrival as the beginning of a new utopian future, where greater social inclusion for minority groups would be realised (see, e.g., Rheingold, 1993; Turkle, 1995). These ideas were gradually dismantled, however, as the importance of place, space, embodiment and everyday life in the development of digital cultures became evident. Through their examination of various queer technocultures, several have authors demonstrated, for example, that while impediments to accessing community support can certainly be diminished for GLBT people through the affordances of the internet, social, cultural and material contexts cannot be simply erased or transcended (see Berry, Martin & Yue, 2003; Campbell, 2004; Gray, 2009; Kuntsman, 2007; Lin, 2006; McLelland, 2002; Mowlabocus, 2004). Also putting an end to simplistic utopian visions of universal equality and community that accompanied the internet's arrival was the rapid commercialisation of the technology during this period.

The newly developed 'World Wide Web' of the early 1990s amplified and extended many of the features of physical gay villages to greater numbers of GLBT people. While largely a directory of sorts at the time, it also offered text-based message boards around which communities could flourish. Postal, faxback and telephone classifieds lists typically found in the queer press were digitised into online classifieds and bulletin boards, such as Pinkboard Personals and the gay

Telecafe (Fitch and 'Out' Magazine Editors, 1997). Internet Relay Chat (IRC) was also a key site for gay men to meet and exchange ideas during this period, with thousands of GLBT-oriented channels helping gay men to understand that their own thoughts, feelings and desires were not only real and expressible, but also shared by others as well (Campbell, 2004). By the end of the 1990s and early 2000s, however, the community-driven nature of the internet was changing, and the online spaces where gay men interacted with each other were becoming increasingly commercially oriented, as had already happened with the queer press. In this way, the 'metropolitan' (Sinfield, 1998) model of homosexuality – and its hallmark focus on youth, sex and urban hedonism – brought to life in gay villages and the publications, products, and advertising campaigns made to capitalise on this market over the previous decade, was the model of identity imported into the first commercial spaces aimed at gay men to emerge with the arrival of Web 2.0 technologies. Accordingly, particularly in regard to issues of identity, these spaces have generated both positive and problematic outcomes for gay male communities resembling those experienced at a broader scale within urban gay villages.

As a key precursor to a wide array of today's online GLBT spaces, Gaydar has illustrated many of these outcomes from its very outset. Described by internet researchers as an 'online community', a 'social networking site', a 'dating site' and, sometimes, as various combinations of these terms, Gaydar arrived as Web 2.0 technologies were first becoming available and prospered by translating the commercial successes of the GLBT press during the 1990s into the more participatory environment emerging online at the dawn of the new millennium. In situating physical interaction as the primary motivation for use, Gaydar facilitated a shift in gay men's digital culture from being focussed around a set of practices and interactions occurring mostly alongside, or in relation to, the physical lives of gay men (as in the case of earlier IRC channels) to something that directly permeates, and is necessarily embedded within, the immediate physical world (Mowlabocus, 2010, p. 13). Hence, the arrival of Gaydar had a large and instant impact on gay life, shaping gay men's perspectives on their own bodies and the ways to go about finding partners for sex and relationships. Research on the cultures and practices surrounding the site demonstrate that Gaydar's impact in this regard has been divergent. For example, the site has been found to assist gay men with navigating important decisions regarding sexual activity and sexual health (see Race, 2010) and to provide an important social and support space for gay men via its capacity to facilitate a wide range of relationships and interactions (see Murphy, Rawstorne, Holt & Ryan, 2004, p. 8). At the same time, however, the design of the site's profile templates and search tools, in creating certain typologies of gay male identity (Payne, 2007), have also seen

Gaydar pointed to as a driver of exclusion and homogenization. Writing about the shift to Gaydar from earlier spaces of gay men's online interaction, such as Usenet groups, Kate O'Riordan (2005) noted, for instance, that Gaydar's arrival in November 1999 prompted the fragmenting of gay male communities "into prescriptive identity menus", which, just as the queer press had done before it, assisted in creating particular niche markets, and thus, the promotion of particular gay lifestyles and identities over others. In his 2007 paper 'Introducing Masculinity Studies to Information Systems Research: the case of Gaydar', Ben Light also reflected upon this situation while looking at the process of technology facilitated identity categorization in online communities – or what Nakamura (2002) would call 'menu-driven-identities'. Through a deconstruction of Gaydar, the process of profile configuration, and the phenomenon of users' resistance to various aspects of the site's infrastructure, Light highlighted how Gaydar is implicated in shoehorning members into being and desiring very specific masculinities (p. 663), such as 'bear' or 'twink', despite the fact that gay men are far more diverse than such terms indicate. In a later paper Light and his co-authors took this idea further, suggesting that Gaydar's income generation tactics were based upon the deployment of strategies that may ultimately serve to reinforce gay men's marginalization in society through the 'commodification of difference' (see Light, Fletcher & Adam, 2008). This commercial imperative to promote certain identity categories and stereotypes has embedded homogenisation and exclusion into Gaydar's very fabric, pushing users to engage in self-surveillance and bodily regulation to best align their own identities with idealised models of gay masculinity (see Gosine, 2007; Mowlabocus, 2010; Payne, 2007).

As Mendelson and Papacharissi (2011) have noted, when put most simply, people use social media to "share aspects of themselves with their networks" (p. 251). These spaces are about establishing, presenting and negotiating identity through the expression of individual tastes and interests (Liu, 2007), the people we choose to friend and otherwise foreground on our profiles (Donath & boyd, 2004; Walther, Van Der Heide, Kim, Westerman & Tom Tong, 2008), the various pages and applications we add (Pearson, 2007), the pictures of ourselves and our friends that appear (boyd, 2004; Donath, 2007; Mendelson & Papacharissi, 2011) and the comments we make to and receive from other users (Mendelson & Papacharissi, 2011). In short, social media are tools of identity management. Through them we engage in the process of 'writing ourselves into being' (boyd, 2006). For minority groups especially, spaces in which to freely express one's identity have always been important. From telephone help lines, to secret warehouse gatherings, to 'gayborhoods', the gay press and early internet communities, social media are simply the latest in a long line of efforts amongst GLBT individuals to identify and connect with likeminded others.

While there is academic work on the role of identity in contemporary GLBT migration in the physical sense, charting a growing shift away from gay villages towards neighbourhoods defined by much greater diversity of sexual orientation (Brown, 2014; Ghaziani, 2014), far less exists concerning how this shift may or may not be playing out in gay men's digital cultures. With the recent development of a raft of mobile social networking applications aimed specifically at gay male users, such as Grindr, Hornet, Hanky and many others, research on gay men's digital cultures has increased sharply in recent years. Focusing on Grindr in particular, as the leading location-based service for the Western gay male demographic, much of this research is focused on public health implications arising, or potentially arising, from the capacity of the service to easily facilitate risky sexual activity (see, e.g., Goedel, Halkitis, Greene, Hickson & Duncan, 2016; Winetrobe, Rice, Bauermeister, Petering & Holloway, 2014). From a technosocial perspective, work in this area has tended to focus on the ways that the location-based aspect of Grindr impacts on understandings of intimacy (see, e.g., Stempfhuber & Liegl, 2016) and the experience of public space (see, e.g., Blackwell, Birnholtz & Abbott, 2015). Excepting the work of Gudelunas (2012) looking at what services form gay men's overall social media ecologies, we know little, for instance, regarding the flows of activity between these niche services and more mainstream social media in gay men's digital culture. Indeed, while the number of items focusing on Grindr showing up in my university's library database has effectively doubled in volume every year since 2012, and there is a growing body of work around GLBT uses of mainstream social media platforms (Duguay, 2016; Raun, 2014; Wuest, 2014) – as well as an established history of scholarship considering the use of previous digital technology by GLBT, and particularly, gay male users (Campbell, 2004; Light, 2007; Mowlabocus, 2010) – there has been no detailed consideration as yet of if, and/or how, these services, and the cultures surrounding them, might fit together.

This void is significant given the importance of understanding the impact of new media use in the embedded realities of daily life; a point which scholars such as Jones (1999), Hine (2000), Di Maggio, Hargittai, Neuman and Robinson (2001) and Baym (2011) have all foregrounded for some time. The lack of attention paid to how membership of multiple SNSs in a converged new media environment impacts upon users' experiences with and understandings of these sites is also a significant issue given the rise of the real-name web, cross-platforming and the current tendency towards compulsory online publicness in both social and professional settings (see, e.g., Gregg, 2011). In the context of gay men's use of social media, for example, it means that we know little about how gay men's experiences of more mainstream SNSs, where real-name policies may be in place and where 'context collapse' (Hogan, 2010; Marwick & boyd, 2011) brings diverse members of users' networks into the mix, might intersect with niche sexually specific sites, such as Gaydar or Grindr.

While there is some research that looks at how Grindr sits alongside other niche dating applications (see, e.g., Quiroz, 2013), work focusing on its place within users' overall social media ecology or within gay men's digital culture more broadly is still lacking. In fact, despite danah boyd (2007) noting in her Study on Friendster's rise to popularity during 2002/2003 that gay men were among the first group to make use of Friendster, and that many of them perceived of it and approached it like a gay dating service, the ways mainstream social networking sites might directly connect with niche services like Gaydar and Grindr and manifest themselves within a broader narrative of gay men's digital cultures has not yet been addressed in any great depth. This is despite the fact, as noted earlier, that a reconfiguration of GLBT identity has been playing out in the realms of social media for several years now, via sites such as Facebook and YouTube. And, moreover, that it is precisely in these environments that young people are now exploring their sexualities (Simon & Daneback, 2013).

The current study, in focusing on the use of both niche and mainstream social networking sites among young gay men in Brisbane, picks up these intersecting threads of concern. Building on the work of Gudelunas (2012), in looking at how different service types fit into the broader ecology of gay men's engagements with social media, this project takes research on gay men's identity management processes in social networking sites and places them within a specific ongoing lineage of gay men's digital cultures and GLBT history. It looks not just at how gay men use niche or mainstream social media platforms, but how their use of these services might fit together into a larger picture about gay men's digital media history and shifting models of identity.

Brisbane's GLBT History

Although there is significant evidence to suggest that, at least in urban areas, there exists a global gay culture of sorts (Sinfield, 1998), before examining how issues of identity, technology and social change have played out in the cultures and practices surrounding young men's use of sites such as Gaydar and Facebook, which will be addressed in the coming chapters of this project, it is appropriate that particular attention be paid to how Brisbane's GLBT past – and present – fits into the above history, given its place as the city in which this research was conducted.

It is important for readers to be aware, for instance, that the Australia Institute's study, 'Mapping Homophobia in Australia' (Flood & Hamilton, 2005), lists Queensland as one of the two most homophobic states in Australia. Until very recently it was the only state or territory in the nation with differing ages of consent for homosexual and heterosexual intercourse (see *Queensland Criminal Code, s208*), laws expressly prohibiting adoption by same-sex couples, and the 'gay panic' defense[7] for murder. While there were gay rights and law reform movements active in Brisbane from the mid-1960s to the late 1980s (Moore, 2001), the state of Queensland did not decriminalise homosexuality until 1990.[8] This was 23 years after the 1967 *Sexual Offences Act* legalised consensual sex between men in England and Wales, and much later than the date of repeal for anti-sodomy laws in the vast majority of other Australian states (see Bull, Pinto & Wilson, 1991). As the capital city of Queensland, with a total population of just 2.2 million (Australian Bureau of Statistics, 2014), Brisbane therefore has both a relatively new and relatively small publicly visible gay community. *Queensland Pride*, the city's first official gay and lesbian newspaper, for example, only began publication in 1991 – some 20 years after GLBT periodicals emerged in Australia's southern states (Robinson, 2007, p. 59). Prior to this time, during the height of the HIV/AIDS epidemic of the 1980s, there were newsletters attached to a university-based gay group being printed, a weekly radio programme called *Gaywaves* airing on 4ZZZ (a small community radio station based at The University of Queensland) and a few small social gatherings occurring, but very little in the way of openly gay venues or professionally produced media. The state government thwarted such efforts through legislation. In 1985, for instance, the Queensland Parliament passed amendments to the *Liquor Act* forbidding licenced premises to allow 'drug dealers, sexual perverts and deviants and child molesters'[9] on licenced premises, effectively prohibiting the lawful operation of gay venues (Van Amsterdam, 2007, p. 57). Today, while the operation of gay venues is entirely legal in Queensland, the recent closure and rebranding of some former gay establishments as non-GLBT-focused venues suggests that commercial incentives to operate them appear to be waning. Hence, Brisbane (and Queensland more generally) has a GLBT history, which seems to be following a pattern set in other Western cities, where homosexuality has gone from a clandestine subculture subordinated by legal, religious and social repression to a celebrated identity via the establishment of beats and commercial gay venues, a GLBT press, community organizations and support groups. And, where, most recently, it seems to have become not unlike other markers of difference, necessitating increasingly less legal and social demarcation.

Due to the timing of these respective shifts, perhaps more so than other cities in Australia, where homosexuality has been legal for far longer, Brisbane's gay community has tended to be structured largely around age-based groupings. Given its decriminalization in 1990, for instance, there is a sizeable proportion of the GLBT community in Brisbane who are old enough to remember a time when homosexuality was still illegal in Queensland, and GLBT people faced high levels of oppression. According to Robinson (2007, p. 71), this created a situation during the 2000s where the state's queer press struggled with striking the correct balance between serving the interests of younger readers – who were more ambivalent about or did not identify with earlier GLBT rights movements – and the interests of older readers who had perused the press since it first emerged as a political force. Given recent events in Queensland, which saw the passing of legislation allowing for same-sex civil unions in 2011, and then its subsequent repealing in 2012 following the election of a new state government,[10] it might equally be argued, though, that the present generation of gay youth (whose age prevents them from having experienced the same kind of validation that older men may have experienced from the commercial gay scene during the 1990s when it first provided gays and lesbians with opportunities for recognition, identity and lifestyle following years of legal repression) is simply bearing witness to a new chapter of the GLBT rights movement based around securing the legalisation of same-sex marriage. Regardless of the specific role of the GLBT rights movement in its origins, however, anyone who has ever spent long enough in Brisbane in the past two decades to become familiar with the city's gay culture will know that a generational division of sorts has been particularly present here. Until very recently, in fact, it was effectively mapped out in physical terms in the three main commercial gay venues that, during the 1990s and 2000s, served as centerpieces of the city's gay community – The Beat Megaclub, The Wickham Hotel and The Sportsman Hotel.[11]

While the newly modelled websites of these venues might now belie this history, crudely speaking at least, for the best part of the past 25 years most young gay men in Brisbane have begun their foray into the physical world of the GLBT community at The Beat – a club in the centre of the city's entertainment precinct with multiple dance floors and bar areas, and where the number of male and female patrons was often relatively even. Sometime between approximately the end of their 20s and the start of their 30s, however, much of The Beat's male clientele would then 'graduate' to The Wickham – a venue which had slightly less dance space and more of a pub/bar culture, where men easily outnumbered women and patrons were predominantly aged between 30 and 45. 'Sporties', as it is affectionately known by locals, lies just outside the city's main entertainment precinct and is organised around a pool table and a small collection of poker machines on one level and a Karaoke stage on another. This venue, while it is certainly welcoming to all ages, genders and identities, has typically been the preserve of gay men 35–40 and beyond. Outside of these key venues, the gay community in Brisbane is also catered to through a small number of temporal spaces, where typically heterosexual venues temporarily transform into gay spaces for one night per week (as in the case of Fluffy) or one night per quarter (as in the case of White Wolf). While these occasional gay spaces tend to draw slightly more diverse crowds than their permanent counterparts, they are also largely oriented around age: White Wolf, for example, is a quarterly, male-only dance party that openly markets itself towards the '30+' crowd.[12] Thus, although there is some level of intergenerational mingling at Brisbane's GLBT venues, the city's gay male culture has tended to be organised in such a way that special events like the annual Brisbane Queer Film Festival and Big Gay Day celebration are often the only places where men of all ages are co-present. This is particularly the case given that the city's gay neighbourhoods, like many others around the world (see Nash & Gorman-Murray, 2014), have also been reshaped into largely heterosexual areas in recent years, as non-GLBT people move into urban villages once dominated by GLBT residents that have been gentrified into desirable places for upper-middle-class living. Given this situation, and the fact that the already limited number of permanent physical venues catering to the gay community in Brisbane is declining, with the recent "evolution" of The Wickham into a non-GLBT venue,[13] the place of technology in generating opportunities for cross-generational interaction and awareness and in simply acting as an additional/alternative gay 'space' for this particular community cannot be understated.

It was partly for this reason I began this book by signalling a possible shift in gay men's *digital* culture via relaying events which occurred at The Beat, a physical space deeply embedded in Brisbane's gay community. Both of these stories – my own experience of being recognised from Gaydar as 'Brista' and my friend 'Sam's' experience with 'Matt' and his Facebook invitation – highlighted immediately the lack of distinction that has always existed between the physical and the virtual in gay men's culture (see Campbell, 2004, p. 14; Mowlabocus, 2010, p. 14); thus, foregrounding the importance of both place (Brisbane) and space (e.g., commercial gay venues) in this project from the outset. More importantly, though, these events also highlight the shift occurring in gay men's digital cultures over the past several years, from something conducted primarily in niche spaces, such as Gaydar, to something much more present across a range of emerging social media platforms, including Facebook and others. This book argues that the repositioning of gay men's digital culture in this way has to a large extent both fostered and been fostered by the emergence of participatory reluctance around digital spaces designed specifically for gay male users – which has, in turn, been driven by technological development and rapid social change with regards to gay male identity and a subsequent shift away from the 'metropolitan' model of homosexuality in gay male subculture.

The next chapter takes up this issue by looking at how the cultures and practices surrounding identity management on Gaydar, as an example of a key community-specific SNS, fits into this history. It demonstrates the ways that shifting ideas about gay male identity and the inability of Gaydar's technological infrastructure to accommodate such ideas combined during the late 2000s to foster a culture of participatory reluctance amongst young users of the site in Brisbane, Australia.

Notes

1 See, for example, the kind of messaging used to support the campaign for marriage equality in Australia at www.equallove.info.
2 See, for example, the NOH8 campaign – www.noh8campaign.com, the It Gets Better project – www.itgetsbetter.org and the GetUp run Marriage Equality 'love story' campaign – www.getup.org.au/campaigns/marriage-equality/love-story/watch-the-video.
3 More information about the It Gets Better Project can be found at www.itgetsbetter.org.
4 These figures are sourced from ABC/Washington Post run polls that coincided with the US presidential election of 2012. See www.langerresearch.com/uploads/1144a1SocialIssues.pdf.
5 For a full list of the years and jurisdictions in which same-sex marriage has been legalized see https://en.wikipedia.org/wiki/Same-sex_marriage.
6 'On the internet nobody knows you're a dog' is a popular idiom emerging from a 1993 Peter Steiner cartoon published in the New Yorker that commented on the nature of privacy and anonymity on the early internet. For more information see http://knowyourmeme.com/memes/on-the-internet-nobody-knows-youre-a-dog.
7 The 'gay panic' defense was a legal argument allowed under QLD law that could be used by men accused of murdering homosexual victims to appeal for the downgrading of their charges to manslaughter on the basis that the accused, rather than acting in a premeditated fashion (as is the case when convicted of murder), committed their crime in the state of panic experienced when being flirted with by a gay man – or when believing he has been flirted with by a gay man. See https://en.wikipedia.org/wiki/Gay_panic_defense.
8 *Criminal Code and Another Act Amendment Act QLD 1990, No. 93.*
9 *Liquor Act and Other Acts Amendment Bill QLD 1985* Item 16 47A.
10 For an overview of Queensland's GLBT rights history see Moore (2001) and https://en.wikipedia.org/wiki/LGBT_rights_in_Queensland.
11 See venue websites for further information. The Beat Megaclub (www.thebeatmegaclub.com.au); The Wickham Hotel (http://thewickham.com.au); The Sportsman Hotel (www.sportsmanhotel.com.au).
12 See www.whitewolf.net.au/about.
13 See http://thewickham.com.au/our-story/.

3 Gaydar Cultures

The Only 'Good' Gay in the Village?

> I am a professional with a job that I do like. I live in the city in a flat that I like. I have friends that do not cause problems, lead dramatic lives or ever want to borrow money from me. I can drive but do not have a car. I like to converse over good food and wine (not in that order) but beer, spirits and takeaway or delivered pizza would do also. I have a great sense of humour and nothing offends me. Because of this I upset people that are sensitive easily, although I do not try to on purpose. I am also clever and smart (perhaps in that order, perhaps not) and quite ambitious. It makes me wonder why I am putting a profile on here.
>
> —Joe Blogs (Gaydar)

Over the many years that I have used gay men's digital services and the thousands of profiles and user interactions I have observed in these spaces, the one idea that I have come across more than any other is the sense that use of these technologies is a futile endeavour. As the first social platform designed specifically for gay male users, Gaydar is, in essence, where this attitude first took hold. Like "Joe Blogs" above, for example, Gaydar users have wondered with an almost predictive repetitiveness, "why [am I] putting a profile on here?" Despite the site marketing itself as a place where users would find "what [they] want, when [they] want it",[1] many of them have flatly stated, as participants in this study did, that what they are looking for quite simply "is not on [Gaydar]". Accordingly, since at least the mid-2000s, Gaydar has tended to function amidst a culture of what I call 'participatory reluctance', where, amongst members themselves, a primarily dismissive attitude towards the site and its users dominates. So strong has this culture of participatory reluctance been, in fact, that with the arrival of newer alternatives in the shape of Grindr and other geolocative apps for gay men in 2009/2010, Gaydar's popularity and market hold spiralled, until the site was completely sold off in 2013 to CPC Connect.

Just prior to this event in 2010, however, Gaydar's original parent company (QSoft Consulting) published an "insider guide to the pleasures and pitfalls of 'The Dar'" (JockBoy26, 2010) full of advice for men on how best to use the site, which often appeared directly aimed at ameliorating this destructive culture. Much of the advice provided, for example, was designed to discourage users from utilising their profiles either to condemn Gaydar or to denigrate other members of the site – both of which were happening frequently in this space. The book urged users to be open to opportunities to make new friends from Gaydar (p. 38) and discouraged any form of negativity. "Nobody cares about what you DON'T like", it said in a section on how to fill out the profile template, "it makes you sound jaded and seriously negative" (p. 8). It also warned, for instance, that "bursting into a chat room and going on and on about how everyone online is shallow and into dangerous drugs and meaningless sex is not going to make you popular" (p. 38).

While this advice in particular, and the existence of *The Big Book of Gaydar* (JockBoy26, 2010) in general, confirms that the culture of participatory reluctance on Gaydar has certainly been widespread, it also suggests that participatory reluctance has tended to be most prevalent in this environment in connection with issues of profile construction and identity management. Across different demographics, however, there does appear to be slight variance in this regard. Although my work has focused specifically on young Gaydar users, aged 18–28, for example, in the profiles of users older than this cohort that I have seen and in the non-formal discussions with Gaydar users over 28 that I've had since beginning to work in this area, I have found the culture of participatory reluctance amongst this group to be primarily connected to issues associated with labour; with identity-based concerns a comparatively lower-order issue. Time spent chatting in gay men's digital environments that did not produce a face-to-face encounter for these older men, for instance, – whether that be for sex, a more date-like scenario or something else altogether – was considered time wasted, and a significant detraction to Gaydar use. "I use Gaydar with a very utilitarian approach", said one 40-something in 2009, before asking me to find out through my work why so many young users of the site that he had come across would chat endlessly with no intention to meet up for sex, however much of an interest they had initially appeared to show in him. By contrast, perhaps in accordance with findings that social networking sites (SNSs) function for young people as mediated spaces in which to socialize when meeting in offline/unmediated settings is not feasible – or simply as places to 'hang out' (see boyd, 2008b; Ito et al., 2008) – amongst the 18–28-year-old users of Gaydar I have studied, simply chatting and socializing (online) with other gay men has been a core desire. Hence, for these users of Gaydar, the culture of participatory reluctance that has defined their engagements with the site has not been related to labour, but, instead, intensely bound up with issues of identity.

In this chapter, then, given the importance of digital spaces as traditionally empowering environments for gay, lesbian, bisexual and transgender (GLBT) youth (see Brown, Maycock & Burns, 2005; Gray, 2009;

Hillier & Harrison, 2007; McKenna & Bargh, 1998), I examine the culture of identity-based participatory reluctance that still exists in the niche spaces of gay men's digital culture today, by providing a snapshot of how this phenomenon first played out on Gaydar, and its particular presence amongst 18–28-year-old users of the site during 2010–2012. The chapter draws on data collected across this period through unobtrusive participant observation, textual analysis of over 7,000 profile biographies, and interviews with 30 young Gaydar users conducted either individually or as part of a set of four focus groups. It highlights the most central components of the culture of participatory reluctance for the 18–28-year-old cohort of users I studied, and how the phenomenon was manifested within the dominant identity management practices seen amongst this demographic – practices which, collectively, might best be described as efforts to present oneself as being different from and better, or more virtuous, than all other members of the site. How Gaydar's digital infrastructure functioned during the data collection period to help elicit these kinds of identity management practices by contributing to the construction of an imagined user highly disconnected from the individual self-perceptions of the young men for whom the site was created will also be discussed. In this way, the present chapter flags how the circumstances surrounding Gaydar and its use during the late 2000s have helped to shape the applications and user practices embedded in more recent gay men's digital cultures that I will return to in Chapter 6.

Gaydar, Identity and Participatory Reluctance

The culture of participatory reluctance that infused a large percentage of the Gaydar use examined during this study, and by extension, the dominant forms of identity presentation that young gay men in Brisbane adopted in this space during 2010–2012, cannot be explained by a single overarching cause. Three key factors, however, played a central and interrelated role. First and foremost was the perception held by these users that Gaydar could not be used to find anything more than casual sex. Second, building upon the first assumption, was the idea that the kinds of men using Gaydar were the kinds of men who were only after casual sex, and therefore, quite significantly, the kinds who would fit neatly into a stereotype of gay masculinity best described in Sinfield's (1998) 'metropolitan model' of homosexuality. The third, and just as significant, factor was the lack of genuine alternatives available in terms of niche SNSs designed for the gay male community at that time. In order to better understand how each of these factors came together during the final years of Gaydar's market dominance to foster a culture of participatory reluctance and to shape the cultures and practices surrounding identity management on Gaydar amongst its 18–28-year-old users of the site, it makes sense to first address each of them separately.

Point of Reluctance #1 – Key Perceptions about Gaydar's Uses/Gaydar Can Only Be Used to Find Sex

Gaydar took its name from the colloquial term to describe the reported ability to identify people who are gay through visual signifiers and other semiotic codes. At its core, even today, the site is simply a database. It houses information about men in the form of text and images, which hang together as profiles, and it allows users to retrieve this information via set search parameters. And with members registered in over 140 countries around the world, at any one time, thousands of men from around the globe are signed in to their local versions of the site doing just that. However, as anyone who has had even the slightest connection with the gay male community in recent decades will know, describing sites like Gaydar in the language of databases is more than just a little reductive.

For the tens of thousands of users who logged on to Gaydar every day during the height of its popularity in the 2000s, the technical language of databases, as a descriptor of the kinds of activity that occurred in this space, could not be more foreign or incongruous. While 'searching', 'browsing' and 'accessing data' are key aspects of the site's functionality, as Mowlabocus (2010) has noted, users did not engage with Gaydar during this period, or, for that matter, with any of the other gay-oriented databases of its kind, to "analyse data and refine search methods" (p. 83). It was – and is still today – the social and sexual potential of the site that drew in Gaydar's users. A member of the site himself, in his book, *Gaydar Culture* (2010, p. 83), Mowlabocus explained the nature of Gaydar use in this way:

> We don't 'access data' [on sites like Gaydar] – we look at pictures of guys and read about what 'danishot' or 'fuck2006' or 'Bunsboi' is into, and when they might be free to meet up with us...We use them to meet other men, to chat to friends and strangers, to keep in touch with acquaintances and to arrange sexual encounters that might range from a romantic date on a Wednesday night through to a weekend-long P'n'P gang-bang involving two or three 'power bottoms' and a bunch of 'aggressive tops'.

As this description suggests, while the back end of Gaydar might be nothing more than a database, the front end, from which users interact with the site, has functioned as a portal to a world that cannot be summed up so neatly. Friendships can be forged and maintained in this space, social chatter with no particular purpose can be enjoyed and just as easily, alongside all of this, romantic dates and all manner of sexual encounters can be arranged. As a result, Gaydar has been variously referred to as a dating site, a hook-up or cruising site, a lifestyle site, an online community and a social networking site – and sometimes all of these at once (see, e.g., Dugdale, 2007, p. 74). I noted in the introduction to this book that, as a young adult, Gaydar had been central to my own life in an array of different ways also: as a tool with which to test the waters of the gay world and my own identity within it; to assist with navigating various physical spaces and real-world events designed to cater for the GLBT community; as an information repository and source of cultural capital and as a tool for simply bonding with my peers. The multiplicity of the potential uses for Gaydar and the roles that it has played in the gay male community seen in this description, and in Mowlabocus' above, have also been confirmed by research conducted on the site by various health organisations, which consistently note the importance of sites like Gaydar as social spaces that have supported a broad range of interactions and relationships in gay male communities (see, e.g., Murphy, Rawstorne, Holt & Ryan, 2004). In short, Gaydar's potential uses, like a great number of other social networking sites', are almost endless. *The Big Book of Gaydar* (JockBoy26, 2010) referred to a gay man's Gaydar profile for this reason as "an essential passport to a world of mates, dates and who-knows-what".

For the demographic studied in this project, however, this description did not ring so true. For these users, the social possibilities encompassed in the site did have limits – and very clearly bounded ones. The gap between what young Gaydar users believed the site could be used for and what they wanted to use it for, it appears, could not have been wider. With Gaydar users observed in this study employing their profiles to express an interest in everything from meeting a gym buddy, to a swim instructor or cycling pal, as well as for finding a flatmate, a travel mate, prospective employees, a tradesman, and local guys to act as a personal tour guide upon arrival in a new city, the notion that Gaydar is a 'who-knows-what' world of endless possibilities seems, at first, quite apt. What's more, these uses of the site give credence to the idea of Gaydar being much more than a dating or hook-up site and help to explain the connections that were so often made during the mid- to late 2000s between Gaydar and more general-purpose or mainstream SNSs, such as Facebook.[2] Nevertheless, there is one crucial thing that younger members of the site resoundingly believed Gaydar could not be used for. While mates, dates and all kinds of 'who-knows-what' were certainly sought after and on offer, committed monogamous relationships were perceived to be well outside the realms of possibility on Gaydar by younger men. Yet, in somewhat of an irony, it was specifically these kinds of relationships that appeared to be highest on the agenda of the site's users in this demographic. In short, amongst the 18–28-year-olds studied here, the site was deemed incapable of being used for that which users would most like to engage with it for. And the key reason that establishing these kinds of relationships via Gaydar was widely perceived to be outside the realms of possibility by these young men, was the deeply held belief that Gaydar is simply a tool for procuring casual sex.

While the site's profile templates have very recently been updated, when signing up to Gaydar throughout the 2000s, there were a number of areas where a user could express to others what they were looking for on the site – or more broadly, why they were using Gaydar. The first area where this information could be found was in two sections of the user profile which showed up to viewers in boxes titled 'Looking For a' and 'For' (see Figure 3.1). The first of these sections appeared at the top of the profile in relation to what kinds of people the user was looking to interact with. It functioned as a drop-down menu with the following choices: 'Single Gay Man', 'Single Bi-Man', 'Gay Male Couple', 'Bi-Couple' and 'Group (Gay Men)'. The 'For' box appeared below this section and, from the back end of the site, also functioned as a drop-down menu: it asked users to choose from a range of activities (including 'Relationship', 'Friendship',

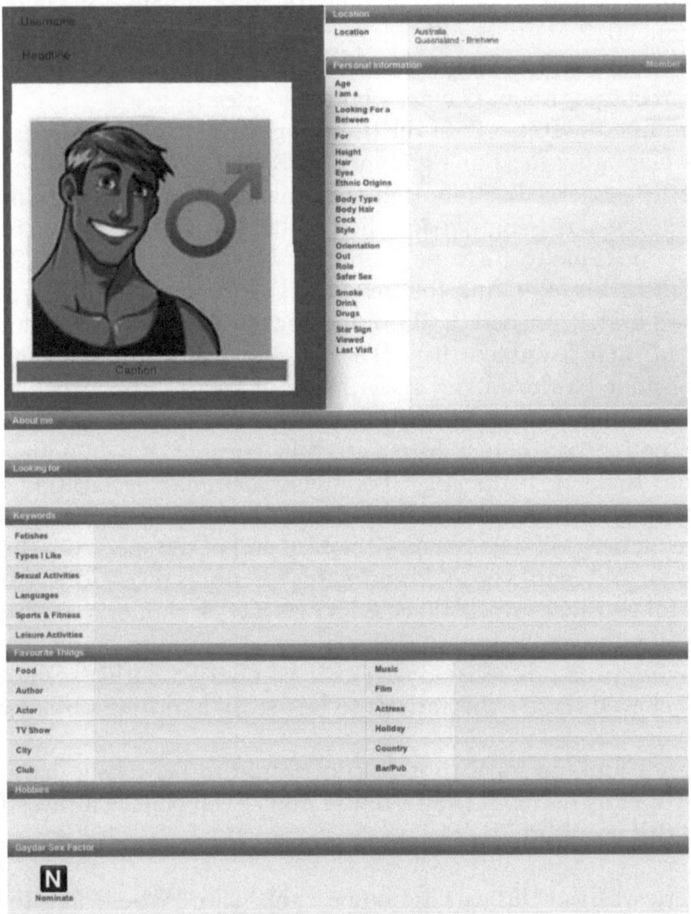

Figure 3.1 Basic layout of a Gaydar profile.

'Email/Chat', '1-on-1 Sex', 'Group Sex' and 'Other Activities') in order to indicate what kinds of interactions or activities each user may be open to engaging in via the site. Each of these menus allowed users to tick as many boxes as they wished, meaning all manner of combinations were possible. Indicating that you were looking for a single gay man for a relationship, for instance, was just as easy as indicating that you were looking to find a gay male couple or a group of gay men for group sex and other activities.[3] Further towards the bottom half of the user profile there was also an open text box titled 'Looking For', where users described in their own words (using up to a total of 1000 characters) what it was they were seeking on Gaydar. Of course, in describing themselves and their hobbies in the two other open text boxes that appeared in a user profile ('About me' and 'Hobbies'), and in choosing a profile name and headline, users were also able to communicate a great deal of information about what it was they were hoping to find on Gaydar – compare, for example, a username such as 'fuckguy2012' with 'boyfriendmaterial'. Undoubtedly, however, it was the open text box 'Looking For' that was most revealing with regards to users' perceptions about Gaydar's potential uses.

Examining the free text of the 'Looking for' box in thousands of user profiles belonging to young gay men in Brisbane during 2010–2012, a clear pattern emerged: committed relationships were highly sought after, but categorised as lying outside the possibility of the kinds of relationships it is possible to forge with another Gaydar user. As one 24-year-old noted in his 'Looking for' text box, "looking for a BF, but don't expect to find it on here". "Looking for a relationship but doubt I'll get one off here" said another. "Ultimate goal is a husband, but this is g*dar L" added a third. And again, "I want friendship, chat, ultimately love. But to find that on Gaydar? Somewhat unlikely, I think", said 'decent4decent', before concluding with, "the number of men on here after no strings fucks is disturbing". Following a similar declaration that he was after love, 18-year-old 'Coolkid' said "but i really don't think i will find love on here lol!". At the more cynical end of the spectrum there was the 23-year-old man whose 'Looking for' section said, "Come off it, it's gaydar. I'll consider myself charmed if i get a cock shot or a one line message and blurry photo from 1999 sent to me." Like so many others, he was looking for a relationship that evolved out of a dating scenario, but clearly believed these expectations to be too high, noting sarcastically:

> I'm not looking for a root & run, would rather a few dates to see how it pans out. Did I say a few? I don't even believe it myself. Let's just call it one and half.

And there was the enthusiastic home cook who "Would like to find a LTR" but was "starting to feel like [he was] the only one genuinely looking (cue violins)." There was the 'outdoorsy' kind of guy who was "happily single", but looking for someone special to change that sometime soon, who said, "though I admit I have my doubts that will occur through gaydar". And there were thousands more, all repeating in one way or another the same chant: 'Gaydar is just for sex; gay men interested in relationships are not on Gaydar – except for me'.

This idea also played on repeat amongst the participants interviewed for the study. While interviewees had successfully used Gaydar for a variety of reasons, including the establishment of friendships and at least two longer-term relationships, the idea that Gaydar is only for finding casual sex partners persisted. One young man who came along to participate in the study, for example, said that he no longer had a Gaydar profile at the time of the focus group he took part in because, "everyone is just on there for sex and random sex doesn't interest me. The kind of person that I want to be with", he explained, "I figure wouldn't use that". "They're just out there for a root", commented another. In a different group, a new arrival to the city who was looking for some local friends and a possible boyfriend noted that he had recently stopped using Gaydar altogether as a means to meet new people in Brisbane because, "most people on Gaydar tend to be sexual. I mean instead of building up friendship and stuff like that", he said, "they prefer to like hook up; 'do you want to meet? Do you want to meet?' That's all." Constructing Gaydar as a failed dating site, another young user in the same group noted,

> I find gay dating websites like Gaydar are more like gay sex websites. There aren't many...out there...[you can use for] actual dating. I mean if you want to date someone it's really hard to find someone online to just date...It's all sex.

The notion that Gaydar was a site for arranging sexual encounters and was therefore a difficult avenue through which to find men interested in relationships was in fact, so strong amongst participants in this study, that two people with Gaydar accounts who separately committed to being involved in the project did not show up for their focus group sessions, citing concerns about being associated with the site due to its focus on sex. "I won't be a good person to interview, anyway, because I don't use the site for sex", they each noted, thinking themselves an exception to the rule. Like Joe Blogs above, who wondered why he was putting a profile on Gaydar, however, these two men were in fact much more the rule than the exception amongst the age group studied here. Socializing in a digital environment that produced opportunities for finding new friends and for going on dates that might lead to a committed relationship were the core motivations for using Gaydar amongst those observed online and in the interview process for this project. Even the one focus-group participant who admitted to using the site solely to procure sex with other men said that he did so understanding that Gaydar could not be used to find anything more than that. Looking for a relationship was something he did elsewhere, offline.[4]

Clearly, these attitudes towards the site and its potential uses are connected to much broader ideas about the diminished capacity for relationships formed via online spaces to be authentic. As Nancy Baym (2010) has written about extensively in *Personal Connections in the Digital Age*, society's tendency to think about new technologies in a deterministic fashion has lead to a number of concerns about mediated communication damaging conversational skills, degrading language and weakening community connections. These kinds of ideas, which are based on the juxtaposition of the online with the offline, collectively create what is referred to as 'the myth of cyberspace'. The notion that technology "replaces meaningful relationships with shallow substitutions" is another one of these myths (Baym, 2010, p. 150). And it ran deep amongst young users of Gaydar. Despite being part of what is often labelled the most technologically savvy generation yet (see, e.g., Heath, 2006; Huntley, 2006; Palfrey & Gasser, 2008; Thornham & McFarlane, 2011), and despite their own experiences often providing evidence to the contrary,[5] the 18–28-year-old Gaydar users observed in this study consistently noted that what they were looking for would not be found on the site. In the words of these users themselves, what they were looking for was more 'substantial', more 'normal', more 'real', more 'genuine', more 'authentic' and 'less superficial' than the hook-ups and sex-based relationships that they perceived to be the only things available on Gaydar.

While general concerns about the authenticity of online relationships played a key part in these perceptions, the digital infrastructure of Gaydar itself, like all technology, is not ideologically neutral (Akrich, 1992; Latour, 1997; Lessig, 1999). The kinds of advertising, competitions/promotions, imagery and profile elements foregrounded on Gaydar at the time of data collection, for instance, certainly also contributed quite significantly to constructions of the site as a space oriented towards the sexual and the superficial. While the kind of banner advertising that occurred on Gaydar during this period sometimes included GLBT community organisations, Pride-style events and GLBT-friendly travel companies, the advertising most commonly found on the site, for instance, came from the pornographic industry and online sex stores.

The kind of imagery found in these advertisements was also replicated in Gaydar's own branding across the site. The rolling images that greeted users throughout the 2000s at both Gaydar's home page and sign-out screen, for instance, were highly sexualised, with models rarely wearing many clothes and often pictured engaging in (or about to engage in) sexual acts (see Figure 3.2). While it has since been removed from the site, a selection of pornographic products (including image and video galleries) and an online sex store were also packaged together in an area of Gaydar called Manzone, which also worked to foreground sex. The intense focus on all things erotic that was so deeply embedded in the infrastructure of the site through these kinds of features also extended to the forms of self-presentation encouraged via the site through the framework provided for profile construction purposes (see Figure 3.1). Whereas other social networking sites that support dating, such as R.S.V.P, routinely ask users to indicate their height, body type, hair and eye colour, Gaydar asked for a physical description of its users which included all of these categories as well as extra ones dedicated to body hair and the user's 'Cock' size and circumcision status (choices being 'Small', 'Average', 'Large', 'Extra Large', 'None' and either 'Cut' or 'Uncut'). The site also asked for users to indicate their preferred sexual role ('Active', 'Active/Versatile', 'Versatile', 'Passive/Versatile' or 'Passive') and attitude towards the practice of safe sex ('Always', 'Sometimes', 'Never', 'Needs Discussion'). The provision of detailed information about sexual practices and preferences was also encouraged through profile sections titled 'Fetishes', 'Types I like' and 'Sexual Activities', where a large array of tick boxes and predefined answers were provided (see Table 3.1), and which showed up on profiles as searchable 'Keywords'. For many years, including the period in which this study was conducted, Gaydar also further reinforced its focus on sex and physicality inside users' profiles through the inclusion (and promotion) of the site's 'Sex Factor' feature, where users were encouraged to configure their profiles to allow themselves to partake in a monthly competition which awarded prizes in various categories to the guys whose profiles had the greatest 'Sex Factor' (calculated by the number of users who had clicked to vote on each nominated profile). Of course, Gaydar also allowed users to upload their

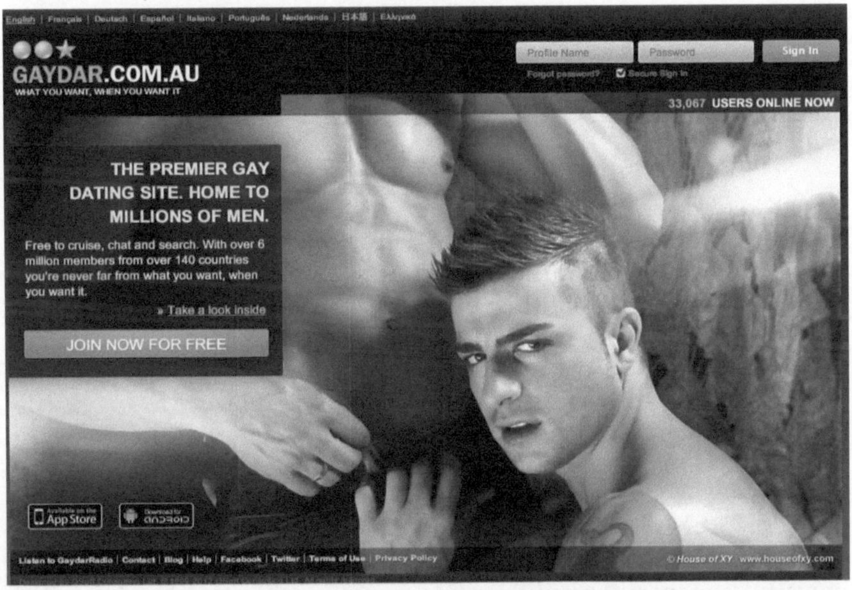

Figure 3.2 A Gaydar cover image from 2012.

Table 3.1 'Keywords' options presented during Gaydar profile construction

Fetishes				
☐ Select all	☐ Body Hair	☐ Boots	☐ Chaps	☐ Cut
☐ Armpits	☐ Drag	☐ Facial Hair	☐ Feet	☐ Frottage
☐ Denim	☐ Hands	☐ Hoods & Masks	☐ Jocks	☐ Kilts
☐ Fur	☐ Lingerie	☐ Lycra	☐ Muscle	☐ Nipples
☐ Leather	☐ Piercing	☐ Rubber/PVC	☐ Smoking	☐ Socks
☐ Nipples	☐ Sportswear	☐ Suits	☐ Tattoos	☐ Toys
☐ Speedos	☐ Uncut	☐ Underwear	☐ Uniforms	☐ Waders
☐ Trainers/ Sneakers				
Types I like				
☐ Select all	☐ Bikers	☐ Builders	☐ Chubbies	☐ Clubbers
☐ Bears	☐ Firemen	☐ Footballers	☐ Geeks	☐ Labourers
☐ Farmers	☐ Married Men	☐ Medical (Uniforms)	☐ Military (Uniforms)	☐ Muscle Men
☐ Leather Men	☐ Policemen	☐ Preppies	☐ Punks	☐ Rugby Players
☐ Older Guys	☐ Skins	☐ Tall Guys	☐ Transvestite/ Transexual	☐ Truck Drivers
☐ Short Guys				
☐ Twinks				
Sexual Activities				
☐ Select all	☐ Bondage	☐ Breath Control	☐ CBT	☐ Cottaging/ Tea Rooms/ Beats
☐ Anal	☐ Electro	☐ Exhibitionists	☐ Fisting	☐ Glory Holes
☐ Cybersex	☐ Kissing	☐ Masters & Dogs	☐ Masters & Slaves	☐ Medical
☐ Groups	☐ Oral	☐ Outdoor	☐ Phone Sex	☐ Rimming
☐ Naturist	☐ S&M	☐ Sauna/Bath Houses	☐ Shaving	☐ Spanking
☐ Role Play	☐ Tickling	☐ Vacuum Pumping	☐ Vanilla	☐ Verbal/Gob
☐ Threesomes	☐ Wanking	☐ Watersports	☐ Wrestling	
☐ Voyeurs				

own X-rated pictures and videos into their profiles during this period. At higher commercial membership rates, it also enabled male escorts to operate from within the site, even providing a specialised chat room for these members. All of this, but particularly the provision of tools to facilitate the inclusion of male escorts, implied, as Light, Fletcher and Adam (2008) have also argued, that sex and the selling of sex in general (and male-male sex in particular) is considered unlikely to be morally concerning amongst gay men; that this demographic is more likely to tolerate and even purchase such services.

To anyone who has ever used an SNS designed for gay men, the appearance of these features and this kind of profile template in Gaydar will be unsurprising. As Mowlabocus (2010) has argued, one of the most powerful metanarratives influencing gay men's digital culture, in all its multifarious iterations, has been the discourse of 'cybercarnality' – a key aspect of which is the "pornographic remediation of the gay male body" (p. 58). Of course, however, as Mowlabocus (2010, p. 60) also points out, "it did not take digital technologies for men to become objects of a homoerotic gaze". Investment in this kind of aesthetic has characterised the gay press since its early beginnings in the pages of publications such as *Physique Pictorial* (1951), and it is still evident today in contemporary gay men's lifestyle magazines such as, *Attitude*, *Blue* and *DNA*, where cover images and fashion spreads tend unapologetically towards the pornographic. Indeed the work of gay historian Tom Waugh (1996, 2002) indicates that gay men have been looking at each other, as Mowlabocus puts it (2010, p. 60), 'in this way', for decades, using every medium available. Accordingly, erotic codings of gay male bodies, such as those woven into the fabric of Gaydar, have been historically significant in the gay community's struggle for social recognition. The importance of gay pornography as a legitimiser of homosexual desire – and therefore as a highly political text – for instance, has been well documented by scholars such as Dyer (1989), Clark (1991), Williams (1992), Strossen (1995), Waugh (1996), McNair (1996), McKee (2001) and many others. As McKee (2001, p. 3) indicates, "[p]ornography is never only about sex. It also presents images of the society in which it is produced, the identities which are available in that society and the forms of behaviour which it deems acceptable". Therefore, against a backdrop of long-standing and ongoing legal and societal discrimination, pornographic materials depicting and exploring gay male sexuality have provided information, entertainment and validation for gay men, and thus, as Strossen (1995, p. 167) notes, have served to 'educate, liberate and empower'. Hence, the discourse of sex that enveloped Gaydar in its original incarnation was part of a long and much broader history of gay male culture in which pornography had been a constitutive element of gay male identity. Indeed, in so far as it predates the establishment of metropolitan gay male subculture in Western societies, gay pornography, in all its forms, helped to "produce the 'homosexual'" (Mowlabocus, 2010, p. 66) – or, in the style of Foucault (1980, p. 43), 'transpose' it from simply a sexual practice into a social identity. 'Cybercarnality' (Mowlabocus, 2010) simply extended this process into new (digital) spaces, making it more visible and explicit.

The material reality of late capitalism has also been central to this process, expediting the transformation Foucault (1980) speaks of, by creating, as D'Emilio (1992, p. 269) argued, the conditions during the 1990s "for homosexual desire to express itself as a central component of some individual's lives". Although not unique to gay male subcultures, the culture of conspicuous consumption, for instance, has developed and flourished in these conditions. And in this environment, the gay male subject – produced as it was through the lens of pornographic imagery – was increasingly commodified. "The ideological dimension of capitalism", as Mowlabocus (2010, p. 70) argues, "interpellate[d] the gay male subject, both producing him and instructing him in the modes of consumption appropriate to his newly recognised and validated lifestyle". The shift in focus of GLBT publications from predominantly political issues associated with the liberation movement, to matters more focused on lifestyle and consumption during the late 20th century is indicative in this regard. Robinson, in her 2007 article on Queensland's queer press, noted that it was precisely this shift that had allowed for GLBT magazines to remain relevant to younger generations of gays and lesbians who did not identify with the GLBT rights movement of previous decades. She cautioned, however, that this relevance would continue only so long as "the queer press recognises that…society is in a state of flux and that ideas about sexuality and identity politics are constantly evolving" (p. 71). Failure to act on this principle and evolve quickly enough in line with changing social attitudes towards homosexuality during the 2000s is at the heart of the kinds of complaints, identified earlier, that young Gaydar users in this study made about the site being overly focused on sex. "The primary difference between existing media forms that incorporate the eroticised body of the gay man, and newer, digital environments", argues Mowlabocus (2010, p. 60), offering an explanation for this stagnation,

> is that while the former have evolved and adapted according to changing consumption practices and socio-political contexts, the latter are founded upon such processes; they are built out of, and cannot be imagined outside of, this erotic economy of gay male corporeality.

This economic aspect of the continued focus on sex and eroticised male bodies in gay men's digital spaces, at a time when the GLBT rights movement had begun to concentrate on issues such as gay marriage, was clear within Gaydar in 2010–2012. There is no doubt that Gaydar's evolution from a small start-up site in 1999 to a hugely successful marketing machine and award-winning global brand by 2007[6] was reliant on the commodification of metropolitan gay subculture and the ideas, aesthetics, identities and practices that go along with it. Prior to being bought by CPC Connect in 2013, even a cursory look at the website of Gaydar's parent company, QSoft Consulting, indicated that Gaydar was not just a social networking site, but a recognisable global brand. Full of statistics and marketing rhetoric, the site sold Gaydar to advertisers as a "one stop shop" for direct access to the lucrative gay and lesbian market and foregrounded its affiliations with a number of world famous brand names such as Harrods, British Airways, Sony, Gillette, Budget and many more.[7] In the interest of strengthening its own brand image and increasing market share, during the height of its popularity in the mid-2000s, Gaydar also elevated its level of integration in the everyday world of urban gay male culture through a range of digital and nondigital enterprises that surrounded and supported its central functioning as an SNS. Gaydar had its own award-winning digital radio station (Gaydar Radio) which played contemporary dance music and featured gay-oriented news and chat; it launched an iPhone app and android equivalent to incorporate smartphone availability; it started a blog; a Facebook page; Twitter, YouTube and Instagram accounts and, as noted above, also ran Manzone – a selection of pornographic products (including image and video galleries) and an online sex store – as an offshoot of its base SNS. In the UK, where Gaydar originates, a bar and a club ('Profile' and 'Lo-Profile', respectively) were also owned and operated by the site in London's gay village until 2013, and Gaydar has had a visible presence at major GLBT events, such as London Pride and Manchester Mardi Gras since its inception. In addition to sponsorship, as Mowlabocus (2010, p. 85) notes, this presence at UK GLBT events often came in the form of "a gang of muscle-bound men wearing white briefs and sporting the Gaydar logo on their bare chests, who g[a]ve out lanyards and whistles during the parades". While there have been no Gaydar-related bars or clubs to speak of in Australia, the site has been just as deeply embedded in traditional forms of metropolitan gay male subculture – and it's attendant focus on sex – in this country. For many years, we have seen, for example, the half-naked men Mowlabocus (2010) speaks of at our own Mardi Gras, fair days and other events. Thanks to Gaydar's success at geo-targeted advertising, as well as the clubs, GLBT health organisations and various products pertinent to this region, those events have also been consistently advertised to us in the banners and borders of the site itself.

Gaydar then has always had an unmistakable interest in the continuation of traditional forms of gay male subculture associated with the 'metropolitan model' (Sinfield, 1998) of homosexuality and in the existence of 'gay' men as a specific marketing demographic. It has been in the site's interest, as Light et al. (2008) explain, to commodify gay male sexuality and the series of normative identity constructions it encompasses. This is not, however, as Light et al. (2008) also note, any kind of conspiracy to "simply part gay men from their money" (p. 306), but more the reality of running and monetizing an SNS of Gaydar's scale. One of the side effects or byproducts of this situation, however, has clearly been the inscription into the platform of an implicit message about the place of sex in gay men's lives that, by 2010, when I began collecting data on Gaydar, did not resonate with the demographic of users studied in this project. It was there in the brand's types and styles of advertising, and moreover, in the existence of a digital infrastructure that organised user profiles around penis size, sexual fetishes and the like. It is not surprising therefore, that frustration with this element of the site's design was a central component of the culture of participatory reluctance that has shaped so many young Gaydar users' engagement with the site, influencing key aspects of the identity construction and participation styles observed among this cohort of users. Many of the focus group and interview participants in this study noted, for instance, that they purposely did not include anything overtly sexual in their Gaydar profiles – they uploaded only 'G' rated, or as they often referred to them, 'lifestyle' types of images; did not answer questions in the profile template about, for example, penis size or sexual fetishes and moreover, refused to acknowledge or reply to messages sent to them which directly offered or asked for sex, contained explicit images or were from users whose profiles were based on such images.

In a number of profile categories Gaydar offers users the option of selecting 'Rather Not Say'; it also allows for some categories that have not been filled out to be 'hidden', or effectively removed. For users in the current study, this was a popular mode of approaching the profile template. "[T]here's certain things that I don't click on", said one participant, "You know how you can hide certain things like cock size, just all different stuff like that? I don't use it in that sense of seedy things. All that's cut out and [my profile is] essentially like brown hair, brown eyes". For the reasons these users were on Gaydar, the 'seedy' categories, as they referred to them (e.g., penis size, circumcision status, sexual role and fetishes) were simply not relevant. As the following interviewee explained:

> [There's] a whole heap of stuff in [my profile about] both what I'm looking for and who I am, and that's often sometimes updated in anger because someone's shit me off…So, often, [the 'Looking For' section has] been: 'not interested in hooks ups', a couple of letters, 'STOP asking'. Even when… you write that, people still don't listen, they're still: 'so are you keen for something later tonight?' I'm like, 'well clearly you're illiterate, I don't know how you're writing to me', but anyway. So yeah, I haven't gone through and filled out like the leisure activities and what I'm into and things like that because, like I said, I'm not using it to hook up, so I don't think that me putting [what I'm into sexually] is going to be pertinent.

With respect to the images used in their profiles, these users took a similar approach: "I put my face pictures and stuff like that, like it's just…normal stuff, nothing sexual about it." "I just put my pictures like from when I'm travelling so it's not really about the sex part of the body", said one young student. "Just [a] genuine face picture, that's all" and "nothing exposed" said others. Their reasons for taking such an approach were mirrored almost exactly by users in other groups who also said they only uploaded face shots, because they, "basically just used [Gaydar] as a social networking tool". They were, "trying to make friends or [go on] dates, and just [meet] people in general, it wasn't so much around hooking up or anything like that". In fact, users in this study generally had a negative attitude towards the inclusion of erotic images in Gaydar profiles. "Photo wise", said one interviewee,

> it's always been a headshot. I think the most revealing photo I've had is I was lying on the beach for my birthday...but I never had my dick out or anything like that. To be honest, I think it's a bit degrading seeing guys that have got all that out on their page.

Erotic or pornographic images in messages from other users were also unwelcome – and in line with statistics from Gaydar itself showing that the average age of users with X-rated images is 64[8] – was often seen as something that only users in much older demographics engaged in. Discussing what kinds of private messages they would reply to, for instance, interviewees said:

> Yeah, I usually respond to everyone, [but] sometimes I won't respond to something, if it's like offering money for sex or something like that....Older people offering money for sex.
>
> It would definitely depend, like you'd get inundated with all of these old people just sending you pictures of their privates and I'd never respond to any of those.
>
> If someone writes and goes 'hey, you want to fuck', then...like I don't write back unless I want to be really rude and I've been drinking and I want to be blunt and [tell them where to go].
>
> **Participant A:** I actually find that a bit of a turn off when I like click on someone's profile [after they've messaged me] and it's just them bent over, picture and all, so yeah.
>
> **Participant B:** ...yeah the position of the cock picture [is an important determinant of whether I will respond or not] because it's like how can I determine whether you're young or not using your cock?
>
> Yeah, I generally ignore the [sexual] ones...I never send a 'no thanks' because, yeah, I think that makes you look better, seem better than you actually are, you're saying 'I'm too good for you'. So I just ignore.

Interestingly, ignoring unwanted messages rather than responding with a polite 'no thanks' was seen as acceptable because, while the interviewees saw themselves as polite people, they saw Gaydar in a very different light. "I understand the politeness thing", said one user, talking about his initial instinct to reply and politely decline, "but I guess" he continued, elaborating on his reasons for not doing so, "... it's not a polite site".

While there was certainly evidence in Gaydar's chatrooms, in users' profiles, in stories in GLBT magazines, on blogs, in academic research and in the many conversations I've had with people about my work on gay men's digital platforms, that Gaydar could be used 'politely' and that it has, in fact, been used for establishing successful long-term relationships, the *perception* that it could not function this way amongst the young gay men studied in this project (derived, rightly or wrongly, from the site's focus on sex and the erotic) had a second, and, arguably, more serious, side effect. Whereas the first symptom of Gaydar's orientation towards the sexual during the 2000s and early 2010s was simply frustration produced by the perception that the site did not function for the purposes that these users wanted it to, the second symptom of Gaydar's orientation towards the sexual during this period was the much more problematic issue of these young users believing themselves to be so unique amongst the gay community that they were, in a sense, alone. In 2010–2012, the idea popularly held amongst Gaydar users in the 18–28-year-old demographic in Brisbane that they were largely unique amongst members of the site was a product of these men holding a particular image of their fellow users that did not resonate with their own self-perceptions. The imagined user of Gaydar for these men was a stereotype of gay identity; he closely resembled the man described in the Sinfield (1998) model of metropolitan homosexuality. And, again, the digital infrastructure of Gaydar was not a neutral player in this situation. Herein lies the second element of the culture of participatory reluctance that surrounded young men's Gaydar use during 2010–2012.

Point of Reluctance #2 – Key Perceptions about Gaydar's Users/All the Men on Gaydar Are Walking Stereotypes – Except Me

When Joe Blogs, who I cited at the commencement of this chapter, noted in his 'About me' section that he wondered why he was putting a profile on Gaydar, he introduced this idea following a description of himself as someone with his life together; a smart guy with ambition, a fulfilling profession, a nice house in the city and a good bunch of friends (who, he made a point of adding, did not lead 'dramatic' lives or ever want to borrow money from him). In wondering why someone with these assets, material and otherwise, would bother putting a profile on Gaydar, this user clearly also turned his 'About me' section into an unambiguous description of his perceptions 'About you' – the imagined audience of Gaydar users. This is a classic example of the way that identity presentation often involves "a process of stereotyping or 'cognitive simplification' that allows people to distinguish easily between self and other, and to define themselves and their group in positive ways" (Buckingham, 2008, p. 6). The prevalence of this kind of approach to identity presentation, which works by stereotyping and implicitly denigrating 'others', is a key factor in explaining why Joe Blogs was not at all alone in filling out his 'About me' box in the manner that he did. In fact, thousands of other users in the 18–28-year-old demographic observed in this study took a very similar approach, indicating in the open text fields of their profiles that the 'group' who they perceived to be the typical users of Gaydar was not one which they themselves were part of.

Close observation of the open text fields in thousands of user profiles, and the dominant discourses found therein, indicates that the millions of words 18–28-year-old Gaydar users enlisted to perform their identities in these spaces during 2010–2012 can generally be summed up in just two: "I'm different". As the previous section indicates, the number one reason users believed themselves to be different to other men on Gaydar was that they were looking for something more than sex from the site. Beyond that however, whether directly or implicitly, over and over again, the main reasons users cited for being different included that they were nicer, more genuine or sincere, more educated or successful, more classy, more happy (or at the very least without 'issues' or 'hang-ups') and more 'normal' than other Gaydar users. These traits, along with repeated declarations that sex was not a motivating factor for using the site, were often given as evidence that a user was different from other men on Gaydar because – by apparent virtue of these traits – they were therefore not a gay stereotype or anything like other men on the gay 'scene'.

With the sheer abundance of profiles on Gaydar belonging to 18–28-year-olds where this kind of rhetoric was employed, choosing just a few to illustrate the above point is difficult. There were users who made these kinds of statements about their perceived differences directly:

> Hi! Nice to meet you. I am a little different to most guys. Class!
>
> I am a guy who likes to meet nie people... please be little sensitive and sensible when you talk to me, I'm not like most of the guys on here.
>
> I'm not 'run of the mill' and won't pretend to be like most guys on here. I'm 'deeper' than most, with a strong sense of reality and what I want out of it. ...I'm intelligent but not arrogant about it. I'm alternative but not for the sake of nonconformity.
>
> I am happy being me...I am not average, I don't fit in to the norm and nor do I want to.

And there were those that took a more indirect route, announcing their perceived point of difference from other Gaydar users through profile headlines framed as rhetorical questions or as remarks directly addressed to the profile reader:

> Where are all the nice guys???
> Is normal too much to ask for?
> Probably too smart for you

Your all a f*ing waste of time!
Are there any guys who aren't cunts?

For the majority, however, the message "I'm different" was spelled out through references (both direct and otherwise) to the various gay stereotypes users believed they were not – which, in turn, clearly illuminated not only the imagined audience of these users, but also the process of "cognitive simplification" Buckingham (2008, p. 6) notes we use when distinguishing ourselves from 'others':

> I don't fit in well with gay people cos I have certain codes I won't break (i.e. don't sleep with a mates ex, don't cheat etc.), 95% of my mates are straight, but also because I believe if you fall in love it shouldn't matter what their gender is.
>
> country bogan boy at heart and…im a hell of a lot hotter then the tragic city faggs in this town who think there the sh*t but are just a sh*t stain of makeup.…I want a str8 acting man, no queens or shoppers, I want strings and lots of them.
>
> I believe in trust, equality, communication and commitment, perhaps somewhat old fashioned in todays gay society, but that's what separates me from all the clone zone ga-ga bois on here.
>
> Love the country, hate small fluffy dogs and hoping to meet somebody (in the long term sense) who agrees with me on both fronts.
>
> Iso genuine, dte, decent guys with depth and substance for mates and dates… Must not be a shallow, two-faced, scene queen. If you're a regular at the wickham/beat we won't get along.
>
> dude that's NORMAL…foreign concept i know. [Looking For] no queens, bitchiness, unintelligent, self-centred Neanderthals… hmm… hang on…that's half the town ruled out :S I would just like ppl to be normal…
>
> Chilled, laid back, fun, sorted socially and professionally…NOT a gaydar freak! [Looking For] Sorted lad with similar interests…has their own "thing" going on. AGAIN…NOT a gaydar freak…!;) My filter is pretty good so best not to try…!:)

As the comments above indicate, the kinds of 'normal' identities that these users described themselves as having and which – to their obvious distress – they perceived to be lacking amongst the 'freaks' of the Gaydar community, were comprised of character traits which fit outside of the metropolitan model of homosexuality. Deriding anything camp or related in any way to typical commercial gay scenes, as portrayed by Sinfield's (1998) model, these users framed themselves as what can only be described as 'post-gay' – where their homosexuality is related (as it was in the times prior to the liberation movement of the 20th century) to sexual desire alone, rather than a particular lifestyle or identity. In vehemently trying to disassociate themselves from stereotypes commonly associated with the gay community, however, the tautological connections that have been forged between orientation and identity were often simply reinforced. 'I am not like most gay people', they argued, because gay people, according to the above comments, are "tragic", "shallow, two-faced scene queen[s]" and "unintelligent, self-centred Neanderthals" who lead "dramatic lives" and don't believe in "trust, equality, communication [or] commitment". In fact, despite their own sexuality standing as proof that not all gay men could be pigeonholed in this manner, characterisations of this kind were particularly common amongst 18–28-year-old users of the site. "I don't define myself by my sexuality" they might say, "...because let's face it, most gays are boring. There's more to nightlife than The Beat. There's more to music than Lady Gaga. And plucked eyebrows...No. Just no".

Carrying out this research as a 20 something gay man, it saddened me to see so many young Gaydar users making these comments. Firstly, because it indicated that the opinions my peers were inclined to hold of each other were incredibly low. And secondly, because it indicated that there were many young gay men feeling othered and isolated in a community that they initially sought out to provide them with a sense of belonging. One hundred per cent of the men interviewed in this study, for instance, noted that they had signed up to Gaydar as teenagers (either before or around the required age of 18) because, at the time, they simply did not know any other gay men. After announcing that he had originally lied about his age to sign up to Gaydar in his early teens, for instance, I asked one of the focus group participants what he was using the site for at that time. Twenty years of age at the time of the focus group, he replied: "Just because I was uncomfortable and because I lived in a small town and knowing I was gay...just so I could talk to people, find out stuff". One user who had attended a male-only boarding school had a similar story. He had signed up to the site in the mid-2000s whilst underage for what he called "accessibility reasons" as well, and noted that he used the site much more frequently during that period than he did at the time of the focus group, as an adult. "I went to a boarding school. So my [only] access really to other gay guys was on Gaydar", he said. And in every focus group, as these kinds of stories were relayed, participants around the room would concur, chiming in with their own tales of how, in the years prior, they too had signed up to Gaydar in the search for like-minded others.

The user comments cited earlier that quite acerbically claim each of their author's dissimilarity from all other members of the site, however, suggest that very few of the young men who signed up to Gaydar with these intentions ever found that kind of connection. When focus group participants were asked if they had found that sense of belonging on Gaydar – if the site had helped them to feel part of a 'gay community' – the response was also a resounding 'no'. Interestingly, though, this 'no' was generally preceded by examples of how Gaydar *had* helped plug these men into the local gay community. For example, one participant said that Gaydar did not help him to *feel* connected to Brisbane's gay community but that it did help him to "pinpoint it". When asked to clarify this statement he said, "Like you know, oh look, thousands of people are online. Wow, I didn't realise there were that many gay people in Brisbane. There are more of us than I thought!" In addition to helping users "pinpoint" the city's gay community, participants noted throughout the focus group discussions that they had made new gay friends via Gaydar; that they had bonded within their existing friendships over discussions of the site and its users; and that they had attended GLBT events sponsored by the site. These apparent benefits, however, were easily forgotten or deemed as being outweighed in discussions of the site's community bonding credentials by what interviewees referred to as the site's "counterproductive" elements. "There's definitely a Brisbane gay community that I am part of I suppose", said one man, "because I've got other friends that are gay and we've all had similar experiences... but yeah, I don't think that has any relation to Gaydar or what Gaydar's purpose is". Gaydar's purpose, he said, was "for people to have sex". In terms of its ability to foster a sense of community belonging, he later added, "I think it can be a bit counterproductive". Referring to the fact that Brisbane is a small city and that use of Gaydar during the height of its success quickly ensured familiarity with many of the men both on the site and in the local gay community, he argued that users' openness to new people in general was stymied by the site in Brisbane.

> [Y]ou've got a pre-conceived notion in your head about what that person is and then you know so much about someone...from their pictures and what they've written, you've created your own opinion of them, so therefore you're not as likely to go and engage with them [if you saw them in public ordinarily], but you might have if you hadn't already got that.

Because of its apparent tendency to encourage users to prejudge and evaluate each other in this way, and because users' impressions of the site's purpose lent themself to the construction amongst this cohort of an imagined audience of sexual deviants, for the men in this study, the benefits of Gaydar membership certainly did not include feeling part of a community of like-minded people. As one interviewee put it, "as much as [it is] part of the gay community, I don't feel a part of a gay community on Gaydar".

In fact, feeling othered in this space was a much more common outcome. Take, for example, the user below who indicated through his profile blurb that he felt unique within the gay community as it was embodied on Gaydar at the time to an extent that the idea of resigning himself to a traditional heterosexual life seemed like a more amenable option:

> My sexuality is the least interesting thing about me. I'm sick of fag boys who behave like girls...you know, the ones who idolise Britney Spears and pluck their eyebrows and think The Beat is cool? Gaydar and its similar sites [are] somewhat depressing...as are gay bars. Is this all there is if you want to find companionship? If so, time to give up. You know get married, have 2.4 kids, a mortgage and a holden...

What is most unsettling about this situation, of course, is that the young man above was not at all alone. The sheer number of users whose profiles suggested feelings of significant isolation and frustration stemming from perceptions of themselves as entirely different from all other gay men was, in fact, evidence that this demographic of Gaydar users actually had much more in common than they tended to believe. At the time of data collection, there were thousands of 18–28-year-old gay men using Gaydar, for instance, in the hope of finding a committed relationship. There were also thousands of 18–28-year-old gay men in Brisbane using the site whose lifestyles and identities were far removed from those stereotypically associated with gay male subculture. In most cases, though, these users simply failed to see this reality. It was a situation that reminded me in many ways of the hugely successful sketch comedy show *Little Britain* (2003–2007), where the character Daffyd Thomas wanders around his local town, Llanddewi Brefi, constantly deflated because he perceives himself to be "the only gay in the village" – a lament he defiantly repeats to anyone and everyone who will listen. What Daffyd, in his hilarious collection of tight PVC and rubber clothing, fails to see as he repeats his catchcry ad nauseum is that his local village is actually full of GLBT characters just like him. Numerous attempts from Daffyd's lesbian friend Myfanwy to encourage him to meet other gay men or join gay men's groups in the area all fall flat, as Daffyd's insistence that he is the "only gay" in Llanddewi Brefi sees him constantly rejecting and insulting the village's other homosexual characters – and, more often than not, flatly refusing to acknowledge their gay authenticity amidst a barrage of ridiculous stereotypes. In short, Daffyd's loneliness is a product of his own inability to see that which is actually all around him. And it is a situation not too far removed from that of many of the Gaydar users I have quoted above.

This is not to suggest that in seeing themselves as exceptionally different from their peers, young Gaydar users in this study were simply ignorant or unperceptive. Again, the site's digital infrastructure played a large role. Given that Gaydar is a cultural artefact that both influences and is informed by contemporary social and cultural attitudes and beliefs (Light, 2007), while it would be foolish to blame the site alone for the culture of participatory reluctance and the "Am I the only good gay in the village?" attitude that has tended to appear on the site, the identity templates provided for users have certainly been a contributing factor. As Ben Light (2007) has argued, the software used within Gaydar to construct user profiles during QSoft's ownership of the site contributed to the "shaping of a particular range of masculinities" as the only ones available to gay men and resulted in the "intended and unintended categorisation of members" into groups with identities that were already "well known within the gay community" (p. 661). Standardised versions of these masculinities, based on differences in age, body type, clothing, lifestyle and sexual activity preferences were evident in many areas of the site, but were most obvious, as Light (2007, p. 661) also notes, where 'Keywords' categories and subcategories were implemented. The 'Types I Like' section of the profile template, for example, was the most explicit in terms of offering particular kinds of masculinities that gay male users might express an interest in being, and being associated with (see Table 3.1). Some of the categories offered in the 'Types I Like' list, such as 'Bears' and 'Twinks', are quite specific to the gay community, but most others (e.g., Builders, Footballers and Policemen) can be linked to more mainstream notions of what it means to be masculine, particularly in the Western world (Light, 2007). Hence, in this one element of the site alone, it is possible to see how the digital infrastructure of Gaydar functioned to preference certain masculinities and forms of identity, which could directly and indirectly subordinate and marginalize those within the user community. Although based on practical considerations to create the most efficient marketplace for both advertising and consumption, as Payne (2007, p. 532) notes, by operating in this fashion Gaydar worked to fix the possibilities of gay identity and desire "to an easily legible typology" where various kinds of 'gayness' were "discursively set up oppositionally or competitively".

This mechanization of identity performance, where Gaydar users were supposed to choose menu-style a particular kind of 'gayness' that they most identify with from a reductive typology of identities (which, as Light (2007) has also argued, are not presented as equally valid) is at the very root of the culture of participatory reluctance that has appeared throughout the site since the mid-2000s. It helps to explain the approach to identity presentation taken by users who choose to simply leave large portions of their profile blank – as many interviewees in this study noted they did for the purpose of resisting or defying the site's focus on sex. And it also underpins the tendency of users to approach the few free-text elements of Gaydar profiles with the aim of professing their individuality; usually by making claims such as "probably too smart for you" and utilizing the kind of antagonistic rhetoric employed by Joe Blogs and other users who I have cited above. These approaches to identity management and the kind of hostile rhetoric used to indicate difference, which is entwined in these performances, can be read as discursive attempts to resist being simplistically categorized. Simultaneously, they also produce, as Payne (2007, p. 532) indicates, "identity territorialism that requires the negation of other claimants to the grounds of gayness and masculinity" (Payne, 2007, p. 532). Given that the site's design has constrained people's abilities to control their own identity performance through the heavy use of drop-down menus and tick-box categories, it is possible then to better understand why users of Gaydar at this time might have made a point to indicate that they did not define themselves by their sexuality, or why a teenager might have noted on his profile that "I'm not a queen or a butch homo im just me". It also helps to explain, as Payne (2007) has argued in his paper on the phenomenon of "str8acting", why users who rejected the identity labels offered via the site itself, often then asserted themselves and their own identities by denigrating others using references to yet more reductive labels and stereotypes: in some of the text quoted from user profiles above, for example, it is evident that labels such as 'scene queen', 'clones' and 'ga-ga bois' featured prominently on the site during this study as descriptors of users' interpretations of negative gay identities. The circulation of labels such as these also ties in to another reason that Gaydar users in this study resisted the reductive typology of masculinities offered to them via the site's profile template. To put it most simply, interviewees saw the subsets of gay identity (e.g., 'Types I like' categories) offered to them via Gaydar as being outdated, as labels belonging to a different generation. "[Y] ou used to be gay and then belong to a subsection of the community", noted one focus group participant, discussing the redundant nature of terms like 'bear' and 'twink', "but now it's not really the case", he said. Making a similar point about both the site's focus on sex and its use of reductive identity labels, another young user, clearly accusing the site of being dated, wrote in his profile, "You'd think by now being a new century and millennium we'd overhaul these sites...".

This user's reference here to the plural 'sites' is also significant. Gaydar's similarity to other niche SNSs designed for the gay male community was the third major factor that contributed to the culture of participatory reluctance that defined use of the site by 18–28-year-olds in this study. Having no genuine alternative in terms of niche SNSs designed for the gay male community, the frustrations that these users already experienced as a result of the site's implicit focus on sex and its championing and of a limited range of highly commodified gay male identities, which did not resonate with their own self-perceptions, were simply magnified.

Point of Reluctance #3 – No Genuine Alternatives among Existing Niche SNSs Designed for Gay Men

In *The Big Book of Gaydar* (JockBoy26, 2010), published by Gaydar's founders QSoft, there is a series of different chapters dedicated to advising users on how to best go about filling out the site's profile template: 'Who Do You Think You Are? Selling Yourself in Words?' and 'What Do You Look Like? Selling Yourself in Pictures'. In the former, QSoft advises users against including any kind of negativity in their profiles and tries to discourage leaving parts of the template blank. In the camp tone that runs through the entire publication, they also note that, "Slagging off Gaydar is funny. But it's sort of like standing in a club talking about how much you hate it. If you hate it that much," they argue, "go home! And if you don't," they add, "shut up and stay and say something nice, you bitchy little queen" (JockBoy26, 2010, p. 8). All jokes aside, the problem with this statement is that, during the 2000s, leaving the metaphorical 'club' that was Gaydar in search of a genuine alternative really did mean effectively going home. As Mowlabocus (2010) has also pointed out, although gay male digital culture is far greater than Gaydar alone, the many other sites that sold themselves as its competitors during this period were in fact "peddling the same types of experiences, the same types of bodies and the same ideological messages" (p. 84). Indeed, 'cybercarnality' (Mowlabocus, 2010) would not have worked as a framework through which gay male digital culture could be understood if this was not the case. Hence, while it is certainly true that not all gay men use these kinds of SNSs, the level of integration that they have enjoyed in wider gay male culture (as discussed in Chapters 1 and 2) does suggest that opting out during this period was, in many ways, akin to choosing to isolate oneself from that community. For this reason, users in this study continued to maintain profiles on Gaydar, despite their relationships with the site often being defined by abhorrence – both of the site itself and its imagined audience.

As these feelings percolated down into users' identity management techniques and interactions with other users the culture of participatory reluctance became cyclical, as users read and responded to others on the site in a manner that matched their already low expectations. Excusing their own failures to be polite because "it's not a polite site", for instance, simply created this reality. Not all Gaydar users were unaware of this irony either. "I think anything you do on those websites is self-inflicted..." said one interviewee, "It's the way you represent yourself really." There were also users who employed the free text of their own profiles, writing, for example, "let's be nice to each other!", to implore civility on the site. Interestingly, however, the few users who made these kinds of statements during the interview process conducted for this study also admitted to ignoring messages from other users and to judging others differently for performing/presenting their identities on the site using similar techniques that they themselves had employed. Leaving areas of their own profiles blank, for example, was a means for interviewees to resist the site's structural focus on sex. When other users left areas of their profiles blank, however, interviewees noted that this was obviously an indication the profile's owner was using the site simply as an avenue to procure sex – their profile left unfilled because it functioned simply as a means of gaining access to the site's erotic images, and the men attached to them. An explanation for this situation, these seemingly obvious double standards, and this tendency to slip into the roles and behaviours which defined the culture of the site, but which they themselves detested, can be found in Butler's (1990) discussions of performativity.

Drawing on Foucault's rejection of the 'sexed' body, Butler (1990, p. 92) argues that the 'body gains meaning in discourse only in the specific context of power relations' and that 'sexuality is an historically specific organization of power, discourse, bodies and affectivity'. That is, when we perform/present our gender and sexuality – and indeed any other aspects of our identities – whether that be offline or via the 'curation' (Hogan, 2011) of various images and elements of text in an online social networking environment, we are engaging in a dialogue/discourse that precedes us, or which is not all our own making. Butler's theory of performativity "does not assume that there is an original which such parodic identities imitate...[i]ndeed the parody is *of* the very notion of an original" (p. 138). Hence, when Gaydar users are performing or presenting their identities within the bounds of the SNS they are engaging in an already existing dialogue about gay male identity established by the infrastructure of the site, and even before that – because Gaydar is a cultural artefact also embedded in a much larger social and cultural context. Through Gaydar's reinforcing of the metropolitan model of homosexuality in its very digital infrastructure during the years of its market dominance throughout the 2000s, users' presentations of identity in this space were necessarily produced in response to the ideas about gay male identity encoded in that model. In this context, the identities and identity management practices most commonly seen in this study within Gaydar amongst young users, defined as they were by the culture of participatory reluctance and by frustration with and rejection of stereotypical gay male identities, make sense. This also indicates, however, that without a significant change in the discourses about gay male identity embedded in the site by its new owners CPC Connect, the kind of identity territorialism that arose from clashes between young users' self-perceptions and their perceptions of the imagined audience of Gaydar in the 2000s will likely continue, meaning that so too might the sense of isolation many young gay men feel when using the service.

So Where to from Here?

Whether it was Gaydar's focus on sex and the erotic, or its implicit indication that there exists a limited range of reductive and outdated identities available to contemporary gay men, during this study, young users of the site in Brisbane were clearly logging on and engaging with Gaydar in a state of participatory reluctance. They would much rather not have not been on it: evidence of dismissive and hostile attitudes towards the site and its imagined audience were found at every turn. Users suggested repeatedly, for example, that mere association with Gaydar could be damaging to one's reputation. One 23–year-old user I came across during the site analysis phase of the project, who did not have a picture on his profile, for instance, said that he had made the decision not to identify himself because he "[didn't] wanna be 'that gaydar guy' you see at Coles".[9] This was not about ensuring he was not 'outed' as a gay man, but in aide of preventing others from knowing that he used the site. Simply being recognized as a user, for instance, opened one up to being labelled – as the discourse employed by interviewees in this study suggests – a "tragic mole". In fact, so ingrained in these users was the idea that Gaydar was not a positive site to be associated with, that the need to justify one's own membership was not uncommon. "Please don't ask me why I'm on this site," wrote one young professional in his profile's 'About Me' section,

> I usually date locally but I'm pretty busy and it allows me to meet people from different parts of the world. Just because you are on a site doesn't mean that you are desperate or that you are a jerk. I've never had a problem dating but I'm serious about settling down. I'm just a regular boy next door type.

In *Gay and After* (1998) Sinfield wrote of the metropolitan model of homosexuality that "we have to entertain the thought that 'gay' as we have produced it and lived it, and perhaps 'lesbian' also, are historical phenomena and may now be hindering us more than they help us" (p. 5). By perpetuating the ideas, aesthetics, identities and practices associated with this model of homosexuality during the 2000s through its own infrastructure, Gaydar too may have been hindering us more than it helped us. The cultures and practices most common amongst young people using the site examined in this study, for example, suggests that Gaydar's infrastructure promoted "identity territorialism" (Payne, 2007), and encouraged users to be dismissive not just of the site itself, but of each other and the broader gay community in general. As one interviewee put it, "all I ever read is people's profiles saying how much they hate other gay people". At a time when bullying and suicide linked to one's sexuality is becoming a topic of great concern in many Western nations and GLBT people in Australia still suffer from anxiety and depression at rates much higher than the rest of the population (Leonard et al., 2012), this is a significantly problematic situation. As noted earlier, every person interviewed for this study said that they had used Gaydar well before the age of 18 to explore their sexuality and to try to connect with a community of like-minded people. Whether the reason they gave was because they had grown up in the country, were attending boarding school, or were simply living in the suburbs but unable to access local gay venues because they were yet to hold a driver license or turn 18, they all revealed, in one way or another, that they had originally signed up to Gaydar because, "I was young [and] didn't know a lot of gay people". That is, they had all originally signed up seeking to find a sense of community. Instead of the site working to provide them the kind of "identity demarginalization" that McKenna and Bargh (1998) found Usenet groups provided for homosexuals in the late 1990s, though, it appears from these findings that Gaydar may have simply been fostering yet more feelings of isolation.

While the arrival of more mainstream SNSs, such as Facebook, did not simply put an end to this situation by providing an all-encompassing alternate space (or 'new Gaydar') for these men, as I noted in the introduction to this book, it certainly worked to alter and extend the ways that they could participate in gay men's digital cultures. In the next chapter, we will therefore examine how the identity management and community engagement practices these young men had employed within Gaydar fit into and informed their experiences with Facebook. And, importantly, how the culture of participatory reluctance within the Gaydar was not ameliorated, but rather magnified, by the converging of the user cultures and practices surrounding these two platforms.

Notes

1 "What you want, when you want it" was Gaydar's marketing slogan throughout the 2000s until its recent takeover by CPC Connect.

2 Connections such as those described in the anecdotes that began this book; in the December 19, 2007 entry, 'Is Facebook the new Gaydar' on Awkward Sex in the City (E, 2007); and, on the cover blurb for The Big Book of Gaydar (JockBoy26, 2010).

3 Interestingly, during the data collection period, in the 18–28-year-old demographic, users interested in 'group sex' returned less search results than any other (older) age category, suggesting that group sex is an activity much less sought after by younger Gaydar users than it is by their older counterparts.

4 This is not to say that interviewees had never had sex with men they had met from Gaydar. More than half of the focus group participants in this study reported that they had used Gaydar (whether successfully or unsuccessfully) to "hook up" on at least one occasion. This, however, was not their core reason for using the site. Overwhelmingly, the core reason for using the site was reported to be finding new friends and going on dates that might lead

to a committed relationship. Interestingly, the focus group participants who noted that they had used Gaydar to find a 'hook up' were also slightly older (i.e., closer to 28 than to 18) than those who said they had never used the site in this way.

5 Two focus group participants had forged long-term relationships as a result of interactions on Gaydar, for example. In line with statistics provided by QSoft, which suggests that 88 per cent of users have made friends through the site (JockBoy26, 2010, p. 37), most interviewees also noted that they too had expanded their social circles as a result of using Gaydar.

6 In 2007 Gaydar was awarded a spot on the British 'Cool Brands' list alongside other premium brands such as Aston Martin, Bang & Olufsen, Apple, Mini and Google (QSoft, 2010).

7 While the website of QSoft consulting no longer exists in the form described here, the website of CPC Connect (www.cpcconnect.co.uk) corroborates this information in its telling of Gaydar's history.

8 See QSoft's list of user statistics on pages 24 and 25 of The Big Book of Gaydar (JockBoy26, 2010).

9 Coles is a leading Australian supermarket chain.

4 Facebook and Its Role in Gaydar Cultures

In her early discussions of social networking sites (SNSs) in the context of the rise (and fall) of Friendster, danah boyd (2008c) wrote about gay men's tendencies to use mainstream SNSs as 'gay dating sites'. Being amongst the earliest adopters of Friendster, during its initial growth period, gay-identified users in New York perceived gay dating to be the site's purpose and invited other gay men (boyd, 2008c). While Friendster itself did not last, due, among other things, to a crumbling database and large-scale user abandonment, the extension of gay men's networks into mainstream social networking did not stop there. The expansion of Facebook beyond collegiate boundaries in the mid-2000s allowed for a very similar pattern of behaviour. Indeed, as I noted in the introduction to this book, when Facebook began achieving popularity in Australia, for example, it was initially touted amongst some in the gay community as 'the new Gaydar'. Encouraged by my peers, I first signed up to Facebook under these assumptions.

By signing up to Facebook in 2007, I took my (then) total number of social networking profiles to five. Like many others in the gay male community,[1] I was already a member of multiple niche SNSs designed for gay men. In addition to Gaydar, I was also on Manhunt, Manjam and Gayromeo. Each of these profiles had been progressively established in line with the also expanding social media portfolios of my close group of gay male peers. Progressively signing up over the previous years to each of these sites was always an act of hope for something different – that the newest site and the newest bunch of users with whom we could then interact would be somehow different from the last. Namely, less oriented towards (casual) sex and the erotic. Regardless of the site, however, this was never the case. As noted in the previous chapter, and, as argued by Mowlabocus (2010), niche social networking services designed for gay men throughout the 2000s were incredibly similar in their tendencies towards the 'cybercarnal'. Hence, despite their different names, claims and branding strategies, and from wherever in the world they originated, underneath it all, the assortment of gay-oriented SNSs my friends and I continued signing up for during this period all offered essentially the same experiences. The digital infrastructure on which they were built cultivated the same cultures and practices with regard to identity management that proliferated on Gaydar, and the same culture of participatory reluctance too. With no real alternative, however, we nevertheless kept them all; using the more populated sites with greater frequency than the others, and always hoping that, collectively, these spaces would offer us a better chance of happening upon the kinds of people and interactions we sought than they each did alone.

Facebook, though, was – and is – genuinely different from these sites, both culturally and in terms of its mechanics. For starters, as opposed to online 'nicks' or handles, it is based around real name profiles. Just as significantly, it is also a mainstream social networking site designed for no particular group of users. It is intended, as its tag line indicates, to help users "connect and share with the people in [their] life" (www.facebook.com). Given these features, adding Facebook to the mix of social networking sites my friends and I already used quickly impacted upon the way I perceived and engaged with SNSs, both as they are used in the gay male community, as well as in a more general sense. It also had tangible implications for my interactions in the broader gay community offline, at GLBT venues and events. Data from this study suggests that I was certainly not alone in this experience.

As important social spaces deeply embedded in gay male culture (Mowlabocus, 2010), any change – however slight – in users' engagements with and understandings of SNSs designed for the gay male audience is significant. While Facebook is certainly not, as it was once imagined in some quarters, 'the new Gaydar', exploring the roles that mainstream social networking services now play in gay men's digital culture will help us to better understand the ways that this community is changing and how SNSs and other online services aimed at this demographic can best change with it. This chapter contributes to that project by providing an in-depth discussion of some of the ways that Facebook has shaped the perception and experience of identity management work in social networking environments for gay male users of these technologies. To this end, it first provides an examination of Facebook's affordances with regards to identity management options as they stood in 2010 – in particular, vis-à-vis GLBT-specific SNSs from the same period, such as Gaydar. It then looks at how the service was immediately taken up and embraced by the 18–28-year-old gay men in Brisbane who are at the centre of this study, to extend, verify, connect with and navigate gay men's social networks. Based on the experiences of these users, the chapter argues that Facebook's digital infrastructure has functioned to open up niche SNSs designed for gay men, such as Gaydar, to further criticisms of the kind described in the previous chapter, already levelled at them by their users. It contends that, for those with experience of both sites, Facebook simply exacerbated Gaydar's emphasis on sex, its implicit championing of a few particular forms of gay male identity associated with the Sinfield (1998) model, and thus, the culture of participatory reluctance underpinned by these aspects of the site. As I will show here, this is because Facebook's arrival provided a framework in which a much wider range of GLBT identities could be expressed in a fashion that makes homosexuality, ostensibly, banal.

Facebook's GLBT-Friendly Credentials

In June every year, the Gay and Lesbian Alliance Against Defamation (GLAAD) hosts its annual Media Awards in San Francisco, California. Now in their 27th year, these awards recognize those people and organisations that produce and promote "fair, accurate and inclusive representations" (GLAAD, 2016) of the GLBT community in television, journalism, music and other media outlets. In 2012, a Special Recognition Award was presented at this event to Facebook for its efforts in support of GLBT-centred anti-bullying campaigns and initiatives and for its inclusion of various profile options – such as same-sex-relationship statuses – to accommodate GLBT users of the site. In receiving this award, Facebook became the first social media company to be honoured by GLAAD.

Over the preceding two years, Facebook had indeed done much to increase its standing as a GLBT-friendly service, both creating and supporting a number of initiatives that helped promote and enable GLBT rights and equality. In 2010, in light of a recent spate of youth suicides in the United States as a result of anti-GLBT bullying, in conjunction with GLAAD (www.glaad.org), MTV's 'A Thin Line' (www.athinline.org/) campaign, the Human Rights Campaign (HRC) (www.hrc.org/), the Trevor Project (www.thetrevorproject.org/), the Gay, Lesbian and Straight Education Network (GLSEN) (www.glsen.org), and Parents, Families & Friends of Lesbians and Gays (PFLAG) (www.pflag.org), the company launched the 'Network of Support', to help them "effectively address issues faced by the lesbian, gay, bisexual and transgender community", and to work together with these organisations to "provide better resources for GLBT teens and everyone who wants to keep the Internet a safe place" (Facebook, 2010). Soon after, Facebook launched the 'Stop Bullying: Speak Up' campaign with Time Warner,[2] which aimed to empower students, teachers and parents to help prevent bullying. The company also added Help Centre content to its site that provided guidance on how users could assist a GLBT person who had posted suicidal content on Facebook (Facebook Help Centre, 2010).

While these kinds of high-profile, official initiatives likely hastened the arrival of greater rights for GLBT people in many jurisdictions by helping to keep such issues on the public agenda, according to the data gathered for this project, it is primarily what the company has not done with its service that has made it a leading avenue for "fair, accurate and inclusive representations" of the GLBT community online. In short, the most inclusive aspect of Facebook's service for young members of the GLBT community appears to be that it is an environment where people need not label their sexuality at all – the site simply does not ask its users to do so. Thereby, Facebook leaves the option of if, and or how, to express one's sexuality largely up to individual users.

When filling in the template to create a Facebook profile at the time data for this project was gathered there were a series of areas where users could provide information about themselves in predefined categories and subcategories. Using a combination of drop-down menus and free-text boxes, these categories included 'Work and Education'; 'Living' (where users could indicate their current city and their home town); 'Relationships and Family'; 'About You' (a text box where users were invited to simply write about themselves); 'Basic Info'; 'Contact Info'; and 'Favourite Quotations'. Beyond providing Facebook with a name and email address, however, 'Gender' and 'Birthdate' (both subcategories of the Basic Information section) were the only required elements for a profile to be activated. Sexuality, was, arguably, not ever addressed. As seen below in Figure 4.1, for instance, the 'Basic Information' subcategory 'Interested In', which provided the two (non-mutually exclusive) options 'Women' and 'Men', can be interpreted in a number of ways. Almost half of the interviewees in this study commented, for example, that they presumed the template was inquiring about the kinds of people they were interested in networking with – and therefore, that, despite being gay men, they had ticked the boxes for both men and women, as they were happy to socialise and network through Facebook with people of both genders. "I'm interested in men and women, well not sexually, but I don't think that was the purpose of the question", said one interviewee, "…If it says who do I like to root [then that would be different]".

Other users in the focus groups conducted, however, did presume that the 'Interested In' subsection of the profile template related to sexuality. For these men, the option to identify as homosexual in this way was either left or taken up depending on a whole host of social factors,

Figure 4.1 Facebook profile template 'Basic Information' and 'Interested In' subsections.

including where they worked, whether or not they had already come out (and to who they had come out), who they had 'friended' on the site, and to what extent they believed that directly announcing or broadcasting one's sexuality is necessary or appropriate. One interviewee who worked in politics, for instance, linked his Facebook to his partner's profile and happily listed himself as 'In a Relationship With' another man (via the 'Relationships and Family' section of the template), but chose not to identify himself as 'Interested in' men via the tick box provided. "Well, I never put anything controversial on there" he said.

> I find that working in politics like I do, you can't really put anything controversial on there. So the next best thing is just to let people know that you're still alive, just mention small ironies and day-to-day things that you do that nobody could ever possibly be offended by.

The act of linking to his partner's profile, "probably does the trick in terms of letting everybody know", he later added, suggesting he preferred this means of identifying himself as same-sex attracted to overtly claiming an orientation by selecting it from a box or drop-down menu. Other interviewees made similar choices based around concern and respect for their families. Speaking about his reasons for not filling in the 'Interested In' element of his Facebook profile, for instance, one user who had grown up in a conservative country town and who had family members in his Facebook network said that,

> [E]ven though [my family] all know [that I am gay], I just don't like I guess rubbing in their face that I am – I mean, every now and then I'll make a comment on something that would indicate that I am [gay], but I don't have the Pride flag on my profile like some people do.

For other interviewees, who had no problem with claiming or expressing their homosexuality on Facebook in the presence of connected family members, and who also presumed the 'Interested in' box relates to sexuality, ticking 'Men' was done without a second thought.

Whether interpreted as relating to one's sexuality or simply to whom users would prefer to network with, Facebook's use of the polysemic phrase 'Interested in' is important. So, too, is the fact that this section of the profile is entirely optional. As boyd (2002, p. 31) has argued, "[t]he intricate processes that comprise all social interaction are embedded in the underlying assumptions that can be made about the environment in which the interaction occurs". Hence, within the Facebook environment, underlying assumptions about the site, based on users interpreting 'Interested in' in a non-sexual manner, may include the idea that one's sexuality is largely irrelevant in social interactions occurring therein.[3] This is simply due to the fact that this non-sexual interpretation of the phrase erases Facebook of any concern for users' sexuality entirely. Quite significantly, for users interpreting 'Interested in' in a manner *directly* related to sexual orientation, this assumption about Facebook's positioning of sexuality as largely irrelevant in social interactions occurring via the site can be taken one step further. Assumptions about the site based on this interpretation, for example, may include, not only the idea that sexual orientation is not a crucial factor in social interactions occurring in this environment (due to the optional nature of the question), but also the additional idea that particular forms of sexual attraction are not tautologically linked in Facebook to a specific lifestyle or identity. Unlike Gaydar, for instance, which compels users to identify as either 'gay' or 'bisexual' – and, of course, presumes such identification through its very name – Facebook does not implicitly link interest in either men or women (or both) to a particular identity label or brand of sexuality. By extension, the site is therefore also precluded through its own design from legitimizing any one particular form of gay male identity; or, indeed, from taxonimising it at all. The kinds of identity subcategories utilized in Gaydar, such as 'Twinks', 'Bears' and 'Leather Men', for example, which have worked to implicitly construct and define the boundaries of available gay male identities in that space, simply do not fit within Facebook's digital infrastructure. The only way that these identities can appear on Facebook is via user-generated groups and pages. That is, they are not part of the actual infrastructure of the site and users need not negotiate their identities in relation to these labels.

The kind of assumptions that can be made, as a result of Facebook's 'Interested in' subsection of the profile template, about the importance (or, more accurately, lack of importance) that the site places on users' sexuality, and on the categorisation of such aspects of identity, are also reinforced by the already mentioned 'Relationships and Family' element of that template. Without further comment or qualification this element of the profile template allows all users to list their relationship status as any one of the following: 'Single', 'In a relationship', 'Engaged', 'Married', 'It's complicated', 'In an open relationship', 'Widowed', 'Separated' or 'Divorced'. In 2011, Facebook also added 'Civil union' and 'Domestic partnership' to this list. In addition, users may choose to elaborate on their relationship status and directly link to another person's Facebook profile using one of these labels as a descriptor. Regardless of the listed sex of the users whose profiles are being linked, Facebook treats all of these relationships as equally valid. Hence, despite the fact that it was legally impossible during my study for two men to be married in Queensland (or anywhere else in Australia), it was quite simple for two men living in this state to list themselves as being 'Married' to each other on Facebook. In fact, in 2012 Facebook even created same-sex icons to allow two male or two female icons to appear in users' news feeds when this option is selected (see Hern, 2012).[4] Facebook users are similarly free to list any other user (regardless of sex) as being part of their 'Family', by employing any of the terms offered by the site as descriptors for typical familial roles;[5] for example, a male user is free to list another male Facebook user as their 'Partner' or 'Husband', regardless of their listed (or legal) marital status.

For those Gaydar users who indicated either in focus group discussions about the site, or in comments in the free-text areas of their profiles (sometimes quite emphatically), that their identity is not defined by their sexuality, these aspects of Facebook's design instantly established it as a more open, less restrictive environment than Gaydar in which to "hang out" – as Ito et al. (2010) found most young people do in SNSs. As discussed in the previous chapter, in the process of looking for date-style scenarios that might lead to longer-term relationships, chatting, hanging out, passing the time and socializing with other gay men were the core types of activities interviewees in this study engaged in on Gaydar. Their attempts to use the site in this manner were hampered, however, by users' presumptions that most Gaydar members were simply seeking casual sex on the site. And these presumptions were deeply connected to Gaydar's design – with its emphasis on sex and eroticized male bodies, and its imbedded taxonomy of gay male identity. By contrast, Facebook's basic infrastructure at the same time was entirely free of the kinds of sexualized rhetoric and identity categorizations offered in Gaydar that often link homosexual desire to the forms of gay male identity commonly understood to exist within Sinfield's (1998) model of metropolitan homosexuality. Moreover, as its use of the polysemic phrase 'Interested in', and its approach to the representation of families and relationships indicates, Facebook's underlying code fundamentally conditions the site as a space where sexuality is not a key concern, but rather, something that individual users can choose to claim or not claim and express or not express in a manner that best suits their own life circumstances. Combined with Facebook's real name policy – see Facebook's 'Statement of Rights and Responsibilities' section 4.1 (Facebook, 2015) – this radically alters, in comparison to Gaydar, the approach to identity management that gay male users adopt in this space.

As we saw in Chapter 3, the identity management work that occurred on Gaydar amongst the 18–28-year-old cohort of users, that is the focus demographic of this study, produced identity territorialism within that site which worked to reinforce the very stereotypes against which these users often railed. With Gaydar restricting access to individualizing social cues and invoking particular social identities for its users through a plethora of reductive drop-down menu selections, as Lea and Spears (1991) found often happens in anonymous contexts, users resorted to stereotyping behaviours. "I don't define myself by my sexuality" they would say, because, as profile after profile would advise, gay people are, "tragic", "shallow, two-faced scene queen[s]" and "boring", "unintelligent, self-centred Neanderthals" who lead "dramatic lives" and don't believe in "trust, equality, communication [or] commitment". Within Facebook, however, in an environment that does not work to classify its users in terms of sexuality, and where the imagined audience of each user is already known to that person, these same men managed their own online identities without resorting to the practice of denigrating others or drawing sharp distinctions between themselves and any particular sexual identity labels. The understanding that those who are part of one's Facebook network already have at least some prior knowledge of us (including our real name), as well as the fact that Facebook foregrounds users' individuality,[6] negates the need for identity territorialism. Hence, instead of concerted efforts to present themselves as being different from and better than other users of the site, as they did on Gaydar, in this environment, users typically took an approach to profile management that made their homosexuality banal. That is, it was alluded to, mentioned, depicted and discussed only in the context of their everyday interactions. Users in this study noted for instance, that their Facebook profiles were used for and defined by "day-to-day" events in their lives. For some users, this meant having a profile where pictures of a newborn niece, status updates complaining about work, and links to the latest weather forecasts and movie previews all appeared alongside discussions, photographs and check-ins related to a trip to Mardi Gras or to the new gay night at a local club. For others, whose everyday interactions may not include trips to local gay venues or events, it meant that information about what they ate for lunch, pictures of a newborn family member, how much they wished they could go home from work, and where they wanted to go on their next holiday, was simply presented within the framework of a profile which, for example, linked them to a male partner, a gay male interest group, or listed a gay icon as their 'Religious Views'.[7]

In short, on Facebook, where there is a much less constraining meta-narrative about sexuality in place than on gay-male-oriented SNSs, such as Gaydar, and where focus is directed towards day-to-day events via features such as the 'News Feed', a user's homosexuality is never categorised or defined – the same way that heterosexuality or bisexuality is not categorised or defined. Instead, it enjoys the simple possibility of being able to flow through each person's profile to the degree, and in the manner, that it otherwise shapes and informs that person's daily activities and engagements; the same way that any other character trait would. On Facebook, then, the possibility exists for representations of what it means to be homosexual to be not only flexible and consistently updated in line with social change, but also, as numerous as there are same-sex-attracted people on the site. The act of creating a Facebook profile, or "writing oneself into being" (boyd, 2008c, p. 119), as a gay man in this space, therefore happens within a narrative shaped much more by the life experiences, social connections and circumstances of the site's individual users, than by its underlying code. This situation offers users the capacity to create and access a significantly broader range of gay male identities than exists in Gaydar, where male homosexuality has been commoditized, defined and pre-categorised within the infrastructure of the site itself. Testament to Facebook's potential in this regard, was the sheer number and diversity of the variations of gay male identity visible at the time of data collection within the site's range of 'groups' and 'pages' dedicated to GLBT-oriented organisations (see, e.g., Queensland Association for Healthy Communities (QAHC), GLBT Historical Society, GLOE: GLBT Outreach and Engagement), websites (see, e.g., Brightest Young Gays, Mybig Gaywedding) identity-based groups (see, e.g., Gay Geeks, Str8 Acting Gay Guys, Gay Boys with Beards, Gay Doctors, Real Gay Bears), location-based groups (Gay Australia Connect, Gay Thailand, Gay Somerset), interests and activities (Gay Sports, Top the Chef: Gay Cooking Club, Gay Men's Opera Club), venues (The Wickham Hotel, The Beat Megaclub, Fluffy) and causes (Gay Marriage Rights in Australia, Gay Equality in Schools, Support Gay Adoption & Gay Parents). It was clearly evident in the dozens of these spaces that I examined for this study, particularly in the profiles of their members and contributors, that the finite list of gay male identities available in Gaydar is highly reductive. By contrast, the fact that these groups are optional, user-generated and number in their thousands – and that there are multiple slightly different versions of the same or similar group present – prevents these groups from generating a situation where gay male identity is taxonomised in the same way that it is on Gaydar.

Facebook as an Authentic Environment

The number and diversity of available gay male identities visible in Facebook, and the fact that these identities do not present a collective image of homosexuality as highly sexualized as the one presented within Gaydar, is one of the most crucial aspects involved in understanding how Gaydar and Facebook fit together in the late 2000s and early 2010s within the broader ecology of SNSs used by the young gay men in this study. As described in the previous chapter, this cohort largely saw Gaydar as outdated and disconnected, both aesthetically and ideologically, from the kinds of post-gay identities and desires that they most related to. By comparison, these users perceived Facebook as a much more authentic environment. Whereas large areas of their Gaydar profiles were often left blank (in order to resist the kinds of highly sexualised discourses about homosexuality embedded in the site's infrastructure that did not mesh with their own self-perceptions), their Facebook profiles were described, for example, as completely 'honest' and 'normal' and like an exact 'record' of their lives. When participants were asked to describe their Facebook profiles in focus groups, for instance, one interviewee said,

> It's just, it's really me, down to the essence of me. I've got family members and stuff on there and I don't care, I'll put on there that it's the third weekend in a row that I've been out three nights in a row, and stuff like that. It's me.... Facebook now, for me, is, it's me. If you want to know what Toby's about, read through the last 10 minutes of my status updates.

Other members of Toby's focus group answered very similarly. The younger participant sitting to his direct right, said, for example,

> Mine's completely honest too. It's me to a tee. Photos, I don't really care what goes up there. I try to limit friends on Facebook to who are actually real friends, or people that I talk to and want to see what's happening in my life. So that said, pretty much anything goes. I've got a lot of family on there, but everything that goes up is pretty tasteful mostly. It's something I use a lot.... It's honest, open and something that it's great to catch up or to see what everybody else is doing.

Even those users who admitted to heavily censoring their Facebook profile described the site as being more authentic than Gaydar – or, as one of these men put it, more "normal oriented".

As the quotes above indicate, the comparative levels of comfort and openness that defined these users' Facebook profiles was not solely related to the site's laissez-faire approach to constructions of sexuality, which made that space feel more 'normal' to these users. It was also a direct result of the way that Facebook enmeshes each user's individual identity, through their personalized social network, in a wider social identity. The reason the above user said that his Facebook profile was "completely honest" and a space where "pretty much anything goes", for example, was because he had limited his connections on the site to people who were, as he described them, his "actua[l] real friends". As this comment indicates, these users were highly aware that grounding online self-representations in explicit connections with identifiable others, makes it, as Baym (2010, p. 115) puts it, "difficult to create online selves that wander too far from the embodied ones." They were highly cognisant, that is, of the idea that having friends and family bear witness to one's interactions on Facebook makes it more difficult to be deceptive in this setting. While there is significant research to suggest that anonymity in online environments, as exists in Gaydar, for example, does not necessarily encourage dishonesty (see Baym, 2000; Henderson & Gilding, 2004; Rutter & Smith, 1999), this perception of Facebook as being more authentic than niche gay-oriented SNSs on this account had nonetheless taken hold amongst this cohort. Combined with the site's reluctance to classify sexuality, this perceived authenticity made the experience of using Facebook in many ways a much more comfortable and relaxed one than the experience of using sites such as Gaydar for this group. It had ensured that, since its very arrival, Facebook had been a key facet of these young men's efforts to connect with, engage with, establish friendships and relationships with and generally socialize with and amongst, other gay men.

Facebook as a Gaydar Supplement

Although Facebook had certainly not usurped the role of Gaydar in gay men's digital culture in Brisbane by 2010, data from this study clearly indicates that young gay men in this city were using the site for purposes that overlapped with their reasons for using Gaydar from as early as 2007, when Facebook first became popular in Australia. In fact, the frequency with which these men used Facebook to supplement, extend and enhance their engagements with Gaydar and its users, and the significance that they placed upon the relationship between these two sites, is evidence that Facebook became an important aspect of gay men's digital culture for this cohort very quickly. The participants in this study, for example, routinely used Facebook:

- as a space to shift acceptable interactions with other Gaydar users away from the Gaydar environment;
- as an important connection point for and verifier of the identities presented in Gaydar; and
- as an alternate avenue to access likeminded gay men.

The remainder of this chapter will be therefore be devoted to chronicling these uses of Facebook – and their implications for Gaydar – in more detail.

Facebook as an Alternate Venue (With Home Ground Advantages)

The use of Facebook by participants in this study as a space into which to shift interactions with other Gaydar users that they deemed acceptable or promising was very much like the act of leaving a popular old gay bar that's not really your cup of tea to, instead, head to your new favourite local coffee shop with a stranger that you just met at the aforementioned bar. For the men in this study, Gaydar could well be described as a tired old gay bar that was not really their cup of tea. While it was still popular at the time of data collection (i.e., there were thousands of users in Brisbane – and around the world), and had long been part of the landscape (i.e., around since its launch in 1999), the old décor and the usual crowd (i.e., the site's digital infrastructure and its imagined audience) simply made them feel uncomfortable and out of place. Given there were no real alternatives amongst the other gay bars in town, though, these men still showed up (or logged in) to the old gay bar whenever they felt like heading out to meet and socialize with new people who were also gay. For the most part, though, they found themselves disappointed and wondered why they bothered turning up again, and eventually, ended up leaving (or logging off) at the end of the night convinced that no other gay men out there with goals and interests like their own existed. However, every so often, these men did find themselves at the old gay haunt in the company of someone with a similar interest, or simply, in whom they had taken an interest, superficial or otherwise, and with who they would like to properly chat (i.e., there were odd occasions where these men did identify other Gaydar users they believed might be worth getting to know better). In this situation, the first thing these men wanted to do was explain to that person (as is typically done pre-emptively in Gaydar profiles) that the old gay bar is not really their scene; that they are different from most of the guys there. The second thing these men wanted to do in this situation, was to go somewhere else more conducive to conversation where they would be more comfortable, and where they would be able to find out more about the other person in whom they'd taken an interest, through simply chatting with them. Accordingly, they would invite their new acquaintance to their favourite coffee shop just down the road, where the owners did not care if the clientele were gay, straight or otherwise; the regulars were all friends; and the lighting (or digital infrastructure) made it much easier to see each other than it was in the club. That is, they invited them to connect profiles on Facebook, where conversation could flow more freely and individuating social cues were much more prominent.

This metaphoric version of events is, of course, not a perfect descriptor of how things happen online. However, in essence, this is indeed how, and why, the practice of shifting interactions with people from Gaydar to Facebook played out for the cohort studied here in 2010. It was about shifting to another environment that users found more comfortable and accommodating than Gaydar, and which provided opportunities for relationship development through greater self-disclosure. Haythornthwaite (2005) refers to this phenomenon in terms of "media multiplexity" – a concept she uses to describe the tendency of people to add more media to relationships as we grow closer. Prior to Facebook's arrival, interactions on Gaydar were routinely shifted to MSN messenger in line with this pattern, often, prior to any other form of interaction. It was not uncommon, for example, for an opening (private) message on Gaydar to be either (a) simply an email address to be used to add the sender to one's MSN list, or, (b) a request to *reply* with an email address for use on MSN. This is because, on Gaydar, which works according to a freemium model, users of the site without a paid-for membership were limited to sending eight messages per day, and private chats with other users needed to be initiated through an arduous process that required repeating with each new conversation.[8] On MSN, however, the linking procedures necessary to chat occurred just once, the number of messages that could be sent and received was unlimited, and conversation always happened in real time. For these reasons, participants in this study rarely mentioned the practice of chatting with other Gaydar users via Gaydar itself. When asked which features of the site participants typically used, for example, consistent with the patterns of use seen in Gaydar's Queensland-based chat rooms,[9] only two men noted that they used the site's chat feature on occasion. Shifting interactions initiated in Gaydar over to MSN in order to avoid the limitations of Gaydar's chat feature and to find out more about a new acquaintance from the site, however, was frequently discussed as a normal part of Gaydar use. With the arrival of Facebook, though, the popularity of MSN as a go-to destination for Gaydar users in this demographic had somewhat waned. With Facebook offering the same unlimited messaging capacity and possibilities for real-time chat as MSN, but the additional benefit of much more abundant social cues (e.g., images, real names and network information), Facebook quickly became an equally popular destination for these users to shift interactions away from Gaydar in the hope of aiding relationship progression. In fact, so common had this practice become, and so accustomed had many of these young men become to interacting with relative strangers via Facebook, that participants in this study noted how Facebook had also developed into the go-to medium for extending interactions that were initiated in GLBT spaces offline. Instead of swapping Gaydar profiles[10] or phone numbers with a new acquaintance, for example, participants said adding each other to Facebook was becoming a much more common practice; often noting – despite their own relative youth – that the practice was growing increasingly popular among "younger people" at night clubs. "[L]ike, you meet them and they're like, 'oh, do you have Facebook?'", said one 26 year old.

Since the publication of Fiske and Taylor's (1984) book on social cognition, social psychologists have described people as "cognitive misers", because we make sense of the world around us largely through mental shortcuts that enable significant amounts of information to be extrapolated from minimal social cues. As Ellison, Heino and Gibbs (2006) have found, in mediated environments where there are considerable blanks available for people to fill, this tendency results in the placing of greater significance on other's social cues than would typically occur in face-to-face settings. In the context of SNS profiles then, as Baym (2010, p. 119) notes, "an ambiguous subject line, a single photograph, a short self-description, or a shared interest leads us to infer other information based on our stereotypes and assumptions about how social reality works". With Gaydar users in the 18–28-year-old range often leaving areas of their profiles blank and the site's infrastructure limiting users' access to individuating social cues, the practice that developed of shifting interactions that might have otherwise occurred via Gaydar or MSN to Facebook (as well as the practice of swapping Facebook profiles instead of phone numbers) therefore makes sense as a timesaving, heuristic exercise. Because Facebook interactions take place in an environment where social cues are more abundant than in Gaydar, the kinds of mental shortcuts that these cues facilitate occur more quickly, allowing users to expedite the process of deciding whether, and how, to proceed or withdraw from any further relationship development. Particularly in the case of swapping Facebooks before phone numbers, it also limits the amount of effort or social investment necessary to make such decisions.

Facebook as Identity Verification Tool and Ancillary Filtering Device

As discussed in the section above, shifting interactions from Gaydar to MSN in order to circumvent some of the niche SNS's limitations was part of the culture of Gaydar since its inception. Users typically organised these shifts through (private) messaging each other in order to send and request email addresses, which could then be added to one's MSN chat list. With the arrival of Facebook, as the shifting of Gaydar interactions into that environment gained popularity, this practice by no means disappeared, but it did take on an important new significance. Whereas, once, requests for email addresses were, in essence, simply a request to open a dialogue in another venue, and the addresses provided were used only to that end, with the arrival of Facebook, the request and provision of email addresses also started becoming associated with the running of Facebook searches on people. As one focus group participant explained, "when you've…got a message like 'add me on MSN' from Gaydar or whatever and they give you like an email address… you just take that email address and put it into Facebook to see if they've got a profile." In 2010, at the time when the focus groups for this study were conducted, not all participants I interviewed were aware of this practice. Others had only thought to run Facebook searches on Gaydar users via the input of a real name – if they could manage to secure one. Moreover, Facebook's privacy settings were also different then than they are today. I will discuss some of these issues (e.g., awareness of privacy settings) in more detail in the following chapter on safety and privacy. For now, however, it is simply important to note that, at the time of data collection, the very possibility of being able to covertly access information about Gaydar users, via their Facebook profiles (either through the provision of an email address or a real name), had encouraged the majority of participants in this study to view and approach Facebook, in relation to Gaydar, not only as a useful alternate venue for interacting with other gay men, but also as an important identity cross-checking or verification tool, and an ancillary filtering device.

More than 80 per cent of participants interviewed in this study discussed Facebook as a tool that they utilized to covertly check up on the identities of those people they had either observed or interacted with on Gaydar. Searching the corresponding Facebook profile of Gaydar users to try to ensure that photos people had posted on Gaydar were genuine and recent, for example, was a popular activity independently brought up by participants in all focus groups conducted for this study. Explaining why he engaged in the process of cross-checking, or verifying, Gaydar users' identities on Facebook, one young professional simply said, "you're not really trying impress anyone [on Facebook]. You are, but you're not [to the same] extent that you are on the other websites". This comment, and the level of agreement which emerged amongst participants on this point, indicates that the widespread use of Facebook as an identity verification tool amongst this cohort could largely be attributed to the fact that, as I discussed earlier in this chapter, these men considered Facebook a more authentic environment than Gaydar. Accordingly, they deemed the identities presented within that space to be truer representations of the embodied selves connected to them. For this reason, it was also not uncommon at this time to find Gaydar users pre-emptively offering access to their listings on Facebook via the free-text areas of Gaydar profiles (a practice that had evolved from the pre-emptive listing of email addresses in these boxes for the purpose of chatting on MSN). As the following comment from a member of focus group four indicates, not only did this practice fulfil the purpose of inviting Gaydar users to cross-check or verify one's identity prior to any interaction (thereby signifying honesty and openness), but it also allowed users to resist or circumvent the need to characterize themselves according to the model of identity classification prescribed within Gaydar:

> Some people obviously have their email address in Gaydar so that you can – you don't have to message them, so you can go up there and go straight in. Or, they don't have things like ['fetishes' or 'favourite things' filled out], but they have [the Facebook] link up.

That is, instead of resisting Gaydar's focus on sex and the erotic by leaving profiles completely blank or engaging in identity territorialism to disassociate themselves from the site and its imagined audience, some users chose to employ their Gaydar profiles to simply cross-reference their profiles on Facebook.

The possibility of verifying or cross-checking Facebook profiles with listings on Gaydar, and the pre-emptive connections to Facebook profiles that some users had provided on account of the popularity of this practice, also afforded participants in this study the opportunity to make judgements about pursuing or reciprocating interaction with other Gaydar users based on criteria outside of those available or immediately visible to them within Gaydar. It had afforded them, essentially, the capacity to use Facebook as an external filtering device. While all participants in this study listed 'age', 'location', or 'online now' as search filters they typically employed when using Gaydar to locate people they might want to connect with, other criteria they highlighted as equally important indicators of social compatibility were unable to be assessed on Gaydar. On Facebook, however, some of those indicators are readily available. For example, one university student mentioned that being able to find information on Gaydar users' religious and political views via Facebook[11] often helped him to decide whether or not he would connect with those users. Cross-checking Gaydar and Facebook profiles was, he said, "a good way to find out…stuff about them because it has like political views and that, religious views and also the kinds of friends they have". "If their political view is like [conservative] and their religious view is like Christian," he added, "then I [can already be aware that I] probably won't belong with them…[because] that means they're most likely a closeted person, which I'm not that interested in meeting". The most frequently discussed way that participants employed Facebook as an ancillary filtering device, however, was, as this user also alluded to, to identify any common friends. On SNSs like Facebook, as Walther, Van Der Heide, Kim, Westerman and Tom Tong (2008) argue, we are all essentially known by the company we keep. While Gaydar technically had the capacity to make visible one's list of 'friends' and 'favourites' at this point, this feature was available only to premium members of the site and was therefore very rarely used. Hence, in its stead, young Gaydar users turned to Facebook to fulfil the role of making visible gay men's social networks.

Being able to view and assess other people's place in Brisbane's gay male social networks was a crucial aspect of Facebook use amongst participants in this study and, as I noted above, was the most commonly discussed way that participants in this study used Facebook as an external filtering device in conjunction with Gaydar. Since the practice of swapping Facebooks had also increased in physical gay spaces, though, it was not only people met via Gaydar that these men were screening in this fashion. Indeed, whether access to Facebook profiles was given preemptively on sites like Gaydar, or offered freely or unknowingly through the exchange of email addresses, names, phone numbers, and the like, using Facebook profiles as a way of mapping people's place in a city's gay male social network quickly became a common part of gay men's digital culture. In 2011, on the popular gay YouTube channel Davey Wavey in the episode titled 'Zero Mutual Facebook Friends: What I Look for in a Guy!' (DaveyWavey, 2011), Davey Wavey took a comedic look at the implications that Facebook's provision of network visibility had on gay men's search criteria when it comes to social compatibility. These implications coincided perfectly with the sentiment of the participants in this study. He says in this episode:

> The gay community is super incestuous with itself, especially if you live in a small town like me. And so here's the deal, if you have mutual friends with someone – let's say that you have ten of them – you best believe that at least half of those people have history with each other. Be it boyfriends, hook-ups, or blind dates gone terribly wrong, it is going to be double dipping your nacho into someone else's salsa.... It's like getting a delicious slice of chocolate cream pie and then fifteen of your friends sneeze on it!...When, out of all the mens, you find someone with zero mutual Facebook friends, it is like when Christopher Columbus discovered America!...It's not even about getting 'sloppy seconds' – I'm fine with that. It's the baggage that comes with all the history and all the drama that you inherit just by virtue of dating that other person.
>
> (DaveyWavey, 2011)

Ensuring that Gaydar users who they would like to connect with came with the least amount of 'history' or 'baggage', as Davey Wavey put it, was an important reason to use Facebook as an ancillary filtering tool for the participants in this study. While Davey Wavey focused solely on avoiding men with mutual friends, however, participants in this study also talked about checking for links to particular people who they themselves were not friends with on Facebook, but whom they knew [also via Facebook] had large friendship networks and/or a particular reputation they wished to avoid being associated with. That is, wherever possible, these men would check the Facebook profile of a person from Gaydar (or from a meeting or interaction occurring in offline gay spaces) for mutual friends, as well as for any links to people in the local gay community who they believed had particular reputations incompatible with their own self-perceptions: they would use Facebook as what Donath and boyd (2004) would call a "virtual compass" to help them navigate the world of Gaydar and the gay male community more generally. "[I]f I see pictures of people [on their Facebook profile] with other people that I'm friends with, I admit I would judge them based on who they're friends with", said one participant, before adding, "[a]lso, Tom Henry, if anyone knows Tom Henry. Tom Henry haunts my Facebook profile because he pops up in everyone's photos...and I'm like, 'wow, this guy must just know everyone' because it doesn't matter who comes up as a friend, like, he'll be in their profile pic." For this user, the negative connotations associated with 'knowing everyone'[12] meant that people he met or had contact with via Gaydar who shared no mutual friends might still have been dismissed as a prospective date or potential boyfriend on account of their connection to Tom Henry. Prior to the arrival of Facebook, however, such information would only be accessible through the kinds of self-disclosure that happens in social interaction over a period of time. Hence, in many ways, being able to use Facebook as a cross-checking tool and ancillary filtering device, had given these men more ways to understand and interact with the people and spaces (both digital and physical) that were closely associated with the city's gay male community. Another user in this study noted, for example, that, because Facebook made gay men's social networks visible, the site played a crucial role in helping him to decide whether to attend events he was invited to. Knowing whether other gay people would be attending and who those gay people might be, he noted, could provide "some incentive to go".[13]

Facebook as an Additional Access Point to Gay Male Communities

Outside of operating as a venue into which users felt they could shift interactions away from Gaydar, and being an efficient filtering tool and source of information, which gave participants in this study a greater sense of agency in their interactions with other gay men, the other key way that Facebook's arrival provided new ways to understand and interact with the city's gay male community was by functioning as a direct access point to a diverse range of people and activities closely associated with GLBT (and GLBT friendly) venues, organizations, events, issues and networks that were not always visible in spaces such as Gaydar. The data from this study suggests, for example, that, particularly for those people who found using Gaydar to be an experience that fuelled thoughts of rarity and isolation, Facebook could provide a range of access points to other likeminded gay men. Indeed, providing support for the notion that Facebook is a less isolating environment for young gay men to network in than niche or gay-specific SNSs, in the interviews conducted for this study, close to 100 per cent of participants indicated that Facebook had helped them to connect with, or stay connected with, other likeminded gay men. Moreover, these men emphasized the fact that Facebook had helped them to do this in a way that fit in with their 'normal' everyday lives and concerns.

At separate points during the focus group interviews conducted for this study, participants were asked directly whether Gaydar and Facebook, respectively, had helped them to feel more connected to the local gay community. While all of the participants noted at some point during their interviews that they had originally signed up to Gaydar in their early teenage years seeking to connect with and explore the gay male community via that site, their experiences therein, as I noted in the previous chapter, generally did not foster any feelings of connection. In fact, on the contrary, Gaydar tended to leave many of its young users feeling different and detached from other gay men. Hence, in response to the question of whether Gaydar had helped them to feel connected to the local gay community, the following answer was typical of participants' responses:

> No…I would say it's not community-based. I think Gaydar themselves as a brand try to connect to the community because of the number of gays that do have profiles and they put their sponsorship and everything out there for things like Mardi Gras, et cetera. But as much as they are part of the gay community, I don't feel a part of a gay community on Gaydar.

In a clear sign that Facebook immediately functioned as a successful alternate access point to the gay male community for these men, however, when asked the same question about Facebook, numerous examples of ways that these men had used the site to connect with, or stay connected with, other likeminded gay men were consistently offered up. For instance, one interviewee who was particularly frank about his aversion to the gay scene, and the nightclubs, websites and individuals he believed defined it, noted that he had used Facebook to track down and join the local GLBT swimming squad. Other interviewees talked about using Facebook to discover and subsequently attend alternative gay music festivals; to increase their number of gay friends by familiarizing themselves with friends of friends that they knew or believed were also gay (and then sending them friend requests); to keep informed about and up to date with the happenings at local gay clubs (even if they did not attend); and to engage with and support GLBT causes they identified with. "I feel as though [on Facebook] the Brisbane gay community keeps me updated on what's going on and asks for my opinion", said one participant. "Because I am a friend of [gay nightclubs] The Wickham and Fluffy and stuff like that, Fluffy sends through the thing of 'what's your favourite Madonna song', and 'final preparations for Fluffy Diva', and 'wait until you hear Jessica Mauboy's new song' and things like that. I feel also the Brisbane gay community and Q News, they do let you know what's going on [via Facebook]. It's just like, 'keep your eyes out for the next edition of Q News'".[14] Focusing his answer on the diversity of the people and activities that Facebook provided opportunities to connect with, another user said that Facebook "definitely…[helped him feel connected to the gay community]… because there's different groups and that – equal rights groups and lots of different things that you can do".

Interestingly, though, given the connotations associated with the metropolitan model of homosexuality (Sinfield, 1998) that the term 'gay community' had for these users, many interviewees stopped short of directly saying that Facebook had helped them to feel connected to the local gay community. Despite all of the examples they listed of connections they had made to other gay men via Facebook, these links were characterized as simply part of their 'normal community' or something they referred to as the 'open community'. Obviously, in these instances, using the term 'gay community' in the phrasing of the question evoked in these participants an image of an identity-based community, similar to their image of the imagined Gaydar audience, that they simply did not feel ideologically connected to. However, as the continual stream of anecdotes offered up in answering the question attests, Facebook clearly offered these people significant new opportunities to access and connect with other homosexual men who, like them, also did not necessarily identify with the model of gay male identity most visible throughout sites such as Gaydar. And in doing so, I would argue, it simultaneously increased the potential for these men to then broaden their own (and others') perceptions, not only of who and what constitutes the local gay community, but also the term 'gay' itself; so that, over time, more young men like them might come to feel less othered by it.

The idea that Facebook's arrival provided an alternative access point to the gay male community, particularly for those people who felt disconnected from the identities available in environments such as Gaydar, was also supported by my direct observations of the Facebook groups and pages associated with the local gay community in Brisbane that were operating in 2010. Most significantly, in line with the grievances outlined in the previous chapter that users harboured about Gaydar and its imagined audience – because of the ideas associated with the metropolitan model of homosexuality (Sinfield, 1998) and the lifestyles associated with it that the site perpetuates – Facebook groups that were simply gay identity markers were largely empty. In 2010, the Facebook group 'Gay Brisbane', for example, was (and had long been) almost completely devoid of any activity. Since it received its first post in September 2007, the group had steadily declined to a membership of just four. Moreover, posts such as "Helloooooooooo? <echo> Is there anybody out there?" typified the kind of activity that had occurred in that space throughout its existence.[15] Likewise, during the same period, the 'Brisbane Gay Men's Facebook Chat Group' had only 133 members, at least 95 per cent of whom were very clearly in the plus 30 demographic. This makes sense in line with the ideas that many young Gaydar users expressed, both on the site itself and in the interviews conducted for this study, about their sexuality being a non-issue, or not definitive of their identity – and with the work of Foth (2003) in 'If you build it they won't necessarily come', where he described how, even in local contexts, the existence of digital spaces designed to foster community does not guarantee user engagement. By contrast, Facebook groups and pages that represented particular spaces and organisations that were gay or GLBT oriented, but that had a clear purpose other than to simply bring gay men together, received high amounts of traffic, and a large degree of involvement from men in the 18–28-year-old demographic. The main Facebook page associated with The Queensland Association for Healthy Communities (QAHC), a small charity group that independently promotes the health of lesbian, gay, bisexual and transgender people in Queensland, for instance, boasted well over a thousand members at the time of this study and had been posted to multiple times almost daily since its inception. Many of the members of the QAHC Facebook group were also part of the 'Gay Marriage Rights in Australia' group, which at the same time had almost 200,000 people on its page – and was, it is worth mentioning, a very commonly supported group amongst the young men interviewed for this study. Also quite popular with these men and the broader demographic to which they belong were the pages of local gay night clubs; at the time of data collection, for instance, the fan page of Fluffy, a weekly gay-friendly night held at an otherwise mainstream club in Brisbane, had over 16,000 likes and 28,000 visits. And in all of the local Facebook groups I observed, this pattern continued. Groups that had a connection to a physical space or organization that served the community, or which worked to keep people informed about issues affecting GLBT folks, were infinitely more popular than those pages and groups which served only as identity markers and as spaces to bring Facebook users together based solely around their homosexuality. Given that being associated with a Facebook page or being a member of a Facebook group only ever represents a small aspect of one's entire Facebook presence, this forsaking of groups such as 'Gay Brisbane', where the focus is on identity rather than activity or interest, speaks volumes about the extent to which young same-sex-attracted men feel that their homosexuality is definitive (or more accurately, not definitive) of their overall identity. Hence, for those men who felt othered by sites like Gaydar and the stereotypes associated with the identities available in those spaces, and for those who, like many of the participants in this study, felt that those spaces tended to force people into being defined by their sexuality, the sheer level of interest and engagement in the range of groups on Facebook which were GLBT related but not definitive in any way of the GLBT community, was evidence that a clear, alternate path to connecting with other gay men was now available to them on Facebook. And moreover, that this path to connection, via Facebook, was one that many young gay men in Brisbane were taking advantage of.

Implications

With Facebook's digital infrastructure being non-prescriptive about how people present their sexuality on the site, its arrival and popular take up immediately afforded gay men the opportunity to manage online identities in a way that made homosexuality banal – something that is not possible on Gaydar. Accordingly, Facebook quickly began to serve as a popular space for young gay men to shift online interactions away from Gaydar; as a connection point for and verifier of identities presented in Gaydar; and as an additional avenue to access a much broader gay male community than was visible in Gaydar. One of the most significant implications that this has had for gay men's digital culture, I would argue, is that it has opened up Gaydar, and similar niche sites designed for gay male users, to increased scrutiny and further criticisms of the kind, discussed in Chapter 3, which were already levelled at them. That is, the simple possibility of being able to compare Gaydar to more mainstream services increased the level of criticism young gay men aimed at the site, further intensifying its underlying culture of participatory reluctance.

In the early 2000s, when I first signed up to Gaydar there were very few alternatives in terms of social networking sites available in which to network with other gay men, either niche or mainstream. Myspace and Facebook were yet to be established, and many other gay-specific SNSs (e.g., Manhunt and Manjam) were not yet popular in Australia. So while the ideological leanings of Gaydar and the gay male identities available therein might not have always matched with the identities and lifestyles of its users, there was, I remember, a distinct sense that you just worked around it. The same way that you just worked around the technical limitations of the site, by using MSN as an ancillary chat feature and leaving parts of your profile blank if need be. But being on Gaydar was simply part of being gay, so you somehow made it work. And when you discovered a new site aimed at connecting gay men, as I mentioned earlier in this chapter, you signed up to that service hoping to find something different. However, while I am personally old enough to remember using niche SNSs designed for gay male audiences well before the arrival of more mainstream SNSs, such as Myspace and Facebook, for some of the younger men interviewed in this study, this was not the case. For them, Myspace and/or Facebook accounts they had established as young teens provided their first experiences of social networking sites. Their Gaydar profiles came a few years after, as they began to explore and discover their own sexuality.

In this context, while all interviewees were, at some point, overtly critical of Gaydar's layout and technical functioning, as well as its focus on sex and the erotic, these aspects of the site tended to appear more outdated and less acceptable to the youngest participants in the study. And while not all men who use Gaydar sign up to the site as teenagers, the tendency of the participants in this study to have done so, injected an almost generational element into the kind of scrutiny and criticism that Facebook had opened Gaydar up to amongst these men – because it meant that participants' ages and levels of experience with Gaydar generally increased in tandem. That is, where participants in this study had spent equal or greater lengths of time as users of Facebook than they had as users of Gaydar, they were generally younger and more critical of Gaydar than those participants who, being slightly older, had used the niche SNS longer and become more accustomed to it. This pattern of being less critical of Gaydar and its focus on sex at an older age was also noticeable in Reynolds (2008) discussion of gay men's internet dating, where he described feeling "out of place and odd" amongst his late-forty-something peers who were enamoured with Gaydar's potential to allow them to 'shop for cock' (p. 10). Hence, while all participants in this study had used both Gaydar and Facebook and were thus capable of comparing the two, the focus and degree of criticism directed at Gaydar tended to change depending on the age of participants. Early indications that generational factors might have been at play in this situation first came to light during my online observations of Gaydar, where I saw over the course of this project an ever-increasing number of young men's profiles being used to criticize the site and its imagined audience.

One of the clearest indications that this situation was not a product of either my imagination or my observational techniques, however; that mainstream social networking sites had indeed opened up Gaydar to an increasingly more intense form of criticism and scrutiny from younger users with more experience using sites like Facebook than niche community SNSs, came in focus group two. In this focus group, two participants had an extended discussion where they vehemently disagreed about the utility of Gaydar for future generations. The older of the two men (at 25 years), who had a Gaydar profile before signing up to Facebook, argued that Gaydar was still needed to prepare young people for the sexually explicit world of gay social networking, and the gay community more generally, that, he said, they would inevitably have to negotiate. Whether one is promiscuous and scene oriented or not, he argued, young gay men would need to be comfortable with and knowledgeable enough of the cultures of those spaces to be safe in the community of gay men (both online and off). At 18 years of age, the younger of the two men, whose Facebook profile existed before he had a presence on Gaydar (and who had since stopped using Gaydar altogether) saw things differently. For him, Gaydar was not about helping people to become comfortable in a sexually explicit environment that already existed outside of the site. The site itself was *creating* that environment; and thus, for him, Gaydar was not at all a positive space for young people to be trying to come to terms with and explore their sexuality or to network with other gay men. Its focus on sex, he argued, would simply instil in young people the erroneous idea that being gay means being promiscuous, and, he added, might land young users in situations where they may be preyed upon by older men.[16]

However moralistic these arguments, both of these men clearly felt that the environment within Gaydar was not a positive one. The older man with more experience using Gaydar was of the opinion that, for lack of a better term, the site was a necessary evil – and he was thus more willing to tolerate its continued existence for the sake of younger gay men 'learning the ropes' and discovering how to best keep themselves safe. Once this learning phase was complete, however, he noted, "You can take some bits from [Gaydar], even people too, into Facebook." The younger participant, whose Facebook profile preceded his Gaydar one, though, was much less forgiving of Gaydar, asking why the service continued to exist at all. In its stead, "[w]hy can't you have a gay based friendship meeting site like Facebook?", he asked. Whichever way one looks at these arguments, and despite the differences between them, they each point towards Facebook as a better alternative to Gaydar in some way or another. In doing this, they also clearly demonstrate how, especially amongst younger demographics, Gaydar's significance in gay men's digital culture had been somewhat diminished by the arrival of Facebook.

While the arguments above point towards Facebook as a better alternative to Gaydar on moral or ideological grounds, other users also made similar points in focus group discussions based around differences between Gaydar and Facebook's respective interfaces. Talking about why he stopped using Gaydar in the months prior to the focus group he participated in as much as he had previously done, for instance, one young user said, "The interface was confusing and that's why I stopped using Gaydar". Asked what particular parts of the site were confusing, to much agreement from others in the room, he responded that the symbols used on the site's buttons (of which there were up to 16 per layer[17]) were especially troublesome; that he did not know what they each meant despite the fact that – at least by his own assessment – he was "quite good with technology and stuff" and, quite significantly, had adapted "easily" to Facebook's frequent changes.

In contrast to Gaydar, as any user of the site will know, Facebook is almost totally devoid of symbol-only buttons. At the time of writing, for instance, I could find only three. As Kirkpatrick (2010, p. 303) points out in 'the Facebook effect', such streamlining of Facebook's design has always been a priority of the Facebook team, who have constantly developed the site to increase the amount of data flowing between users and to make it easier to digest larger volumes of information. In the site's early years, for example, the status update slot at the top of the user profile with the pre-existing framework: "Elija Cassidy is....." was a fixed element and basic, text-only updates were the only option. Post 2008, however, this slot was replaced with the much more open-ended 'publisher' feature, where users were also able to post photos, videos and links to articles and other sites of interest all around the Web. Having become accustomed to this kind of streamlined, open-ended interface from a young age, for those users who established profiles on Gaydar after using Facebook, the busier interface and profile template, clunky chat feature and limited opportunities for user-driven activity (e.g., posting and sharing) appear to have established their perceptions of Gaydar as a much more restrictive and outdated environment. In a sign of the extent to which Facebook's interface shone a light on Gaydar's technical limitations, this perception was also held in the upper end of the 18–28-year-old demographic at the centre of this study, by users who had established (and become familiar with) Gaydar profiles long before the existence of Facebook. Talking about how, in comparison to other sites, Gaydar was much more difficult to use, one participant in his late twenties commented, for example:

> I still have [a Gaydar profile] somewhere out there, like I haven't deleted it but I don't use it because I think it's easier now that I'm a little bit older to meet people, and there's other better sites now as well, such as Facebook and Grindr.

Grindr – the other 'better' site referred to alongside Facebook here – is the all-male geolocative social networking service available on Apple iOS and Android. It was the first application in the iTunes app store to engage the location-based services on users' mobile devices – to show "the guys that are closest to you that are also on Grindr" (Grindr, 2012, np). Established in 2009 during the early stages of my initial project looking at the convergence between Gaydar and Facebook, Grindr rapidly expanded into 192 countries around the world and soon boasted over five million active monthly users (QueerMeUp, 2014). I will come back to Grindr and its role in contemporary gay men's digital cultures in Chapter 6. However, it is important to note here, particularly considering the increased criticism that Gaydar received with the arrival of Facebook, that Grindr works on the same principle of simplicity that has always driven the team behind Facebook. On its initial corporate website the company noted, for instance, with obvious reference to sites such as Gaydar, that "Grindr's different because it's uncomplicated...It's not your average dating site – you know, the ones that make you sit in front of a faraway computer filling out complex, detailed profiles and answering invasive psychological questions (Grindr, 2012, np)."

Without the added features of mainstream social networking sites, however (such as group pages and network visibility), while Grindr went on to take Gaydar's mantle as the leading player in gay men's digital culture, its arrival did not halt the extension of gay men's networks into Facebook. In fact, with movements in Australia and around the globe aiming to secure marriage rights for same-sex couples, Facebook became a key destination to access, promote and organize GLBT and GLBT-oriented networks. A simple search on Facebook of the term 'gay marriage' – or even just 'gay' or 'GLBT' – will confirm as much. Hence, instead of being used by young gay men in conjunction with Gaydar alone, with Grindr's arrival Facebook was then used in conjunction with that service also. Indeed, while I did not specifically ask participants interviewed for this study in 2010 about Grindr, the way they brought it up in conversation themselves and the way that they talked about Gaydar, Grindr and Facebook together demonstrates that Grindr was immediately perceived of as part of the same category of services, and in direct competition with, Gaydar (despite their technological differences). Facebook, however, as this chapter has shown, was not used in competition with these kinds of niche SNSs, but in relation to them, to provide additional or ancillary services that helped young men to better navigate gay men's social networks, both online and off. In this way, it became a significant part of gay men's digital culture.

The next chapter discusses how, in addition to opening up Gaydar to further scrutiny and criticism (related to both its technical and ideological underpinnings), Facebook's arrival and its deep enmeshment in gay men's digital culture also opened up young gay men to a whole host of safety and privacy concerns, which effectively prevented Facebook from functioning as a wholesale alternative to niche services such as Gaydar. In particular, focus is placed on the implications of the site's real name policy and its tendency to collapse social contexts, as well as how these elements of Facebook's design impacted upon the everyday lives of the young men who participated in this study and, at a broader level, further intensified the culture of participatory reluctance within Gaydar. This chapter helps to set the up the final part of the book, which demonstrates how this history has shaped contemporary gay men's digital cultures and practices today, where many of the same issues, like participatory reluctance, appear to exist in similar ways in newer platforms and practices.

Notes

1 The fact that many users have profiles on multiple SNSs designed for the gay male community is evident from the approximately 80 per cent of participants in this study that directly noted they had profiles on multiple sites, or implied that they did via reference to gay-male-oriented SNSs other than Gaydar. It is also particularly easy in a small city like Brisbane to observe, across multiple popular social networking sites designed for the gay male community, an ingrained culture of duplicating profiles (or parts thereof – e.g., a username, a photo) for use across several services.

2 Full details of the 'Stop Bullying: Speak Up' campaign can be found here: www.facebook.com/stopbullyingspeakup

3 Drawing on Byrne's (2007a) work on BlackPlanet.com, Baym (2010) makes a similar point regarding race and the lack of references to race in Facebook's infrastructure.

4 It has been argued by some, however, that these icons represent a case of "one step forward but two steps back" for same-sex couples, as they reinforce the traditional gender roles that often make life difficult for such people (see Hern, 2012) by, for example, representing women with a dress. Although, it must be noted that this complaint is one that is applicable, even if to a lesser extent, to heterosexual men and women also.

5 At the time of writing, familial relationship descriptors offered on Facebook included Wife, Husband, Sister, Brother, Mother, Father, Daughter,

Son, Aunt, Uncle, Niece, Nephew, Cousin (female), Cousin (male), Grandmother, Grandfather, Granddaughter, Grandson, Stepsister, Stepbrother, Stepmother, Stepfather, Stepdaughter, Stepson, Sister-in-law, Brother-in-law, Mother-in-law, Father-in-law, Daughter-in-law, Son-in-law, Partner (female) and Partner (male).

6 By, for example, emphasizing users' real names and not forcing any particular social identity upon them.

7 In one Facebook profile I came across during the course of this study, beside 'Religious views', the gay male owner of the profile had simply listed 'Madonna'.

8 At the time of data collection, to initiate a private chat with another Gaydar user there were two possible ways to go about it. From the point of simply browsing through profiles, the user needed to send a chat request to another person (this was only possible if the other user was also online at the same time). This was an automated process during which the sender was asked to simply choose a 'room' from a drop-down menu in which to chat with the man attached to their chosen profile and click 'send request'. Alternatively, a user might enter a room to begin with and invite one of the men already in that room to 'private chat' – in this case, the sender need not choose a room to chat in, but had to fill in a box to create the text of their own invitation. In both of these situations, Gaydar notified the sender that a chat request had been sent to the other user. The sender then had to wait for the receiver to accept the invitation and activate the chat window. Without a paid-for membership, for two people to have recurring conversations, this process would need to be repeated on every occasion.

9 Chat rooms were not a significantly popular area of Gaydar for users in Queensland at the time data was collected. Of the 10 chat rooms designed for use by Queensland-based members of Gaydar, only one of these was regularly used: 'Australia – Queensland General Chat'. In the years that I observed Gaydar for the purposes of this study I never saw more than 50 users in this room at any one time. Moreover, the Queensland-based rooms designed for 'Cruising', 'Young' users, 'Mature' users, and various subregions of the state were generally empty.

10 A practice that Mowlabocus (2010) also noted occurred in his work.

11 At the time of data collection, Gaydar did have a tick-box menu titled 'Religious Interests', however, it was one of the categories of the 'Key Words' area of Gaydar's profile template that was rarely filled out, particularly amongst 18–28-year-old users of the site. It did not, however, have any area specifically dedicated to political views; although, users were free to express these in any of the free-text sections of their profile.

12 For further information on the negative connotations of large Facebook networks see Tong, Van Der Heide, Langwell and Walther's (2008) paper 'Too Much of a Good Thing? The Relationship between Number of Friends and Interpersonal Impressions on Facebook'. In this paper, the authors show how college students are generally impressed with peers whose Facebook friends numbered up to 302, but how, over this number, the esteem in which their peers with large friendship lists are held falls again.

13 Another user noted that this process also happened in reverse. That is, where his heterosexual friends checked the Facebook profiles of those people who were invited to his parties to ensure that they wouldn't be the only straight person in attendance, or, as he put it, "the odd one out".

14 As noted in Chapter 1, The Wickham and Fluffy are a gay nightclub and a gay night at an otherwise mainstream club. And QNews is a Queensland-based, free, fortnightly GLBT magazine.

15 Since the page received its first post in September 2007, it averaged less than four posts per year until 2011. With only three members (other than myself) when I last checked it for any new activity in 2012, it had by then, in effect, ceased to exist entirely.

16 A full-text of this particular discussion can be found in the appendix.

17 The 16 top-level-only buttons available for use on Gaydar at the time of the focus group interviews, for example, were identified by symbols that came with no further explanation that ranged from flames and steaming coffee cups, to two different pencil icons, letters and punctuation marks, colours and emoticons.

5 Consequences of Convergence – Privacy and Safety Concerns

The history of new media has been one of supplementation rather than supplantion. And in the case of gay men's digital culture, the arrival of mainstream social networking sites has not altered this pattern. As the previous chapter highlighted, the extension of gay men's social networks into Facebook during the late 2000s did not kill off young gay men's use of niche SNSs designed specifically for gay male audiences. Instead, it simply cast Facebook into an equally important role in gay men's digital culture, as a tool routinely used to augment users' experiences of niche SNSs, such as Gaydar. One of the chief consequences of this situation was the opening up of sites like Gaydar to further scrutiny, particularly in terms of the limited range of gay masculinities on offer therein. Just as significantly, though, the supplementary-style relationship that developed between Gaydar and Facebook in gay male communities also had considerable implications for the privacy and personal safety of both users and non-users of these sites. This chapter discusses some of these implications, how they were understood and experienced by the participants at the centre of this study and what sorts of steps these men took to manage their privacy and personal safety in this context. It serves to highlight some of the complexities around gay men's digital culture that drive the continued development of niche services targeted at gay male communities today, as well as their continued use amidst considerable levels of participatory reluctance.

Before launching into any discussion regarding the potential implications Facebook's arrival and popular take-up held for the safety and privacy of this demographic, whether users or non-users of the site, it is important to first acknowledge a few central tenets about the concept of privacy itself. The first of these being that privacy is integral to identity. It is well recognised, for instance, that being able to strike a comfortable balance between disclosing and concealing information about ourselves lies at the heart of all identity management work (see, e.g., Baym, 2010; Goffman, 1959; Schlenker, 1980; Quercia et al., 2012). It is the mastering of this balance that allows us to simultaneously support numerous self-narratives, and to be, in different social contexts, sibling, partner, teammate or colleague and so on. In fact, all human relationships, mediated or otherwise, are built around the disclosure and concealment of information (Altman & Taylor, 1973; Chan & Cheng, 2004) – we are socialised to read the sharing of personal information as an indication of trust and intimacy. In this way, privacy is not only crucial to our identities, but also a key aspect of relationship development. And in all societies there exists complex norms around how much information we ought to be revealing and when, and in regards to all different kinds of relationships. Sharing too much too soon, or sharing something that other people find unappealing or inappropriate, for example, can have significant repercussions. Hence, the third central tenet of privacy pertinent here is that privacy is also a highly contextual concept. What constitutes privacy is constantly shifting, defined both by historical circumstance and social expectations (Prost, Ariès & Vincent, 1991) – which, in turn, are influenced by environmental factors, individuals' personality traits, age, gender, race, sexual orientation, religious background, social status, employment circumstances and all kinds of other variables (see, e.g., Chang, Rosenn, Backstrom & Marlow, 2010; Gilbert, Karahalios & Sandvig, 2008; Quercia et al., 2012; Tufekci, 2012).

With all of these factors at play in human interactions, striking the right balance between disclosure and concealment can be quite complicated, and it requires a high degree of awareness. Of course, in the context of social networking sites, where multiple forms of interpersonal relationships often converge, this requirement is considerably greater still. The environmental boundaries people typically rely on in the physical world to help create discrete social contexts, for example, are removed – generating what leading scholars in this area have referred to as "context collapse" (see, e.g., boyd & Heer, 2006; Hogan, 2010; Marwick & boyd, 2011). In this new situation, people's awareness of social expectations and capacity to act on considered judgement must be essentially learned over, as social norms associated with information disclosure are progressively renewed and re-established. Making the situation surrounding SNSs a veritable "privacy trainwreck", as boyd (2008a) once described it, the capacity to cope with unsettled norms associated with information disclosure is not the only requirement to successfully function in these environments. Success is also heavily dependent on a significant level of technological literacy (boyd & Hargittai, 2010). Managing one's identity and relationships via SNSs by applying restrictions to what information is available and to whom, for example, requires the ability to fully understand and implement appropriate privacy settings: this is a task which is made all the more difficult by the variation in settings available across different services and by the rate at which these are/can be changed.

The following two sections of this chapter will therefore describe the affordances with regards to privacy of each of the respective SNSs discussed so far in this study as they stood at the time of data collection in the late 2000s/early 2010s, showing, in particular, how Facebook's privacy provisions during this period were complex and changing by comparison with Gaydar's simple and stable arrangements. These sections will also look at the norms that evolved during this period around information disclosure and concealment on each service amongst 18–28-year-old gay male users of the sites. How these cultures and practices created new privacy and safety concerns for this cohort, through the coexistence of both Gaydar and Facebook, will be discussed in detail thereafter. 'Safety', it should also be noted, is discussed in this chapter alongside privacy because, in the context of SNSs, the condition of being safe – that is, free from danger, risk or injury – is also heavily dependent upon understanding privacy issues as they arise online, and on having enough technological literacy to successfully navigate privacy settings and other safety-oriented aspects of various SNS interfaces. In fact, much of the research conducted on SNSs in relation to privacy has been driven by safety concerns. In particular, by popular concerns that young people do not care about privacy, are unaware of the potential dangers of SNS use and will therefore carelessly or unwittingly reveal personal details about themselves in these environments; which could, in turn, open up possibilities for them to become victims of online predators and other unsavoury characters. The need to rigorously assess the validity of such concerns, for example, was a driving factor behind the research of Lenhart and Madden (2007), Hinduja and Patchin (2008), boyd and Hargittai (2010), Madden and Smith (2010), Hoofnagle, King, Li and Turow (2010) and Tufekci (2012). Incidentally, in each of these studies, as it is in the present project, the notion that youth do not care about privacy or take steps to protect their personal information is resoundingly challenged.

Gaydar and Privacy – Simplicity and Stability

Despite a number of internationally significant advancements in social attitudes regarding GLBT equality issues in recent times,[1] homosexuality can still be a highly sensitive subject. This, combined with the fact that gay men's social networking sites are often used for intensely personal purposes, such as arranging sexual encounters and seeking intimate relationships, means that it is not surprising that, since its arrival, Gaydar has taken a multilayered approach to protecting the safety and privacy of its users. This approach has included, for example, a detailed privacy policy, which states how Gaydar would collect, store and use members' data in accordance with the terms of the UK's Data Protection Laws and Regulations; the incorporation into the site of a set of adjustable privacy settings for user profiles; a non-restrictive approach to usernames and the role of inter-profile connectivity; the presence of GLBT-friendly police who have acted as safety officers on the site; functions for blocking individual users from one's account; and the provision of advice on how Gaydar's privacy functions work and how to best use the site safely (see Gaydar, 2012). Despite its multilayered nature, however, what really characterised Gaydar's approach to user protection at the time of data collection for this project – and, indeed, for the entirety of the 2000s preceding that – was that the privacy and safety-oriented aspects of the site were resolutely simple, stable and user friendly.

As Table 5.1 indicates, below, the adjustable privacy settings available to Gaydar users, for example, were wide-ranging in scope, yet highly succinct. They were designed to address issues of privacy associated with the external visibility of profile content (e.g., "Can others access your profile externally at this address http://gaydar.com.au/profilename?"), as well as the extent to which profiles and the actions undertaken with them could be viewed internally, by the Gaydar community itself (e.g., "Would you like to hide your profile?" "Would you like to leave a Track when you view other profiles?"). They could be utilised to provide greater protection against quite serious privacy breaches, such as identity theft/the unauthorised use of people's images, and infringements of copyright (e.g., "Would you like to watermark your pictures with your profile name?"). And they could be used to provide a level of protection against more basic privacy concerns, such as those associated with social embarrassment (e.g., "Would you like to display on your profile how many times your profile has been seen by others?").[2] Moreover, all of this occurred within the space of just seven very simply

Table 5.1 Privacy settings available on Gaydar

Privacy
☐ Would you like to leave a **Track** when you view other profiles?
If you leave a public thought (Hot, Nice, Get to Know) they will be able to see you thought in their Tracks
☐ Would you like to display on your profile how many times your profile has been seen by others?
Would you like others to be able to see your Membership status on your profile? ⊙ Always ○ Status visible only to Members ○ Never
Can others access your profile externally at this address: http://gaydar.com.au/profilename? ⊙ Yes ○ Only online Members and Guests ○ Only online Members
☐ Would you like to watermark your photos with your profile name?
☐ Would you like to add the Sex Factor nomination button to your profile?
Other guys will be able to nominate you and you can then decide if you'd like to take part!
☐ Would you like to hide your profile? If you tick this option other guys will not be able to find you. Your profile will always be visible if you are in the Gaydar Chat rooms.

phrased questions that Gaydar did not change or reset. Hence, unless users independently decided that they would like to alter their privacy settings, dealing with this aspect of the site was a one-off concern.

In addition to keeping privacy settings stable and succinct and using language that might help people to easily understand what exactly they were agreeing or not agreeing to, Gaydar put the user in a position to best control the level of privacy they wished to maintain on the site in a number of other ways. The first of these was the actual variations in profile visibility levels it offered via the aforementioned privacy settings. The kind of protection of user privacy addressed via the last option in the adjustable settings shown above in Table 5.1 ("Would you like to hide your profile?"), for example, was the most comprehensive form of blanket privacy coverage available on Gaydar. The hidden profile allowed people to use the SNS completely unseen by all others (users and non-users alike), except where that person chose to send private messages to other users or entered one of the site's chat rooms. That is, it allowed profile owners to exist within the site in the role of 'lurker'. While this option gave people the capacity to have almost complete control over who had access to their information, it also meant that opportunities to engage with other users of the site (who were unable to initiate contact with hidden profile owners) were also severely limited in the name of privacy and safety. Accordingly, very few Gaydar users had this kind of profile.[3]

Alternatively, users could choose to remain visible and contactable via the site and manage any privacy or safety concerns that arose by relying on the safety nets Gaydar provided to them through the blocking function, the 'report abuse' button, the 'hide empty info' option embedded in the profile template, and via the presence of police officers in some of the site's chat rooms. This more nuanced, individualised way of controlling visibility on the site while still optimising opportunities to use Gaydar as a platform to meet and socialise with new people was the approach taken by the vast majority of Gaydar's users during this study.[4] This approach allowed users to have the greatest level of control over their information while still optimising their own visibility. For example, one click and a problem user could be blocked, rendering him unable to see your profile or any of your activities on the site. Equally, a click on the 'hide empty info' box and any (or all) of the non-compulsory information categories in the profile template could be removed from your profile. Quite significantly, though, Gaydar did not favour, promote or legitimise either of these approaches to using the site – or, for that matter, any of the other slight variations on these approaches to privacy protection that it made available to users via its privacy settings.[5] Instead, Gaydar took a design approach that aimed to support users to balance the benefits of visibility with their individual needs for privacy, without impeding users' activities on the site or instructing them to engage with the service in any particular manner.

Outside of the various options it provided users to control their own visibility on the site, through its adjustable privacy settings and the capacity to remove various elements of the profile template, for example, perhaps the most important indications that Gaydar put users in control of their own approach to privacy and safety were its affordances with regards to profile names and connectivity. In both of these areas, Gaydar did not, and had never promoted or legitimised any particular approach to privacy protection. Whether users chose to be highly revealing or intensely private, their capacity to use the service would not be diminished. That is, on Gaydar, openness/transparency and connectivity were not needed to participate. The amount of personal information users wished to share via their usernames, for example, was entirely up to the users themselves, as Gaydar had no policy with regards to profile names. Hence, users could choose to use their real names, some derivative thereof, or create an entirely invented one, being as creative as they liked. Throughout the course of this project, Gaydar made this option clear to users during the registration process where it provided an example username (hot_guy74) beneath the very first registration box that prospective users encountered. Accordingly, while usernames on Gaydar have ranged from the intensely private (e.g., random collections of numbers and letters) to the partially revealing (e.g., the inclusion of first names, birth years, postcodes etc.), and the entirely open (first and last name), the site has always been in nature a pseudonymous environment, with online names that obfuscate user identity (e.g., hot_guy74) dominating. Likewise, though Gaydar provided the tools to allow users to link to other profiles throughout the 2000s, the site was not designed in such a way as to limit user experience if this option was not taken up. While adding 'friends' and 'favourites' is a common activity on all kinds of SNSs – and in many cases a prerequisite to access and participate in the network – this was not the case on Gaydar. Indeed, while the site's infrastructure allowed for this practice, the cultural norms surrounding use of the site – for example, attitudes towards the imagined audience (see Chapter 3) – dictated that, during the period of this study, linking with other profiles was highly uncommon.[6]

This approach to user safety and privacy issues, which through its simplicity and inherent flexibility put users themselves in a position of control, was also evident in the minimalist manner that Gaydar communicated with users about the privacy and safety options available to them on the site. As with the explanations that were offered on the site itself for the various privacy settings available on Gaydar, the chapter on privacy and safety issues in *The Big Book of Gaydar* (JockBoy26, 2010) is demonstrative in this regard. The shortest chapter in the entire book, 'Safely, Safely, Online' (pp. 44–47) identified the key ways that Gaydar worked to make its community of users safe by presenting clear details (in simple, accessible, everyday language) about the range of options for privacy protection that had been built into the site – and it reminded users that the degree to which Gaydar protected the individual privacy of its user community was dictated by the users themselves. The chapter noted, for example, that Gaydar had a strict agreement with the police personnel who acted as safety officers on the site, "not to engage in or interrupt conversations in chat rooms so [users could] chat in comfort and safety" (JockBoy26, 2010, p. 47). These officers were instructed to act only upon request from users: readers were told, "they're not gathering evidence – they're listening to our complaints and protecting our community". That is, the chapter simply ensured that users would have enough information about the site and the privacy and safety options available to them to make informed choices about their own profiles and about the ways that they used Gaydar. It also emphasised the extent to which users themselves were in control of their own privacy and safety on the site. The only instructional-style information or material in the chapter, which suggested a 'correct' way to use the SNS, was a short list on page 45, which contained "things you should never put on your Gaydar profile" (JockBoy26, 2010). That list included the following items:

- your phone number
- your email address
- your actual address (home or work) or pics of where you live/work
- your credit card number
- the name of your employer
- the name of your fave bar.[7]

Given that the focus group participants in this project were all of an age – and from social backgrounds – where they had grown up using online services and had been suitably schooled on 'stranger danger' issues, like many of the young people in the studies of Lenhart and Madden (2007), Hinduja and Patchin (2008) and boyd and Hargittai (2010), concealing phone numbers, home addresses and the like in digital spaces came as second nature to these men. Armed with this knowledge, a set of easily navigable tools to manage the disclosure/concealment of their personal information, and the protective benefits of an essentially pseudonymous environment, the participants in this study expressed very few concerns about their privacy and/or safety being compromised as a result of using Gaydar. Hence, while they had all created usernames that did not include their real names or current locations (e.g., suburb names or postcodes), none of the focus group participants had gone so far as to create a hidden profile. All focus group participants had instead opted for widely visible Gaydar profiles (i.e., accessible to all other Gaydar users) where they comfortably balanced the disclosure and concealment of personal information via the profile template – by removing or leaving blank various categories as they saw fit. And, as noted in Chapter 3, there were clear patterns around what kind of personal information they felt content to disclose in this environment. While all but one of the participants indicated, for example, that they had posted 'lifestyle'-oriented images of themselves where their faces were visible, highly personal information that could potentially associate them with the kinds of sex-oriented stereotypes about gay men that Gaydar tended to perpetuate was left off. The sections of Gaydar's profile template relating to penis size, circumcision status, sexual roles and fetishes, for instance, were largely left blank by these users. In addition to writing very little in free-text boxes, or, as one university student put it, going "super vague", this was the preferred way to balance out the level of exposure received through posting identifiable images. This approach mirrors the findings of Lenhart and Madden (2007), who noted that, among young SNS users, the posting of a photo is 'standard', whereas more detailed personal information (e.g., phone numbers) is much more likely to be withheld.

In my observations of the patterns surrounding information disclosure and concealment on Gaydar itself, this same approach to privacy and identity management (i.e., pseudonymity with a visible face picture) was hugely popular amongst 18–28-year-old users of the site – as was the practice of leaving large areas of the profile template blank, or writing 'ask me' into the free-text fields. This image rich, information light, style of privacy management was common as it allowed for the balancing act between disclosure and concealment to be negotiated on a case-by-case basis, because, through this approach, users needed to actively engage in a dialogue in order to gain access to information about each other. This approach was also a preferred one because photographs on user profiles were much more culturally necessary in this space than text-based information – perhaps on account of the image-driven nature of gay male culture more generally, or, as Mowlabocus (2010) has discussed, because the uploading of a picture demonstrates an investment in the space and its associated community and thus a "willingness to openly identify as gay or bisexual" (p. 103) that also articulates with issues of honesty and integrity. In any case, evidence of the cultural necessity to share images/photographs of oneself could be found, for instance, in the widespread appearance of captions beneath self-taken images (or 'selfies') on the site which read, for example, "everyone has to have one...", "I guess we all need one of these", and "obligatory mirror pic".

Despite the prevalence of this privacy management strategy, where images were more readily shared than written information, however, there were also a smaller number of men in this demographic observed during the site analysis phase of this project who had taken advantage of the capacity to fully participate on Gaydar while completely concealing their identities from other users through their approach to profile pictures. That is, there were a smaller number of people seen on Gaydar during observations conducted for this study who had not officially 'hidden' their profiles via the available privacy settings, but who had created a profile that still offered them complete anonymity. This was done either by posting only pictures from which they could not be identified (e.g., headless torso shots, pictures taken from behind), or by not posting any pictures of themselves on their profiles at all. Of course, in many instances there was evidence that this approach had been taken in order to protect the owners of these profiles from being identified as gay men. At the time of data collection, for example, there were 483 profiles on Gaydar located in the Brisbane area without any images that belonged to 18–28-year-old men who identified themselves as 'not out'. In other cases, it appeared that users without images on their profiles were 'out',[8] but, as some of them put it themselves, were too 'shy', 'inexperienced' or unwilling to be associated with the site to post them. One user with zero images on his profile that I came across during my observations of Gaydar, for instance, noted that the he had face pictures of himself on file that he was happy to share with people who asked, but that he had refrained from directly posting any images of himself to the site in order to prevent a situation where he might be recognised as "that Gaydar guy from Coles".[9] Others had clearly chosen not to reveal their identities by posting images on account of the fact that they were simply using the site to find sex partners – a practice which, at least according to the profiles found on Gaydar belonging to users in the 18–28-year-old age bracket, would be frowned upon by a large percentage of their peers (see Chapter 3).

As the above information indicates, despite all of the privacy-related options and functions embedded into the digital infrastructure of Gaydar – and the simplicity of their design – from a practical perspective, it was the act of posting pictures versus not posting pictures (or posting non-identifying images) that acted as the key determinant of each user's approach to privacy on this site. It distinguished between those comfortable with pseudonymity and those who preferred complete anonymity. As the next section of this chapter discusses, the approach to posting pictures that each user took in this environment was therefore also highly indicative of the kinds of privacy and safety issues that user might face during the course of their interactions with Gaydar. This is because the key privacy and safety issues associated with Gaydar use have largely revolved around the potential consequences of identification and recognition. Indeed, outside of the risks associated with identification and recognition discussed in the next section, the only other risk associated with using Gaydar that came up during focus group discussions was one that participants felt did not necessarily apply to them. In essence, it came to light that a handful of participants believed that the centrality of Gaydar and similar sites to gay male communities had brought about a situation where young gay men and new users of these sites had become dangerously complacent about meeting up with strangers. Speaking about young people in general, one participant said, "because of more social networking and all that kind of stuff, we're more in tune to it and we're more trusting. If someone sends you a message saying, 'let's go out for coffee'...you make a pretty quick judgement call and meet someone that you've never met before because that's the way that we interact with people now." Embedded with the common concerns about young people's naivety and the dangers of new media formats that have shaped public discourse on youth and the media for decades (see Springhall, 1998), this comment was an interesting one because it bared no resemblance to the experience of this particular user or of the wider group of men who participated in this study. Indeed, demonstrating the extent to which this particular concern was more a product of Davison's (1983) third person effect than their own experiences, these men talked about being highly conscious of their safety in the event of meeting someone from Gaydar, and about being particularly reticent with regards to their personal information when using the site, especially during the period in which they were newer users.[10] Moreover, not one of the participants interviewed for this study reported an incident where their personal safety had been jeopardised by meeting another Gaydar user. All of the participants, however, had had at least one experience where being recognised from Gaydar themselves, or conversely, recognising another person from Gaydar, in the course of their lives offline had made them feel awkward or uncomfortable.

Gaydar and Recognition

In 2010, Gaydar put the number of profiles on its site without any images at 2,087,954 – meaning that 75 per cent of profiles on Gaydar contained at least one picture (JockBoy26, 2010, pp. 17–18). They also noted that the number of profiles with pictures had increased steadily since the site launched in 1999, arguing that it was a sign of how far the community had come in terms of its willingness to be open (JockBoy26, 2010, pp. 17–18). In line with this trend, it is perhaps not surprising that the 18–28-year-old men studied here displayed a clear preference towards the posting of images to their profiles – and in particular, towards "lifestyle" or "everyday" pictures, as they described them, where their faces were visible. Indeed, such had been the prevalence of this approach on the site in the years immediately prior to data collection for this study, that those Gaydar users who choose not to post pictures at all were considered suspicious by the openly gay members of the focus groups I conducted. As one of the younger participants put it,

> I know some [people who don't post photos] have the theory that they don't want to be seen or recognised in the community and that. But I figure if they don't have a photo they're either not confident or they're butt ugly.

Not having a photo, and in particular, a 'face pic', was also considered an indication that casual sex was the only goal of such profile owners. So strong was this belief, in fact, that – in an interesting contradiction which again highlights how people judge others differently from themselves (Davison, 1983) – the idea that having no profile pictures indicated that a user was solely seeking casual sex was also expressed by the one participant in this study who had, himself, not posted an image to his Gaydar profile, and who, in explaining his reasons for not doing so, had cited his desire not to be publicly associated with the SNS on account of its inherent emphasis on the sexual.

Hence, across all focus groups, followed by 'age', having a 'face pic' was in fact the number one criterion that determined who these men would message, and/or reply to messages from, on the site. "If they don't have a picture I just ignore them", was a common assertion. And as *The Big Book of Gaydar* confirms (JockBoy26, 2010, p. 18), this tendency matched those also seen far beyond the confines of these focus groups. "The fact is," notes JockBoy26, "the most popular profiles are the ones with pictures". "No pic, no chat, no meet. Get it?" (JockBo26, 2010, p. 18) he says, mimicking a phrase commonly found on Gaydar profiles throughout the 2000s and early 2010s. Of course, in this context, where there was cultural pressure to post images, the role of pseudonymity, the option to 'hide empty info', and all of the site's other privacy and safety provisions discussed above, took on greater significance. In effect, these tools allowed users to partake in the culture of Gaydar more fully by enabling them to maintain some level of privacy while still posting identifiable images of themselves. The tendency of users to "go super vague" in an attempt to manage their privacy via the profile template, whilst still posting an identifiable image, also makes sense in this context. Like much of our identity management work more generally (Page, Kobsa & Knijnenburg, 2012), these tactics were simply attempts to create and preserve relationship boundaries: in this case, for example, withholding information was used as a means to position the boundaries between the profile owner and the imagined audience in such a way as to indicate foreignness/unfamiliarity, and the corresponding lack of trust that often accompanies it (i.e., it said to the audience, "if you want to know more about me, you need to ask").

For the majority of Gaydar users who, myself included, have taken this approach to profile management – uploading a visible face picture, but constructing a pseudonymous username and providing only a smattering of relatively vague personal information – the most common way that one's privacy and/or safety could be compromised by using the site was by being recognised, either online or offline, by another member of the Gaydar community. In the years that I had used Gaydar even prior to conducting this study, for example, thanks primarily to the size of Brisbane and the relatively small number of users situated in this area, I had personally stumbled across several profiles belonging to students and staff members at my university, local businessmen and even neighbours – some of which belonged to people I had not already known were gay. Even in much larger cities, where Gaydar users are more plentiful, this was not uncommon either. Focusing on London's Gaydar community, for instance, *The Big Book of Gaydar* (JockBoy26, 2010) discusses a number of instances where Gaydar profiles belonging to politicians, high-profile policemen and various celebrities became public knowledge in a series of 'Gaydar Scandals' (p. 63). JockBoy26 (2010) recounts, for example, the stories of two policemen, who, in separate incidents in the UK and Italy, were reprimanded when their presence on Gaydar became widely publicised. Similarly, in *Gaydar Culture*, Mowlabocus (2010, p. 99) discusses the situation of British politician Chris Bryant, who, in 2003, was set upon by the tabloid press when they published his Gaydar profile picture, seemingly to inform the public of his aberrant behaviour. In all three of these cases, these men were already openly gay in their respective private lives and had each been long-time members of the site. Of course, what makes such situations in the case of celebrities and other high-profile figures a 'scandal', and in the case of more regular citizens a potential privacy and safety concern, is that the information contained in a Gaydar profile is intended for a particular audience. And while that information might be uncontroversial and entirely appropriate in the Gaydar environment, and even amongst the wider gay male community, in other contexts it could easily become quite problematic depending on an individual's life circumstances and the degree to which their surrounding environment is characterised by homophobia. This situation, of course, is no longer unique to Gaydar. As I will return to in the following chapter, today, similar situations arise through platforms like Grindr – perhaps even to a larger degree due to the geolocative nature of contemporary platforms. However, during the time of Gaydar's market dominance throughout the 2000s, it was through Gaydar and its competitor sites that the gay male community first dealt with these kinds of privacy concerns at a large scale.

Equally, though, being recognised on Gaydar, or alternatively, *from* Gaydar, could have its benefits, in particular, when that recognition remained within the immediate population of Gaydar users. Young (2004), for example, argued that the system of recognition that existed amongst gay men in urban communities as a result of Gaydar offered users of the SNS access to new narrowcast forms of celebrity status – or what Senft (2008) in her work on 'celebrity and community in the age of social networks' later termed 'micro-celebrity'. Beyond micro-celebrity status, however, recognition in this context could also have more practical benefits. One participant in this study noted, for example, that he had become aware of his own housemate's homosexuality by discovering his profile on Gaydar, which then freed both him and his housemate up to talk about their sexualities at home. Likewise, as I noted in the introduction to this book, it was the fact that he recognised me from my Gaydar profile that gave my partner, as a new arrival to the city, the initial confidence/excuse to approach me in a crowded nightclub back in 2007. In the years prior to that evening, regularly recognising the faces in that same venue from my own use of Gaydar (without necessarily knowing many of the people there), had also made my experiences as a young gay man encountering Brisbane's gay clubs and other gay men's social spaces much less intimidating and more comfortable than they might otherwise have been. Indeed, the capacity to recognise people from Gaydar afforded me the kind of informational social capital that allows one to negotiate these spaces with a greater sense of agency and awareness long after I had first encountered them. Hence, for me personally, the potential breaches of privacy that might have resulted from being recognised as a gay man, by another gay man, on, or from, Gaydar, had always been balanced out by the benefits that using Gaydar could also bring. The extent to which this was true for other users of Gaydar, however, would again have depend upon their own life circumstances.

For the particular group of men interviewed for this study, who were comfortable enough with their sexuality to speak about their experiences with Gaydar in a room with other users of the site, the potential risks with regard to privacy and safety associated with using Gaydar were also balanced out against the opportunities or benefits that could arise from using the site. There were numerous discussions across all of the focus groups conducted, for instance, which highlighted what participants saw as both the positive and negative implications of being recognised – be that online or offline – as a result of using Gaydar. Asked if they could discuss the ways that they saw Gaydar intersecting with their lives offline in physical environments, for example, interviewees quickly channelled discussion toward the experience of entering commercial gay spaces and seeing crowds that they recognised to be comprised of Gaydar usernames. Stories of walking into a venue and seeing 'hung-like-a-horse', 'suMMer-Fun' and 'chillivodka', rather than, for example, Mike, Tom and Sam were common across all focus groups. And, likewise, all focus groups discussed reverse scenarios where, during the course of their use of Gaydar, participants had come across profiles of men they had met in various offline spaces and contexts, such as at work, in restaurants and at GLBT events – thereby gaining information about those men they otherwise would not have had access to in an offline setting.

Amongst discussions of these kinds of situations, and the system of recognition surrounding gay men's digital culture that enables them, participants' most serious concern for their own safety and privacy related to the possibility of being stalked. Being recognised via Gaydar could potentially help facilitate stalking in offline contexts they reasoned: in particular, as one man put it, "at a club because [someone] stalked you online". However, none of the participants interviewed for this study had personally been in this situation as a result of using Gaydar, and the time that they devoted to talking about this danger across all focus groups was limited. It was mentioned quickly and casually as if it were an obvious, yet unlikely, potential occurrence; a danger that inherently went along with the use of digital spaces in general. Hence, despite this mention of the risk that stalking via Gaydar may occur in physical spaces, participants' concerns with regard to the possibility of being recognised via Gaydar were actually quite minimal and primarily associated with preserving their own self-perceptions and protecting their reputations as gay men amongst other gay men. The fact that people could readily recognise each other on Gaydar generated the most discussion – and also troubled participants most, or was most seen as a disadvantage of using the site – for instance, because they had found that it occasionally lead to awkward or uncomfortable social interactions in what were sometimes referred to as 'non-gay' contexts:

> It's kind of like you can be somewhere and have been speaking to someone on Gaydar and just completely ignore the fact that you have when you happen to meet them in real life because it's too awkward for them to bring up…it's too awkward for them, so you just don't.
>
> You're serving them and you're like, {imitates thinking} 'I know you', and this is really embarrassing. I've hid at work because I've recognised someone. When you work in a department store you obviously see a lot of people…and because I'm in menswear people come round and I'm like, 'crap', or they've sent me a message and I've declined once again. It would be awkward so I'd quickly go to the changing rooms or something.
>
> I have the worst memory. People walk up to me and they're like, I was chatting to you on such and such. I say, 'you weren't, who are you?' They're like, 'yes, you live in such-and-such [suburb]'. 'No, don't remember you, I'm going back over here now.'

In addition to its capacity to generate uncomfortable offline situations, such as these, where social contexts collapse, the commonplace ability to recognise each other from Gaydar was also condemned amongst participants for what they saw as its tendency to encourage gay men to prejudge each other:

> I know people that go and out and will know everything about different people from what they've read on the profiles and be like, 'he's cheating on his partner. They're with they in an open relationship…'. You automatically can have a judgement on these people.
>
> Like a lot of the people that I work with, we all have it. We'll be at work and you'll see someone walk in and it'll be, 'oh there's that tragic mole from Grindr or Gaydar or whatever'. That happens quite a lot.

> It's awful...you've got a pre-conceived notion in your head about what that person is and then you know so much about someone and you've created – well, sometimes you know so much about them from their pictures and what they've written, you've created your own opinion of them, therefore you're not as likely to go and engage with them, but you might have if you hadn't already got that. So I think it can help you meet people and get involved in different community things and stuff like that, but it can also turn a bit counterproductive.

At the same time that participants labelled the system of recognition surrounding Gaydar as counterproductive, however, in the vein of Albrechtslund's (2008) notion of "participatory surveillance", these men had clearly found a number of ways to make the fact that recognising each other in offline situations from the SNS (and vice versa) was quite common, into a socially productive or advantageous situation for themselves. Being more informed in offline contexts about the kinds of people they might be engaging with, or just considering engaging with, via information available on Gaydar profiles, for example, was a particularly popular byproduct of using the site. "[J]ust for the simple fact that you have seen them", said one participant, "I think that helps you in a way to make a judgement of them, whether you will talk to them or not. When you go on those websites you can see, and if they write different things about themselves, then you can make a judgement whether you'll talk to them, ignore them or snob them or whatever you're going to do". The ability to have some information – however minimal – about people they encountered, either online or offline, was also considered quite productive in the sense that it helped participants to expedite the process of forming friendships with other gay men, by giving them ways to start conversations. "[Gaydar] familiarises you with what type of person they are perhaps before you go and say hi", said one participant.

> Like, I've seen a couple of people on there and I might have said hi or something once or twice and then never said something for a while. But then I'll see them out and I'll go up and say 'blah blah blah' and they'll be like 'oh hey!'.

To this remark, there was much nodding and agreement amongst those in the same focus group and another man added,

> I think it works the reverse way as well. Like when you see someone out or meet someone and then you might be online and you see them and connect with them through that way. It'd be like, 'Hey, I met you on Saturday!'.

Participants also noted, for example, that they had taken advantage of the fact that they could recognise people via Gaydar in order to "suss-out a cheating ex-boyfriend"[11] and to "pinpoint the local gay community". The latter had made a significantly positive difference to the life of at least one participant, for instance, who noted that in aiding him to "pinpoint the gay community", Gaydar had helped him to reassess his own mental image of the size of the local gay male population and to realise that he was not as alone in Brisbane as he first thought. Echoing the findings of McKenna and Bargh (1998) and Gray (2009), who each explain how online services have helped young gay people to experience "identity demarginalization", this participant described his own reaction to logging on to the site and regularly seeing thousands of men online in the following way: "[It's like] 'wow!' I didn't realise there were that many gay people in Brisbane. There are more of us than I thought".

Whether commenting on Gaydar's tendency to encourage prejudgement of others, its capacity to be utilised to "suss out ex-boyfriends", or simply to identify the scope of the local gay community, what was most apparent in discussions of what interviewees perceived to be the pros and cons surrounding Gaydar's system of recognition, was that these young users were highly aware of the potential privacy and safety risks associated with the SNS. This awareness was also apparent in the ways that these men approached their own privacy and identity management strategies on the site. Focus group participants had balanced out concealment and exposure of their personal information via posting identifiable images accompanied by sparse textual cues for instance – and in the profiles observed online there was a similar pattern. As was also noted above, in both contexts, those who opted not to post images to their profiles directly cited specific cons associated with the site's system of recognition that were brought up by focus group participants, such as the tendency to prejudge each other, as reasons for maintaining their anonymity. "I don't want to be that Gaydar guy at Coles",[12] wrote one user without an image on his profile. "Looking for people who won't come running up to me if seen out", wrote another. In short, on Gaydar, these users had an understanding of the site and the risks associated with using it deep enough to ensure that they were able to balance the emotional and social benefits that may arise from using the service out against those risks by adjusting their behaviour and identity management strategies accordingly. As the next section of this chapter details, however, an entirely different situation existed within the context of these users' engagements with Facebook and with the expansion of gay men's social networks into Facebook more generally. The very nature of the mainstream social networking service, its comparatively complex and unstable privacy settings, and the culture of transparency which underpins it, combined in this context to create far more safety and privacy concerns for this demographic than they identified with regards to their use of Gaydar. More significantly, these factors also combined in such a manner as to potentially:

- limit access to many of the benefits associated with use of Facebook;
- heighten privacy and safety concerns related to Gaydar use when accounts were held on both services; and
- create privacy and safety concerns for men part of the broader gay male community but who did not use either Gaydar or Facebook at all.

Complex and Changing – The Facebook Approach to Privacy

As is documented in various accounts of the site's development (see, e.g., boyd & Hargittai, 2010; Kirkpatrick, 2010), Facebook's history with privacy settings has been a tumultuous one, plagued by controversy and constant change. In its early days, when Facebook was university focussed, for example, users' content was essentially protected by the fact that it was visible only to those on the same campus, or registered with the same institution-based email address. By the time the SNS became publicly available and had gained popularity in Australia, around 2007/2008, however, privacy was becoming a matter of much broader concern, and, in response, the site allowed users to limit their information to being shared only with "'Friends', 'Friends-of-Friends', a specific 'Network' or 'No One'" (Zuckerberg, 2009). Soon after, Facebook developed into a platform upon which other companies could create games and applications, leading to the introduction of privacy settings enabling users to determine what level of access third parties could have to their information. In essence, as the size and scope of the service and the range of users it attracts has increased and diversified, the company has needed to expand and update its available privacy settings accordingly. As a result, through a series of redesigns Facebook's functions for controlling privacy have both multiplied and become increasingly complex in recent years.

In 2010, at the commencement my of data collection, in comparison to Gaydar, Facebook therefore sat on the opposite end of the spectrum in terms of the number and complexity of privacy settings it provided to users. Whereas Gaydar had a total of five sections or questions within its privacy settings – seven, if sub-questions are included (see Table 5.1 above) – Facebook had more than twenty. The twenty-plus questions users were first faced with when opening Facebook's privacy settings were arranged into five categories, as seen in Table 5.2 below. Although not shown here, many of the sub-questions contained in this table also had their own multilayered sub-parts. The process of answering these questions, which was done via an assortment of drop-down menus and tick boxes, as well as through free-text areas, could be complex and time-consuming. For example, whereas the largest number of possible options for answering privacy-related questions

Table 5.2 Categories of privacy settings available on Facebook

How you connect	*Timeline and tagging*	*Ads, apps and websites*	*Limit the audience for past posts*	*Blocked people and apps*
Who can look up your timeline by name?	Who can post on your timeline?	Apps you use	Limit old posts	Add friends to your Restricted list
Who can look you up using the email address or phone number you provided?	Who can see what others post on your timeline?	How people bring your info to apps they use		Block users
Who can send you friend requests?	Review posts friends tag you in before they appear on your timeline	Instant personalization		Block app invites
Who can send you Facebook messages?	Who can see posts you've been tagged in on your timeline?	Public search		Block event invites
	Review tags people add to your own posts on Facebook	Ads		Block apps
	Who sees tag suggestions when photos that look like you are uploaded?			

on Gaydar was three, anywhere between two and seventeen[13] choices were available in areas where answers were pre-provided on Facebook. Making the job of sifting through Facebook's privacy settings even more laborious was the level of description and explanation provided to help users grasp what exactly each setting pertained to. Some questions, for example, were accompanied by large paragraphs of text containing links to entire pages of information concerning the operation of just a single setting. Many of these pages themselves also contained links to additional material. On Gaydar, however, the information provided about each of the site's five privacy settings did not exceed one line. Moreover, Gaydar's descriptions of its privacy settings were provided in clear active language (e.g., Would you like others to be able to see your Membership status on your profile?), whereas

Facebook's were comprised of passive, indirect language which required users to consider in some detail how the information in question would travel through their networks (e.g., 'How people bring your info to apps they use'). Hence, by comparison with Gaydar, in 2010, the task of navigating through Facebook's privacy settings was much more arduous. This was even more so the case, as Facebook was regularly changing and updating the layout and content of its privacy controls in a manner that required users to constantly adjust their settings.

As noted earlier in this chapter, privacy settings were generally a one-off concern for Gaydar users. On Facebook, however, even today, adjusting privacy settings with each new update – or as Opsahl (2010) would call it "erosion" – of the settings is essential in order to retain even a basic level of control over one's own information. This is due to the fact that whenever Facebook has introduced new options for sharing content to the site, users' privacy controls are set to the default, which is invariably to share information broadly.[14] By taking this approach, Facebook has on multiple occasions exposed the information contained in users' profiles in ways that they were either not aware of or were not comfortable with. The 2006 introduction of the 'News Feed' feature, for example, collated and published all of the actions taken on a user's profile in one place, in a way that gave others much easier access to it (boyd, 2008a). It was only due to users' protests that Facebook was eventually prompted to introduce privacy settings to control what would be shared on people's News Feeds. Similarly, in 2007, in what was one of the site's most controversial developments, leading to a class action against the company, Facebook introduced Beacon – an advertising platform that shared users' activities on partner sites outside of Facebook on the News Feed. In addition to the obvious economic motivations, what drives the company to constantly develop like this, in a manner that, as Kirkpatrick (2010, p. 201) puts it, sees them "pus[h]...users a bit too hard to expose their data and subsequently have to retreat", is Mark Zuckerberg's unwavering belief that transparency is socially ideal (see Barnett, 2010). "In a more open and transparent world," he reasons, "people will be held to the consequences of their actions and be more likely to behave responsibly" (in Kirkpatrick, 2010, p. 200).

It is based on this premise that Facebook has developed into a platform where privacy settings are complex and constantly changing and where the default position is always to share broadly. It is also based on this premise that Facebook has a real-name policy[15] and, unlike Gaydar, only really works when users are visibly connected to others. In fact, the push to ensure that users share as much as possible on Facebook is evident in all aspects of the site and its design. The introduction of the Timeline-based profile in 2011, for example, centred around enabling and encouraging users to "tell [their] life story". This feature, and all of the material that accompanied its launch (see, e.g., Figure 5.1), along with the site's complex privacy settings, default positions, and real-name policy are clearly geared

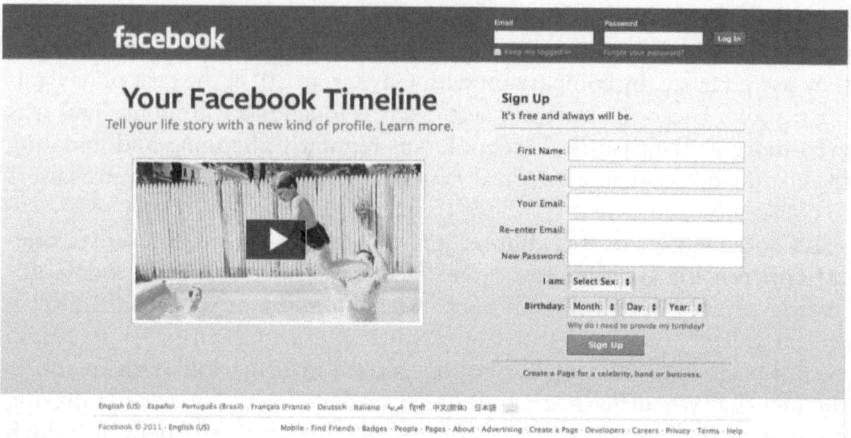

Figure 5.1 'Tell your life story': Facebook cover page at launch of Timeline.

towards ensuring that each user has a singular, transparent identity. "The days of you having a different image for your work friends or coworkers and for the other people you know are probably coming to an end pretty quickly", argues Zuckerberg (in Kirkpatrick, 2010, p. 199). "You have one identity", he says (in Kirkpatrick, 2010, p. 199), and Facebook is designed according to that principle. By contrast, Gaydar has supported much more nuanced and varied approaches to information disclosure. "[C]reate your own profile and let guys know as little or as much about you as you like", exclaims the site's introductory tour (Gaydar, 2010).

Despite conceptualising greater openness as a route to enhancing online safety, the Facebook model, in voraciously promoting one identity tied to our real names, is a system that collapses social contexts (Hogan, 2010; Marwick & boyd, 2011) and raises substantial privacy and safety issues in the process. While social contexts can also be collapsed via Gaydar, of course, in situations such as those mentioned earlier (e.g., where a retail worker is required to serve a customer that he recognises as a Gaydar user he may have previously snubbed online), the collapsed contexts the niche SNS generates in these situations are typically ephemeral. That is, the (socially awkward) moment where the boundary is removed between the retail worker's identity as an employee and as a user of Gaydar lasts only for the duration of time that the other Gaydar user remains in the store. By contrast, the very nature of Facebook as a general purpose SNS, which encourages users to map out their entire social network online, creates a situation where social contexts are more permanently collapsed. Accordingly, as privacy concerns are "just symptoms of a higher level motivation…to preserve one's existing offline relationship boundaries" (Page et al., 2012, p. 266), it follows that the potential for privacy concerns to be experienced in this environment is much greater than it is in the context of Gaydar. Indeed, indicating the seriousness of the potential consequences of a move towards the 'real name web' during this period by mainstream social networking services, such as Facebook, both boyd (2011) and Hogan (2011, 2012) argued that real name policies (which foster context collapse) are an abuse of power and an impediment to free speech. Hogan (2011) argued, for example, that the removal of context and the pushing of singular identity, in effect, also remove the basic right to free speech because real name sites, such as Facebook:

> deny individuals the right to be context-specific….if you don't think that being context-specific is a right, consider what you think 'free' means in the right to free speech. When my speech is necessarily encumbered by a tethering to a single all-encompassing key (the real name) that unlocks whatever I say, I am no longer free to address one specific context and not another one….I am not free to say what I want.
> (Hogan, 2011, np)

As a group that is widely acknowledged to have benefitted greatly from pseudonymous online environments and the freedoms they provide (see, e.g., Campbell, 2004; Hillier & Harrison, 2007; McKenna & Bargh, 2008; Gray 2009), GLBT youth are frequently cited in discussions of how "denying individuals the right to be context-specific" (Hogan, 2010) endangers the privacy and safety of SNS users. *The Wall Street Journal*, for example, in an article titled 'When the Most Personal Secrets Get Outed on Facebook' (Fowler, 2012), published the story of two teens at the University of Texas who had been inadvertently outed as gay and lesbian via the platform by their Queer Chorus choirmaster who added them to the choir's Facebook group. Back in 2009, the Boston Globe also ran an article regarding the "new questions about online privacy" (Johnson, 2009) raised by SNSs by focussing on the capacity to use Facebook to predict whether or a not a person is gay via their online friends list. Discussing the many "victims whose privacy was unwillingly removed" by Facebook's "path to more openness", Kirkpatrick (2010) also turned first to the possibility of being 'outed' as homosexual by the site. "How many openly gay friends must you have on a social network before you're outed by implication?" he asked, quoting an unnamed privacy law expert (Kirkpatrick, 2010, p. 200). However, while this group is often cited as an example in cautionary tales about Facebook's potential privacy risks, how sexuality impacts upon young people's approach to sharing information in mainstream SNS environments had not, at this point, received the scholarly attention that factors such as age and gender had (see, e.g., Graham, Greenfield & Salimkhan, 2008; Lenhart & Madden, 2007; Livingstone, 2008; Manago, Mendelson & Papacharissi, 2011; Stutzman, 2006). In Tufekci's (2012) work on the reasons behind the "striking increase in privacy protective activities" on SNSs, for example, it is noted that the study gathered demographic data in relation to gender, race, age and sexual orientation, but that "the sexual orientation variable was not analysed statistically due to de-anonymization concerns with a small sub-sample." In place of such analysis, it is simply noted that the approximately 5 per cent of participants who identified as gay, lesbian or bisexual "had stronger privacy protections, were more active in privacy-related modes, and had all changed their privacy settings." (p. 340). The following section of this chapter will therefore address how young gay users of Facebook at the centre of this study understood, experienced and managed their safety and privacy on the site, in particular, in relation to the expansion of gay men's networks into that space during the late 2000s – as this is a key aspect of the continued presence of participatory reluctance in the niche (or community specific) spaces of gay men's digital culture today.

Participants' Approach to Privacy and Safety on Facebook

At the time of the interviews conducted in 2010 for the initial project from which this book has emerged, only three participants were aware that the capacity to create different groups, or 'lists' of friends with whom to share different information with, existed on Facebook. Only two of these three had made an attempt to use this feature: neither had done so successfully. There were also participants entirely unaware of the way that their privacy settings were configured. Discussing the level of access that others had to photos on his Facebook profile, for instance, one man said, "I don't really know if it's public or not. I wouldn't be surprised if my whole profile was public for anybody to see".

Unable to make the complex privacy settings provided on Facebook work in the fashion that they desired, or to keep up with their frequent changes, participants in this study tended to invent their own personal privacy strategies to use on the mainstream SNS. Lampinen, Tamminen and Oulasvirta (2009) and Lampinen, Lehtinen, Lehmuskallio and Tamminen (2011) refer to these kinds of strategies as 'mental' privacy protection strategies on account of the fact that they do not rely on the use of the site's features to guide information disclosures to the correct audience/s – as 'behavioural' privacy strategies would.

The privacy protection strategies implemented by participants in this study were geared towards entirely different concerns than those they had in the context of their Gaydar use. As we saw earlier, as a discrete pseudonymous environment where all of the men in this study – and the vast majority of men on the site more generally – openly identified as gay, privacy concerns amongst the 18–28 year old demographic on Gaydar related primarily to protecting their reputations amongst other gay men as individuals unlike those constructed in stereotypical depictions of the demographic. That is, they were relatively minor context-specific concerns. On Facebook, however, in a more mainstream, multi-context environment where individual and networked identities are anchored to real names, the privacy concerns of this same group were significantly greater. For example, following Livingstone's (2008) findings that young people are more concerned about their personal information being visible to 'known others they deemed inappropriate' (e.g., parents) than they are about it becoming visible to strangers, participants across all focus groups in this study experienced privacy concerns related to the potential dangers and/or discomfort that might arise from the crossing over of their engagements with the cultures and communities associated with their lives as gay men, with other aspects of their identities (e.g., family and work lives). Naturally, the nature and scope of participants' concerns in this regard were determined by the extent to which each man was able and/or willing to identify as gay across multiple aspects of his life. And, in turn, these situations determined the extent to which the strategies participants in this study devised and implemented to protect their privacy were geared towards separating the various contexts of their lives within the Facebook environment, where social contexts are collapsed. That is, participants' situations with respect to being 'out' determined the extent to which their strategies for generating privacy were geared towards creating specific contexts or audience groups that, as Livingstone's (2008, p. 404) conception of privacy would put it, would help them to leverage some form of "control over who [knew] what about [them]".

For the approximately 70 per cent of participants in this study whose personal circumstances allowed them to openly identify as gay in all facets of their lives, Facebook-related privacy and safety concerns were oriented, first and foremost, towards concealing or protecting personal information from strangers – as they would be in any online environment. Nevertheless, the majority of these men still expressed the desire to avoid their homosexuality being, as one man put it, "rubbed in [the] face", of their families on the site. The difficulty involved with monitoring this situation using the privacy controls provided by Facebook, however, meant that many of these men had come to take a laissez faire approach to information disclosure on Facebook, relying on the assumption that their audience on the platform would either not understand or politely ignore that which was not directed at them. Explaining why he had stopped censoring the amount of gay-oriented content on his Facebook profile on account of his family's presence on the site, and instead opted to rely on the principle of 'civil inattention' (Goffman, 1963a), one student said, for instance,

> I used to filter mine, but mine's very clear now because I think – with my status updates – if I'm going to make something that's towards my gay friends it will be a joke that they'll understand but the straight community won't.

Hence, amongst these men, for who creating separate contexts on Facebook was not their highest priority, controlling whom they added as friends on the site was generally the extent of their security strategies. For the more than 30 per cent of participants whose personal circumstances dictated that being out in all aspects of their lives was either not possible or not ideal, however, basic concerns about protecting personal information from strangers were also combined with more intense concerns about needing to completely conceal certain parts of their identity from parents, colleagues, classmates and various others. As a result, these men's security strategies were more elaborate. They did not, however, make any additional use of the privacy settings provided by Facebook itself. Indeed, whether directed primarily towards preventing information becoming accessible to an unwanted or inappropriate audience internally or externally, participants in this study tended to invent their own tactics for dealing with privacy concerns as they arose – using, as noted above 'mental', privacy generating strategies. Accordingly, in stark contrast to their approach to managing privacy and balancing the disclosure and concealment of information on their Gaydar profiles, which was done in a knowing, preventative, and almost uniform fashion (using selective exposure techniques), the approach to privacy and safety that participants in this study took on Facebook was haphazard, ad hoc and reactionary. It was also rather ineffective; for some – whose stories I will return to shortly – dangerously so.

Privacy Generating Strategies on Facebook

Given that protecting personal information from strangers external to one's individual Facebook network was a common concern amongst all participants in this study, regardless of the extent to which they were living openly gay lives, the most frequently discussed tactic used by participants to generate some form of safety net around their engagements with Facebook was the implementation of a system for limiting the number and/or type of people they added as friends on the site. Approximately 85 per cent of users who took part in the focus groups conducted for this study had explicit self-imposed friends policies.[16] These policies saw participants add friends to their Facebook networks in a manner that, for example, limited their connections to 100 friends only, or, to take another user's approach, ensured that they added only people they had personally met. One participant had decided that connections must be no more than two degrees of separation, adding only as wide as "friends of friends". On the opposite end of the spectrum, there was also a small group of participants in this study who had added 'friends' almost indiscriminately, accepting "anyone that requests" or "anyone who's hot". One of the men who had taken this approach, for example, reported having over 1100 Facebook friends. This is not to say that these men did not have friending policies that they applied, however. Two participants, who noted that they had taken similarly relaxed attitudes to accepting Facebook friendship by adding "anyone that requests", qualified their positions by saying that they gave all new friends a probationary period of sorts. If a new connection did not add anything to these participants' social lives during that period, or was considered an unsuitable match for them, they were deleted. For one of these men that probationary period was approximately three months. For the other, whose motivation for accepting all friend requests that came his way was to avoid appearing mean or impolite, it was just one week.

Regardless of their level of rigour, though, for those participants in this study for whom their personal set of life circumstances meant that reclaiming some level of contextual separation on Facebook was necessary (or just preferable) due to their sexuality, the implementation of a self-imposed friends policy was rarely the extent of the privacy and safety precautions they had taken. A wide array of ad hoc style initiatives used in addition to the kinds of friending policies outlined above were also brought up during focus group discussions by these men. One user noted, for example, that he had taken it upon himself to create code names for his gay friends and for various locations that he frequented with them in order to ensure his status updates were decipherable only to the small group of people (i.e., his other gay friends) aware of those code names. This form of limiting access to information "based on social knowledge, not structural access" (Marwick & boyd, 2011, p. 24) was also evident in the tactics employed by the teenagers, studied in Marwick and boyd's (2011) project, who encoded or obscured information on their SNS profiles to generate privacy amidst parental surveillance. Another man talked about what he termed 'lagging'. This involved posting information to Facebook about his life and the activities he engaged in days, weeks, or even months, after events had already occurred. He did this in order to keep people in his small hometown relatively unaware of the shape of his new life in the city. A number of other forms of censoring and self-censoring, or what might also been termed "disconnective practices" (see Light, 2014; Light & Cassidy, 2014) were also popular. Habitually untagging and deleting material posted to Facebook by others, for example, was the most common form of censoring that this group of participants engaged in. In one focus group, for example, a young retail worker who was not yet out to all of his family (including his parents) made daily efforts to censor his profile and was often quite stressed by the experience of using Facebook as a result. "I un-tag photos if they're relevant to that sort of [gay] issue and same when I have to be careful when people post things. I have to quickly get on and take it off," he said. He did not join any gay-oriented Facebook groups either, because, as he put it, "it can come back on me". This user had tried his best to operate Facebook's 'Lists' function, or as he put it, the "system where you can actually choose who you can display different things to", in order to automate some of the censoring that he felt his profile needed, but to little avail. The additional work this censoring process created for him on a daily basis in trying to maintain his privacy was something he resented. In a similar vein, self-censoring was also reported amongst these men as a means of simply keeping indicators of one's sexual identity off the everyday Newsfeed of other Facebook users. Primarily, this was done through limiting or avoiding photo uploads and by keeping any posts made to the site thoroughly trivial. As noted in the previous chapter, for instance, one of the young men in this study who worked in politics ensured that his Facebook posts focused only on trivial, noncontroversial issues, such as meals he had eaten and local weather patterns, despite the fact that his profile listed him as in a relationship with another man. Hogan (2010) refers to these kinds of privacy generating strategies as 'the lowest-common-denominator approach', as the individuals who employ them are effectively limiting the information on their profiles to that which they deem acceptable or appropriate for all network members to have access to.

Breaches of Participants' Privacy via Facebook

While implementing various combinations of the different strategies above to generate some form of control over the ways that their personal information would be shared on Facebook, participants in this study had nonetheless experienced considerable privacy and safety concerns as a result of using the site. Though none of the participants interviewed in this study had had their stories published in a newspaper, for many of them, the experiences of the Texas University students discussed in *The Wall Street Journal* (Fowler, 2012) article cited earlier would strike a familiar chord. Out, not out or somewhere in between, the consequences of being caught off guard or unawares of the ways that Facebook use could compromise one's privacy and safety had been felt widely amongst this group, and in a wide range of circumstances. Being outed or being stalked via Facebook, however, were the two most common experiences.

Out of the 30 interviewees who took part in this project, three had been outed as homosexual via Facebook. Two of these had been outed to their parents, and, as a result, had experienced periods of familial conflict. Speaking about this situation, one of these two men said, for example,

> I only came out to my parents a couple of years ago and I've had a Facebook profile for more than that. They're aware that it has that [the 'interested in: men'] box ticked on and they're also very aware that I have pretty much accepted [Facebook] friends of a lot of the sons and daughters of their friends. So they weren't very happy in the fact that I was parading my sexuality around. They were quite honest about that to me, particularly once I came out, [and about] the fact that I've got family members on there who we haven't discussed

it with, but because of Facebook obviously know that I'm gay. So they weren't particularly happy.

Not being concerned that his sexuality was visible amongst his friends on Facebook was a source of conflict between this participant and his parents.

> I'm like, 'so what?'. The only people who are on there are people who I know, so they know [that I'm gay] anyway...So I've ticked the 'interested in: men', and I've got 'in a relationship' with James on there. I've got my profile picture, which is a picture of me and James. So I don't care, but it's my parents who do.

In summing up his story, this participant explained that things had marginally improved between him and his parents, who still disagreed about him 'parading' his sexuality around on social networking sites. However, the period around the time they discovered from Facebook that he was gay, but before they had had the discussion about it, was by far the worst, he said. For the other participant in this group whose parents had become aware of his homosexuality via Facebook, it was linking with his cousins' profiles that did it. Again, while he was open about his sexuality amongst his peers at that time, he was not yet ready to share that information with his parents. When this participant's parents confronted him about material on his Facebook profile that indicated his sexuality, it left him in deep shock. As he explained to his peers in the focus group, this was because he knew that his parents did not actually use Facebook. "I'm just like, 'how the f*$% did you find out about that!?'", he said. Of course, his cousins were friends on Facebook with their respective parents – who then passed on information to the participant's parents.

The third man in this study who was outed via Facebook was an international student, originally from a predominantly Muslim country, who had been outed to his peers back home – and, he believed, potentially also to university officials at his home institution. Facebook was a distressing experience for this student at times, because he had been bullied and verbally attacked with homophobic slurs by those in his home country who had seen pictures of him posted to the SNS by students in Brisbane. In these pictures, he explained, he looked "too feminine" for their liking. Worried that this negative attention may result in the scholarship that funded his studies in Australia being revoked (on the basis that his school's officials might deem him an unfit representative of their institution), he had heavily censored his own profile. This student did not, for example, ever post pictures of himself to Facebook – especially since arriving in Australia where he dressed and styled himself in ways that would be considered inappropriate at home. He also took steps similar to those listed by the young retail worker mentioned earlier who engaged in daily censoring of his profile, by untagging himself in photos and deleting any material posted to his wall by others that might identify him as homosexual.

Beyond the problems associated with being outed via Facebook, though, there were also a number of other quite serious privacy-related concerns that participants in this study had experienced as a result of Facebook stalking (or 'facestalking' as it is popularly known)[17] – including amongst those who were already out in all areas of their lives. One man described a situation, for example, where he was stalked (both online and off) by other young gay men via Facebook due to his work situation. "I had a big problem with my last job", he said

> [M]y name used to be printed on my receipt and everyone found me on Facebook. Probably about each week I had a new story of someone stalking me or sending me quite strange messages, or people that worked across from my work that used to send me a list on Facebook of everything I did all day…I used to have people that came in and just wouldn't leave the store and used to know everything about you.

In a similar situation, there was another man in this study who had received messages and friend requests from a gay male waiter who took the participant's name from his credit card after serving him at a restaurant. "I was actually quite shocked…I didn't feel that that was particularly good at all. I actually felt a little bit stalked," he said. For another participant, there was a situation where he was angrily approached in public by an unknown man who believed him to be the love-interest of a gay male friend he was regularly in photographs with on Facebook. The stranger, who was romantically interested in the participant's friend, had approached the participant to warn him to stay away from that man so that he might have a better chance of starting a relationship with him.

> [I]n the gay community you get a lot of people that might have a crush on someone else or whatever and can get really jealous of who's talking to them and who they are being seen in photos with…people come up and go, 'don't talk to this person, you're in all their photos'.

"There's nothing to it," he explained, "but people do make those assumptions….there's a lot of people that will do a lot of online stalking, that type of thing…that carries on in real life as well and people find you." (Of course, jealousy is not unique to the gay male population; what this participant was getting at here is that, with the relatively small size of the gay community in Brisbane, Facebook has made it much easier than it previously was via niche sites such as Gaydar for people to find the personal details of others and to track them down offline.)

As participants in this study discussed their concerns with regards to possible breaches of privacy related to Facebook and the experiences they had had in this regard, what was most apparent was that these men had experienced significantly more breaches of their privacy via Facebook than they had by using Gaydar. As I also noted earlier, however, their attempts to protect their own privacy and safety on Facebook were much more haphazard, ad hoc and reactionary than their approaches to safety and privacy on Gaydar. Many of the participants' personal friending policies, discussed above, for example, had been developed and implemented simply to counter particular negative experiences these users had already had. Before discussing the specifics of their friending policies, for instance, users would typically talk about how or why they came to implement such guidelines for themselves. "I used to be very indiscriminate about people that I added", they might say, before discussing how they had reigned in their friending practices due an incident like one of the ones just mentioned. "[N]ow when it comes to people requesting me as a friend, I am a little bit more cautious", said one man, capturing the general pattern of use amongst his peers. "I do ignore a lot more [friend requests] than I used to and I'll only add them if they're a mutual friend of somebody else", he noted. Being generally more cautious about whom one interacts with on Facebook, however, does not make for a particularly thorough security strategy if users have no clear idea about how their privacy settings work or are configured – even if this greater sense of caution is combined with tactics such as 'lagging' and the creation of code names for one's friends. Indeed, it entirely underestimates the way that basic properties of the Internet, such as "persistence", "replicability", "scalability" and "searchability" (Marwick and boyd, 2011, p. 9), as well as an essentially unknowable audience, bear on privacy, both individually and in combination with each other.

The underestimation of Facebook's capacity to expose users' information to unknown audiences by participants in this study, like their underestimation of persistence, replicability, scalability and searchability as factors impacting upon user safety in SNSs, was no doubt exacerbated by a lack of familiarity with Facebook's privacy settings and the difficulties involved in coming to grips with their constant changes. Comments about not knowing how profile settings were configured, to what extent a profile was public or private, or how to properly operate the 'lists' function on the site were indicative of this. Demonstrating the widespread nature of the security concerns experienced by the men in this study amongst the broader demographic of young gay men, however, was the abundance of similar incidents occurring in the dozens of Facebook groups oriented towards Brisbane's gay community observed for this study. In the highly patronised Facebook group associated with popular gay night spot Fluffy, for example, cases of unexpected or unwanted results of Facebook's tendency to make information visible in unforeseen ways (and to unknown audiences) appeared almost weekly. Amongst a myriad of other materials promoting the venue, following each Sunday night event held by Fluffy, a collection of photographs – usually somewhere between 200 and 400 – are posted on this page. In the days before mainstream SNSs these photos or 'scene pics' were published only in the local GLBT street press, and due to the limited nature of space in hard copy publications only a very small number (e.g., four or five) were ever published. In more recent years, however, these photos have become a major part of the publicity strategies of commercial gay venues and are posted online to mainstream SNSs, such as Facebook, in pages and groups associated with these venues on a regular basis. The ways that people's private information becomes visible in unexpected contexts as a result are considerable. Fluffy's 'scene pics' on Facebook, for example, appear on the Fluffy page itself, in the Newsfeeds of all those who have 'liked' the page, as well as on the profiles of anybody tagged in the photographs. Hence, when a comment is made on a photo of somebody at Fluffy on that person's wall it can appear to those involved to be an intimate conversation between the person posting the message and the person it is intended for (and/or their mutual group of friends). However, these photos and the comments that go with them, also show up in a very public context on the Fluffy page itself, as well as in the individual Newsfeeds of all those connected to the Fluffy page. In this way, during the course of this study I observed hundreds of users unwittingly publishing details of their relationships, their weekly schedules (including times and locations), and their concerns about tarnishing workplace reputations, to an audience of thousands simply by commenting to their own friends on photos of them at Fluffy. Because of the nature of Facebook as a real name environment, this material is also provided alongside the real names of these users, and with links back to their personal profiles.

While the revelation of such personal information in the comments section of Fluffy photographs can easily convey sensitive information to strangers, the multiple avenues through which photographs taken at a gay club, such as Fluffy, or at any other gay-oriented space or event can appear on one's profile, or on the profiles of one's friends and/or acquaintances, via Facebook groups and pages, also makes it difficult to ensure that such images do not materialise in other parts of one's own network in contexts where users would prefer them not to. When they do, as any close observation of Fluffy's page will indicate, it can, and frequently does, lead to outings and homophobic bullying amongst Facebook friends themselves. The following comments and conversations seen beside photographs of people on the Fluffy page during the course of this project are illustrative in this regard[18]:

Example 1: Beside a photo of four men posing for the camera with arms around each other's shoulders. All four are tagged. Of the commenters below, only John is in the photograph.

NICK: Yeahhhhhhhhh....cause all the "straight" guys that go to fluffy are 100% straight hahaha

TOM: Haha exactly

NICK: Yes John [tagged] you included!! "Straight"
JOHN: You fucker...
NICK: truth hurts;-)

Example 2: Beside a photo where two men are posing together as a couple alongside a heterosexual couple

KEN: [Referring to one of the men tagged in the male/male couple]. Well we all knew it Archy!!!

Example 3: Beside a photo of two young men kissing passionately, apparently unaware of the camera. (Neither man is tagged).

EMILY: ...Just ruined my news feed...
BROOKE: Agreed!!! And you denied being gay Ben! Hahaha

Example 4: Beside a photo of one man (Daniel) and one woman (Tanya) amongst the Fluffy crowd. Daniel is giving the 'peace' sign with one hand and has the other around Tanya's shoulder.

TANYA: Don't even remember this being taken >_<
EDWARD: Dan why are you at a gay bar? –. – Not the way bro. Not cool.
DANIEL: Hey man, didn't find out until I was in line haha
EDWARD: haha i was thinking i have never heard of fluffy and it sounds gay so i looked it up –. – turns out its gay haha not cool man

Example 5: Beside a photo of three men standing near the bar at Fluffy. Only the man in the middle (Todd) is tagged.

BEN: You know how I know ur gay Todd?

Example 6: In a photo of two young men sitting beside each other at Fluffy, an unknown person has tagged the two men as follows –

David Nraw, ugly Jew nose, lots of penises have been in this mouth, Brady Arella, gross hair and too much makeup

On the odd occasion, situations where homophobia is present can also bring forth support from strangers, as was the case in this exchange I witnessed on the Facebook page of gay-friendly venue The Beat when Rachel stepped in:

Beside a photo of a group of four young men posing with a shirtless male promotional model:

NATASHA: [Tagging 3 of the men photographed] ...look what i found...
CAMERON: [Who is friends with both Natasha and two of the tagged men] Isn't the beat a gay club??
RACHEL: [who is not a Facebook friend of either Natasha, Cameron or any of the other men tagged] straight ppl go to gay bars too. usually with their gay friends.

Ordinarily, however, it is the owners/moderators of the pages themselves that must remind users of appropriate group etiquette. The following two posts were made several months apart on the Fluffy page, for example, in response to high concentrations of photos with comments and tags on them such as those seen in the examples cited above:

> [FAN PAGE CODE OF CONDUCT] Please note we have a strict code of conduct on our fan page. Anyone found bullying other members, making racist or homophobic comments will be instantly banned no questions asked. If you are a victim at all on here especially in photos please message us with the link to the photo/comment and we will sort it out asap. There is no room for such behaviour at all anywhere and especially in our club. SHARE THE LOVE. Xxx
>
> CODE OF CONDUCT: Please note we have a no tolerance policy when it comes to inappropriate and nasty comments anywhere on this fan page. If you wanna be a keyboard warrior do it on your own page or profile. We don't have the space for it on ours. Comments will be deleted and you will be banned. Sucks that 99% of people in this world are awesome and 1% really need to get a life. Please send a message to the page with the link to any photo/comments you feel is not appropriate and we will sort it out. Share The Love!

It is worth pointing out here, though, that many of the derogatory comments made on Fluffy photos are not made on the Fluffy page itself, but via the profiles of those people in the photos. And moreover, that by the time the team at Fluffy are able to 'sort it out asap', as they guarantee to do, the photographs and comments at the centre of a bullying scenario can be replicated and re-shared extensively. It is also worth pointing out here that these incidents are not isolated to those groups and pages associated only with commercial gay venues. After joining and posting to the wall of the group 'Gay Brisbane Dating', for example, a young man was chided by his friend in the following exchange in 2012:

JACK: Hi I am a 17 year old turning 18 in November and looking for someone close to my age who really wants to have a good relationship

DAVID: Oh Jack! What are you trying to do!!??

Along with the incidents shown above that occurred on Fluffy's Facebook page and the experiences of being outed, bullied and stalked via the mainstream SNS that focus group participants recounted, this comment from David to Jack indicates how much greater potential there is for privacy and safety breaches to occur on Facebook by comparison with Gaydar as a result of context collapse. It also gives a great deal of insight into how much more difficult it is to manage multiple (often conflicting) self-narratives in this environment, as people's identity management processes are placed in the hands of the network in a way that does not occur on Gaydar. What is not evident in looking at either of these sites in isolation, however, is how using Facebook could also increase the security concerns associated with use of Gaydar, when these sites were used simultaneously.

Facebook as a Multiplier of Potential Security Concerns

Earlier in this chapter, I noted that participants in this study were not particularly concerned about the possible privacy and safety issues that may arise from using Gaydar. The pseudonymous environment of the community-specific SNS and the inbuilt capacity to use the site without creating visible connections with other users meant that participants' biggest concerns with regard to privacy on Gaydar were associated with protecting their reputations as non-stereotypical gay men. Protecting personal details, such as names, addresses, phone numbers and so on from strangers was not an issue, as the profile template and the general digital infrastructure of Gaydar would require people to actively provide that information to others for them to gain access to it. Accordingly, Gaydar users have historically maintained a high level of control over their own privacy. Alongside the arrival of Facebook, with its comparatively greater privacy and safety concerns, and the extension of gay men's networks into that space, however, that level of control was significantly reduced for those men who chose to use both of these sites. Interestingly, during the late 2000s, the extension of gay men's networks into Facebook also raised new privacy and safety concerns for those men who used neither site, but who attended, or engaged in, offline GLBT venues and events.

In the previous chapter, I discussed the tendency of young Gaydar users in the mid- to late 2000s to arrange to chat with each other via MSN, in a bid to escape the technical and ideological confines of Gaydar – and I noted how these arrangements were typically made by asking for, or proactively sending, email addresses to each other in private messages on the site. While this behaviour quickly gave way, at least in part, to the practice of swapping or linking Facebook profiles (see Chapter 4) at the time of data collection, it was nonetheless still recognised as a central cultural aspect of Gaydar use. With the arrival of Facebook, however, the act of swapping email addresses on Gaydar took on much greater significance, particularly with regard to issues of privacy. That is, following Facebook's arrival, when a Gaydar user asked for another person's email address on Gaydar it was likely that that address would be used primarily as fodder for a Facebook search, trying to uncover additional information. Asked if they could identify any ways that they saw Gaydar and Facebook intertwining, for example, 27 of the 30 men who participated in the focus groups for this study noted that they routinely tried to use Facebook to access information about people from Gaydar using email addresses. As the exchange below indicates, the possibility of being able to find someone on

Facebook via the email used as their MSN address was a strong motivator during this transition period for asking people to chat on MSN:

FACILITATOR: Is there anything about Facebook or the ways that you use Facebook that might have changed or impacted upon your use of Gaydar?

PARTICIPANT: ...I probably will try and get someone's email now to check them out through Facebook. You know, 'why don't you add me to MSN?'...so I can stalk them.

In fact, the possibility of being able to glean additional information about a man on Gaydar via his Facebook profile was a strong motivator for trying to find or extract *any* piece of information that might allow for a Facebook search to be conducted. "Yeah if they add me to their MSN, [I'll] check out their Facebook – or if you find out their full name – [I'll] stalk them like that", said one man, "just to find out more about them and not necessarily say, 'hey I'm checking you out on Facebook'." Another participant noted that he tried all avenues he could to find a Facebook match, including running Gaydar usernames through a Facebook search. "[Y]ou can actually just take the user name and put @hotmail.com or @gmail.com, [and] you can check their Facebook. It's the same sort of scenario", he explained.

The possibility to engage in the surveillance of others via this practice clearly yielded a number of positive results for the men interviewed for this study. The ability to predetermine or at least, attempt to predetermine, whether people are worth engaging with before actually doing so was considered especially useful. Participants in all focus groups gave examples, for instance, of how 'facestalking' (searching for information about people via Facebook) helped them to avoid drama in their lives; in particular, drama associated with the gay scene and the relatively small, highly connected gay male community in Brisbane. As one participant explained, having access to people's personal information and a map of their social connections, allowed him to properly consider the question "what kind of impact will this have on my life?", every time he contemplated either dating or making friends with another gay man. The provision of location-based information was also considered favourable by these men as they recognised that it allowed them to connect with friends and/or new acquaintances from Gaydar without necessarily planning a specific meetup, date or other social event. Given the size of the entertainment precinct in which Brisbane's gay-friendly commercial venues operate, tracking down and joining up with people on a night out, who might have 'checked in' at a club down the street, for example, was a considered a real benefit of the way that Facebook made other people's information widely visible.

On the flip side of this scenario, however, there are obvious privacy and safety issues. This was particularly the case for those who were less technologically literate – but also for those unable to keep up with changes to Facebook's privacy policies – as this practice represented a significant elevation of the security issues surrounding Gaydar use. Should one be on the end of the situation where they are being searched on Facebook, or coaxed into exchanging searchable information, for example, not being aware of the need for separate email addresses and/or of how one's privacy settings on Facebook are configured could lead to the exposure of personal details and to the linking of an anonymous or pseudonymous profile on Gaydar with a clearly identifiable one on Facebook. For the three men who were unaware of these dangers at the time of the focus groups conducted for this study, the level of familiarity with this practice displayed amongst their peers lead all three to declare that they would be changing/separating their email addresses immediately following the respective sessions in which they participated. For those who were already aware of the Gaydar/Facebook crosschecking practice, though, there was still a palpable sense of discomfort about its prevalence. This arose from the fact that the balance between the benefits of being able to cross check information about others, and the risks associated with the ability of others to do the same in return, was an uneasy one. The one participant in this project who had not posted an identifiable image of himself on Gaydar (and who had recently stopped using the site) displayed this unease and clearly illuminated its root cause when he noted, for example, that

> you could use the two [Gaydar and Facebook] to double check and so on, but surely there's significant risks there as well, because when I used to use Gaydar I didn't use a face pic…I used a false name and whatever else, and if you used both you'd potentially be letting a whole lot of people that you don't know into aspects of your personal life that everybody puts in their Facebook in terms of who else you know and what's your relationship with them and what you're doing and what you were doing the last time you were drunk and said, 'ah, I'm drunk at whatever club' and that sort of thing.

And one after another, other members of this man's focus group began chiming in also, adding to the list of the kinds of personal information that might be unwittingly revealed via Gaydar members 'facestalking' each other on Facebook. "Yeah, your whereabouts, where you work and what you do," noted one man. "Yeah, well you can like access my siblings on Facebook by clicking on their profile", added another. "So if I don't know you, especially if I met you off Gaydar, and I don't trust you, but then you message [on Facebook after facestalking], like it's just really awkward," he said. "I think it's a security thing too," said a third.

> You might be friendly enough to talk to them [on Gaydar], but you perhaps don't want them to know your location. I think it's a security thing. Just being anonymous [as is the case on Gaydar] is nice…

> Even if you've spoken to them before [on Gaydar]…if you go to a nightclub or something and you don't want to see them and they can track you [via Facebook] that's a kind of danger, I think.

As this last man's comment indicates, Facebook's arrival not only heightened the dangers associated with using Gaydar by increasing the possibilities for pseudonymous Gaydar profiles to be linked with identifiable ones on Facebook, it also significantly changed the nature of the system of recognition that existed around Gaydar, and gay men's digital culture more broadly, by infusing it, including in offline contexts, with extra (quite significant) safety and privacy concerns. As I noted in the introduction to this book and again in an earlier part of this chapter, prior to Facebook's advent gay men regularly recognised each other in offline spaces from their Gaydar profiles. If a man used Gaydar consistently enough, and had a reasonable memory, he could potentially walk into a commercial gay venue and recognise the patrons there as 'hung-like-a-horse', 'suMMer-Fun', and 'chillivodka', rather than, for example, Mike, Tom, and Sam. However, with the extension of gay men's networks into Facebook, and a culture of surveillance that aimed to constantly connect the two of these sites, this system of recognition could then operate around real names. In effect, this removed the capacity of Gaydar users who were also on Facebook to post identifiable images of themselves to the community-specific site whilst still concealing their real names and other personal information in that environment – because other Gaydar users might now find a way to access these details via Facebook. As any attempts to circumvent this situation, by, for example, removing identifiable images from one's Gaydar profile or refusing to provide any information to other users that would enable a Facebook search to be conducted, would detract from one's capacity to participate in the Gaydar community (due to the cultural pressure to post images and the tendency to chat via MSN or shift interactions to Facebook entirely), this effectively removed the control that Gaydar afforded users over their own privacy management. Likewise, attempts to circumvent the situation where one's profiles on Gaydar and Facebook were effectively linked by removing oneself from the Facebook environment would be to limit access to the people and social capital contained within one's own personal networks. As Tufekci (2012) also noted, while simultaneously "pushing its users to broader visibility and disclosure", Facebook had increasingly become a social norm by this time, thus making it difficult to avoid using (p. 345).

Interestingly, observations of Brisbane-based Facebook groups connected with GLBT venues and events during the course of this study, indicated that the extension of gay men's networks into Facebook also extended the system of recognition that existed around gay men's digital culture so far as to include those who may not have had a profile on either of the two sites concerned here at all. With the high volume of photographs posted on Facebook in heavily populated groups of the people and events held at gay-friendly venues, the ability to physically enter these venues without one's photograph being published online was significantly reduced. Even without overtly agreeing to pose for a professional photograph in a commercial gay venue, there is plenty of evidence in the albums of such venues posted on Facebook that simply being in the crowd or in the background of other people's shots is enough to be clearly identified. Hence, in the time that I spent conducting this study I came across several men – just in the course of daily conversations – who had directly noted that their attendance patterns at commercial gay venues had changed as a result of those venues' tendencies to document all of their patrons and events on Facebook. Just as Tufekci (2012) found that 20 per cent of her participants had deactivated their account at least once, some of these men also discussed periods in which they had taken 'breaks' from Facebook (i.e., disabled or not used their accounts) in order to remove themselves from the new system of recognition, based on real names, that surrounded gay men's digital cultures following Facebook's arrival.

Amongst the men who actually participated in this study, however, very few efforts of this kind were made. The one participant in this study who had maintained an anonymous profile on Gaydar, for example, ceased using the community-specific SNS, saying that de-activating his Gaydar profile was the only logical response to its emerging cultural entanglement with Facebook. Nobody from the focus groups conducted had gone so far as to cease using Facebook however. As opposed to the situation with Gaydar, as I noted above, removing oneself from the mainstream SNS (given its overarching purpose to connect users to the people already in their lives) would be to significantly reduce one's access to sociality and to one's own personal network and the social capital contained therein – and, moreover, to the benefits that can also be reaped from the expanded system of recognition surrounding gay men's digital culture noted earlier (i.e., removing oneself from Facebook would also reduce access to information that could inform decisions around engaging with *new* people). So instead, as described during the discussion of participants' approach to safety and privacy on Facebook earlier in this chapter, these men improvised and tried to manage their privacy (and not always successfully) by implementing ad hoc security measures, such as daily censoring and 'lagging' and trying to keep their Gaydar and Facebook profiles as separate as possible by using different email addresses. And if a situation arose where the information about them on Gaydar and Facebook combined in a way that endangered their security, participants in this study tended to feel a deep sense of frustration, but continued on using the sites anyway. One participant, for example, described a situation where a man threatened him on Gaydar because he did not wish to go on a date with him. The man then proceeded to tell the participant that, from seeing him on Facebook, he knew who all the of his friends were and that he would be able to find him while out in public and "just run into him" one day. Despite the situation being "really off putting" and frustrating for the participant concerned, because "everything these days is too intertwined", he clearly noted at the conclusion of this story, that the incident "wasn't enough to make [him] stop [using Facebook]".

This story raises the question then of what would be "enough" to stop this participant from using Facebook. That is, it draws our attention to the potential 'costs' associated with using SNSs. Privacy and safety concerns such as the ones discussed in this chapter that can arise from SNS use, and the 'intertwined' or collapsed contexts that they foster, are by no means unique to the demographic at the centre of this study. Tufekci (2012, p. 344) notes, for instance, that "overwhelming majorities" of the participants in her project had reported "that their profiles were found by unwanted audiences (72.9%)" and that "unwanted photos of them were posted (70%)" on SNSs. Documenting the ways that such conditions bear upon the nature of gay men's digital culture, and gay men's culture more generally, however, is important given that this population has historically been quite skilled at using media technologies to manage identities and to balance the concealment and exposure of personal information across multiple (often conflicting) social contexts (see Gross, 2007, pp. vii–x). What is evident from this study, however, is that many young gay men were finding maintaining an appropriate balance between exposure and concealment of personal information in these environments to be extremely difficult in the late 2000s and early 2010s. Indeed, as was seen in the testimonies of participants in this study who were outed via Facebook or who lived in fear of such an event; in the examples that I presented of the kinds of experiences that young gay men may have encountered in GLBT-oriented Facebook groups; and in the growing number of newspaper articles that tell tales of those who have been outed, bullied and even driven to suicide by the ways that SNSs can reveal personal information in unexpected contexts and in unforeseen ways (see, e.g., Cohen, 2011; Fowler, 2012; Johnson, 2009), the cost of sociality for this demographic in the converged social media environment had the potential to be tragically high.

The cultures and practices surrounding more recent iterations of gay men's digital culture that exist today have been forged in response to these issues; in response to the continued shifts in gay male identity models discussed earlier in this book, and in relation to the much broader range of social media – both niche and mainstream – that is now available. Hence, it is to these subjects, and the part they have played in bolstering the place of participatory reluctance in contemporary gay men's digital culture that I will turn in the following – and final – chapter of this book.

Notes

1 Take, for example, the recent vote to implement same-sex marriage in the UK (Simons, 2013); the constitutional recognition of same-sex marriage rights in the United States in 2015 (Obergefell v. Hodges 2015); and the success of the Irish marriage equality referendum in 2015 (McDonald, 2015).

2 Many users choose to remove the number of views their profile has received lest it be considered a social index of, for example, their unpopularity or lack of desirability.
3 While there is no way of knowing this directly, during the data collection process for this study, the number of users that Gaydar regularly advertised as 'online now' and the number of visible profiles was always very similar, suggesting that the number of hidden profiles on the site was limited during this period.
4 Contrarily, in the vast majority of online communities that existed prior to the arrival of social networking sites, the role of 'lurker' was much more common (see Baym, 2000; Hansen, Ackerman, Resnick & Munson, 2007).
5 Between the two extremes of a hidden profile and a visible profile there was also the option to have a profile hidden to those outside the site but visible to all other users of the site, or even only to (paying) members. This setting could be activated by adjusting the settings for the question, 'Can others access your profile externally at this address?'
6 Only one participant in this study had ever experimented with the friending option on Gaydar, for example.
7 'Bar/Pub' is nonetheless included as one of the sub-categories of 'Favourite Things' in Gaydar's profile template.
8 That is, they identified themselves as 'out' by answering 'yes' in the field of the Gaydar profile template corresponding to this question.
9 'Coles' is the name of a leading Australian supermarket chain.
10 For example, participants talked about their profile pictures and personal descriptions becoming more 'honest' as they became more comfortable with the site over time, and less concerned for their safety. More than one participant explained, for instance, how they had originally posted a photo taken from behind their back, or some other obscure angle, and then eventually graduated to an identifiable face pic.
11 Suspecting his partner was cheating on him, the participant in question here created a completely anonymous profile on Gaydar (with no images) and searched the site to see if indeed his partner was using Gaydar to arrange sexual liaisons with other men. Recognising his partner in a picture he had posted to a profile on the site effectively ended their relationship.
12 Coles is a leading chain of supermarkets in Australia.
13 'How people bring your info to apps they use' had 17 tick-boxes to consider.
14 A close inspection of Table 5.1, which has the same default choices selected as per Gaydar's arrangements at the time of data collection, will reveal how, by contrast, Gaydar set the default options on its privacy settings to the highest level of protection available.
15 See Section 4 of Facebook's 'Statement of Rights and Responsibilities' (www.facebook.com/legal/terms).
16 The other 15% simply added friends on a case-by-case basis. There was no particular 'rule of thumb' or set of guidelines they routinely applied.
17 See the entry for 'Facestalking' on Urban Dictionary at www.urbandictionary.com/define.php?term=facestalking.
18 Screenshots of the actual photographs and comments concerned can be produced upon request. They have not been included here, however, in order to protect the privacy of the people in the photographs. (Note – anonymising the photos was not considered an available option here, as the amount of blurring necessary to appropriately obscure the identities of those involved would make publication of them redundant.)

6 Participatory Reluctance Post-Gaydar

In early 2013, Gaydar was sold to boutique investment company, Charlie Parsons Creative (CPC) and a new range of branding was released for the site, to reflect what was described as a 'less sleazy' image (Gaydar, 2013). While CPC promoted this moment as the beginning of a new exciting future for Gaydar (CPC Connect, 2013), it would be more accurate to describe this period as the definitive end of Gaydar's reign at the centre of gay men's digital culture. Gaydar radio was shut down at this time, and the two entertainment venues owned by Gaydar in London's Soho were also permanently closed. While new banner material and cover pages incorporating language such as 'love' and 'Mr Right' were rolled out to reorient the site's focus and branding away from earlier stereotypes about homosexuality, the profile template and other elements of Gaydar's highly sexualised original digital infrastructure remained in place. Indeed, the full-scale redesign necessary for Gaydar to keep pace with the changing nature of gay male subculture and identity that was promised by CPC did not materialise. Already significantly weighed down by these issues, Gaydar was unable to compete with the wave of mobile phone applications that had been arriving to serve its user base since the late 2000s and the site effectively slid into insignificance. When I began writing this book, in 2015, Gaydar remained operational, but largely unchanged since CPC's takeover in 2013 and was a veritable shell of its former self. Users – especially in younger demographics – had become increasingly scarce and it was no longer central to discussions about gay male culture in the broader mediasphere. It had been replaced in this respect by newer, more agile, geolocative mobile phone applications, such as Grindr.

Facebook, by contrast, has continued on as a central player in the world of social media and remains part of gay men's digital cultures, particularly with regard to the circulation of materials concerning gay, lesbian, bisexual and transgender (GLBT) equality issues. With a raft of new mainstream social media platforms now available, though, its role today is much more that of an ensemble cast member than the critical niche-service supplement it has previously been (see Chapter 4). Alongside Facebook, for example, there is also a growing amount of gay male interaction and activity occurring across spaces such as Instagram and Snapchat, and on predominantly heterosexual dating services, such as Tinder and RSVP-type applications.

Despite considerable technological differences between the services available today and in the mid- to late 2000s, at the height of Gaydar and Facebook's success, there is much continuity to be seen in the ways that these services (both niche and mainstream) have been approached by gay male audiences. Indeed, in the ways that issues of identity, privacy and participatory reluctance play out in these spaces history seems to be, in many ways, repeating.

Gaydar, Grindr and the Continued Culture of Participatory Reluctance

Established by Joel Simkhai, Grindr was the first location-based mobile social networking application designed to help facilitate engagement between gay and bisexual men. It was first released in the iTunes app store in 2009 and was adapted for Android in 2011, by which time the service had already become the largest mobile app community for gay men around the world, with users in over 192 countries. In addition to its game-changing geolocative functions, and unlimited real-time messaging, Grindr initially distinguished itself from Gaydar and other earlier social networking sites for gay men by focusing on images, a clean, simple interface and the provision of a profile template non-taxonomising of sexuality or sexual identity. Indeed, when Grindr was first launched its company website noted (with obvious reference to sites such as Gaydar) that "Grindr's different because it's uncomplicated… It's not your average dating site – you know, the ones that make you sit in front of a faraway computer filling out complex, detailed profiles and answering invasive psychological questions" (Grindr, 2012, np).

For the young men who took part in this study however, while Grindr's interface may have offered them new ways to interact with other gay men and the gay male community around them that they enjoyed and made use of, these benefits were largely offset by concerns about privacy and the app's implicit focus on sexual activity. In terms of Grindr's benefits, focus group participants noted, for example, that they used Grindr as a means to communicate with gay friends in place of other messaging services and as a tool to map and observe the gay male community around them.

With focus groups for this study conducted in the days prior to the widespread take-up in Australia of mobile messaging apps such as Whatsapp, Line and, more recently, Snapchat, participants noted, for example, that Grindr worked as a mobile replacement for MSN messenger (which, as I noted in Chapter 4, had been a central part of Gaydar culture prior to Facebook's arrival on account of Gaydar's daily message limits).

"Grindr's pretty much the same thing [as Gaydar], except I just use it as MSN because all of my homo friends are on there", said one participant. Mirroring this comment in a later focus group another man said, "I use [Grindr] for like MSN because I have so many gay friends that are on there." Similar points were also made about using Grindr to interact with existing acquaintances by participants who indicated they did not use the service to "talk to randoms" (interact with strangers) and by men who noted that the 'favourites' feature on Grindr was more useable than the equivalent feature on Gaydar – making it easier to build or map a network and maintain ongoing conversations with existing friends.

When it came to the geolocative aspects of Grindr, as Blackwell, Birnholtz and Abbott (2015) also found in their work, participants were quite positive about the opportunities this feature created to visualise a proximate gay community, even in heteronormative physical space. One participant who worked in retail noted, for example, that he used Grindr constantly while at work because he was interested in meeting men who did not fit within the realms of typical gay stereotypes. He figured Grindr would help in this regard by identifying gay men in his shop that he might not recognise as being gay on his own accord. Others noted that they used this feature for fun, "to perv" and to bond with existing gay peers through what one participant termed group "gay hunting" expeditions – which were basically small groups of gay male friends travelling around the city using Grindr "just to see who's around". That is, while participants employed language suggesting using Grindr in this way was something of a game, one of the key draw cards of the service for these men was clearly that it offered them the capacity to witness the existence of, and to feel connected to, a community of others with similar sexual identities. While young GLBT people have been flocking to the internet for this purpose since it's very inception (see, e.g., Hillier, Kurdas & Horsely, 2001), unlike Gaydar before it, Grindr offers these visualization capacities in real time and the convenience of unlimited instant messaging all within the one mobile phone application.

One of the biggest downsides of Grindr for these men, though, was their awareness that the geolocative aspects of the service – and the uses they could be put to – could also be applied in reverse, by other men in relation to them. This caused some participants to have significant concerns about the safety and privacy aspects of Grindr use. "It's fun to go on and see how close people are to you, but I would never approach anyone. That's fucked", said one participant before recounting one of his many experiences of feeling surveilled by the Grindr community. "The other day I was sitting at Starbucks with one of my friends in the city," he said.

> We were both on there and then some guy started talking to us and then he literally came from where he was and walked outside the Starbucks and just sat there watching us…Then after 20 minutes he just got up and left. It was so creepy.

Other men had similar thoughts about Grindr's geolocative feature.

> If you really want to meet somebody and they want to meet you, it's not that hard to agree on a specific place and time. I don't want to know that they're five metres away from me the whole time while I'm talking to them.
>
> I just think location based social networking…is a big chance for people to stalk you.
>
> I think it's a security thing too. You might be friendly enough to talk to them, but you perhaps don't want them to know your location. I think it's a security thing. Just being anonymous is nice. Or, even if you've spoken to them before….[and are connected with them somehow/have favourited their profile] you still don't want them to track you, like if you go to a nightclub or something. For me, that's kind of a danger, I think.
>
> [W]henever I'm in my bed there's this one guy on Grindr who's always zero metres away from me whenever I'm in my bed and he's like 56. It's just so weird. And creepy! Every time I'm in bed, *zero* metres. It's so strange.

To counter some of these issues, several participants noted that they chose not to use identifying images on Grindr – particularly since their main reason for using the service was to talk to friends and to be able to visualise the gay community around them. "On Grindr," said one man, for example, "I actually don't have a photo of my face and I just use it talk to my friends, like Bradley, because he's always on there". His peer in the same focus group agreed, adding "Yeah, I have a picture of – well, it's like a distance picture, so you can't actually see my face, but it's still me on there". In a different group, another man with similar reservations about the tracking element of Grindr who worked in politics said he chose not to have a profile at all and instead purposely only ever used Grindr "on other people's phones…just to have a look". In addition to trying to carve out personal privacy, not having a face picture was also seen amongst these men as a means to disassociate oneself from Grindr entirely: an action which some participants indicated they took on account of the service's apparent promotion of sexual promiscuity – which, as with Gaydar previously, they felt linked Grindr together with outdated ideas about gay male identity.

While Grindr's profile template does not itself address users' sexuality, sexual activity preferences, or, for example, ask for information about users' genitals in the way that Gaydar does, other features of the service have been read as equally focused on sex and encouraging of sexual promiscuity. Studies of Grindr have identified its geolocative features and capacity for real-time engagement in rapid text-messaging format (neither of which were part of Gaydar's remit), for instance, as constructing in person meet-ups as the core reason for Grindr use (see

Licoppe, Riviere & Morel, 2016; Race, 2014). These in person meet-ups are then further framed as being for the purpose of 'no-strings-attached' casual sexual encounters, due to factors such as the service's streamlined interface and visual focus, and the scarcity of information required in user profiles, which connote superficial interaction (see Licoppe et al., 2016; Race, 2014), and even via perceptions carried over to it by users from predecessor services, such as Gaydar. Indeed, citing Grindr's mobile enabled user-friendly interface as a motivating factor for disconnecting from Gaydar and switching to Grindr, participants in this study seemed to perceive of Grindr as superior to Gaydar technologically, but otherwise no different. Asked why (at the time of the focus groups) he had recently stopped using Gaydar, for instance, one man replied simply, "isn't Grindr the same thing?", as if to suggest it was well known that the service was not exceptional, but just less bad than Gaydar on account of its greater simplicity.

Although technologically more advanced than Gaydar, however, Grindr's assumed implicit focus on sex made it equally inconsistent with the self-perceptions of participants in this study, and thus, also a space in which they participated reluctantly. As with Gaydar, the culture of participatory reluctance that infused these men's engagements with Grindr was evident in the way participants spoke about the service itself, their imagined audience of co-users, and their sense that no real alternatives existed. Speaking about their disappointments with Grindr as an application, for example, participants in this study honed in on the role they saw it playing in perpetuating outdated stereotypes about gay male identity. Explaining why he did not enjoy using Grindr, for instance, one 20-year-old participant said, "it's just the whole stereotype of the gay community that has been built that gay men are promiscuous and go out looking for sex and stuff like that." Asked if Grindr itself had created that situation, another man chimed in, "I think it encourages it. I don't blame the site for that, as such, but I think it encourages people to be promiscuous which keeps that [stereotype] going". And in other focus groups the same ideas arose also. Comparing Gaydar and Grindr for instance, one man said, "It's just like Gaydar, I hate being on there [Grindr], and that's why I don't show my face, because I know that people just use that [Grindr] for sex as well." His friend in the same focus group concurred, explaining his own dissatisfaction with Grindr was a product of the service "insinuating, I think, more or less, the whole booty call thing, which isn't what I'm looking for on those sites".

With regards to the ways participants saw themselves as different from the imagined audience of Grindr users, perhaps the most telling comments were about how these men automatically assumed other users were not worth engaging with – on mere account of their using a service such as Grindr, and despite these participants' own use of the very same service. One 19-year-old university student, for example, noted that he never bothered to speak to people on Grindr he didn't already know. If he received messages from unknown users of the service, he said, he automatically responded in dismissive ways designed to belittle others; both to prevent the need for any further engagement and to distinguish himself from "typical" Grindr users by strongly signalling his lack of interest in casual sex. "If random people talk to me on Grindr", he noted, "I act like a dickhead just for fun and say all random sarcastic things to them. I don't lie about stuff. I just say stupid things. Like, I don't know, if they ask, "What are you doing? Wanna meet up?" and stuff like that, I just say stupid snarky things to stop them." This tactic, of pre-emptively attacking or condemning other users, is, of course, the same kind of identity territorialism (Payne, 2007) that these men often used in Gaydar profiles (see Chapter 3) to present their identities as divergent from the typical imagined user of that site, simply adapted for the real-time engagement that occurs on Grindr. And, as the material commonly found across the various incarnations of Douchebags of Grindr (see www.douchebagsofgrindr.com and @grindrdouches) indicates, participants in this study are by no means alone in taking this approach. Indeed, the enormous success of Douchebags of Grindr – a site to which Grindr users upload screenshots of 'douchebag' profiles they have encountered on the app – has occurred precisely because thousands of men on Grindr take a pre-emptively confrontational approach to engaging with other users; often by pointedly distancing themselves from stereotypical models of metropolitan homosexual identity by denigrating and dismissing them. As with Gaydar before it, however, this creates a cycle whereby Grindr users tend to read and respond to each other in a manner that matches their already low expectations of other gay men in these spaces.

At the time the focus groups for this study were conducted, the possibility that users could avoid this environment, by leaving Grindr altogether, for a better alternative was not an idea that participants ascribed to. These men wanted a space where they could enjoy the benefits of having access to an online community of local gay men, the capacity for unlimited messaging/real-time engagement, and options to avoid the pitfalls of location-based services, such as surveillance and potential stalking, but most importantly, a space devoid of traditional stereotypes associated with gay male identity and, in particular, ideas about gay men's relationships with casual sex. With Tinder still months out from launching at this point, participants thoughts turned to predominantly heterosexual dating applications, such as RSVP. However, most men were doubtful that these services would have enough gay male users to make them viable alternatives. The conversation between participants below, for example, is indicative of what was said on this issue across all focus groups.

PARTICIPANT 1: Do the actual, like RSVP, have like 'men seeking men' sort of...

PARTICIPANT 2: Yeah, I think it actually does.

PARTICIPANT 3: Yeah, but I don't think many people would use it.

PARTICIPANT 1: Yeah. I wouldn't sign up to a dating website. It'd be all girls.

As the research of Brubaker, Ananny and Crawford (2016) suggests, those users who leave or disconnect from Grindr often do so on account of the issues discussed here so far, regarding disillusionment with the application and its user base. Given the perceived lack of alternatives to Grindr, however, as with Gaydar before it, many men who do engage with the service tend to do so reluctantly – like the active users seen in this study who said they "hate[d] being on there" – creating a broader culture of participatory reluctance within the application.

The Arrival of Today's (More Mainstream) Alternatives

In 2013 Grindr introduced the capacity to formally integrate 'social media links' into user profiles suggesting that, "linking to Instagram from your profile is a great way to provide more pics to that hot guy you're chatting up" (Grindr, 2013, np). Among a raft of other changes, it also made the 'About You' section of user profiles bigger so users could "have more room to describe yourself and what you're looking for" (Grindr, 2013, np). In the media release that accompanied these changes, Grindr CEO, Joel Simkhai, indicated that the "new Grindr" had been designed and implemented to improve user experience (Simkhai, 2013). However, the introduction of "Grindr Tribes" at this time which allowed users to align themselves with particular identity-based groups or communities, suggests that creation of identity-based marketing categories was also a key motivator for updating the Grindr interface. A rapid increase in competition from other social media may have equally played a part. Indeed, during the period from 2010 to 2014 a wave of new mobile social media applications emerged that were quickly taken up as alternate spaces in which gay men could engage with one another – in a similar scenario to the activities which saw Facebook integrated into Gaydar cultures several years earlier.

As Grindr's own mention of the service in its media release indicates, chief amongst these has been image and video sharing application Instagram. While Instagram has been showcasing users' photos to their followers in mosaic-style across members' profiles since it first launched in 2010, its later addition of features to better enable community formation and engagement appear to have been the main impetus for it becoming a key part of contemporary gay men's digital cultures. In 2011, for example, Instagram added the capacity to hashtag posts, opening up opportunities for material on the site to become more widely visible and for hashtagged posts to behave like nodes in a larger network, around which hashtag communities (see Bruns & Burgess, 2015) or networked publics (boyd, 2011) might form. As a demographic well-known for its tendency toward early adoption (see Florida, 2002; Gross, 2003; Warren, 2000), gay men began taking advantage of this possibility almost instantly, tagging posts with hashtags referencing not just gay male identity itself (e.g., #gay, #gaydude), but the existence of Instagram-based communities of gay men (e.g., #instagay, #gayinstagram, #gaysofinstagram). Such hashtags, as Duguay (2016) has written about in relation to queer women, can function as important acts of personal identification for individual users, allowing for banal everyday activities to be recontextualised as constitutive of contemporary homosexual identity. As noted above, these hashtags also help to make visible much larger networked publics based around the shared interest of a common sexuality. Given that at the time of writing some of the most popular hashtags on Instagram that relate to homosexuality have close to 40 million posts, however, the sheer volume of materials and users involved in these spaces, and their dispersion across the global population of Instagram users, means that these more generic hashtags (e.g., #gay, #gaysofinstagram) hold limited potential for user interaction and engagement to proceed to offline face-to-face contexts when compared to more specific localised ones. Accordingly, city-centric Instagram hashtags such as #gaysydney and #gaybrisbane have become an important element of contemporary gay men's digital culture in recent years for their capacity to both visualise gay male communities *and* facilitate in-person contact amongst users.

My analysis of the concerns of participants in this study regarding the tendency of services such as Gaydar and Grindr to promote stereotypes about gay male identity (see Chapter 3), together with a critical reading of content posted to the hashtag #gaybrisbane, suggests that the impetus for gay men making use of Instagram in this way appears to be primarily related to identity issues – and, in particular, the less restrictive ways that the digital infrastructure of Instagram shapes possibilities for identity management.

In addition to the capacity to simultaneously visualise a range of gay male communities (e.g., based on locality and/or subcultural identity), Instagram gives users an almost endless range of possibilities in terms of how they can position themselves in relation to these. Whereas Gaydar's 'types I like' and Grindr's 'Grindr Tribes' limit options available for identity expression and construct a particular set of gay male character types for users to identify with, hashtags can, of course, be designed and implemented by users themselves. In this way, expression of gay male identity is not restricted within Instagram to any particular set of 'types' or categories. Indeed, even when modified to engage local communities, hashtags related to long-standing gay identity types on

Instagram, such as #brisbears, are far less popular than hashtags, such as #beardedhomosaustralia, which focus on a particular trait or feature, like a beard or tattoo.[1] Instagram also gives users the ability to present complex, dynamic identities – and not just by permitting the use of up to 30 hashtags per post. Whereas niche services for gay male audiences, such as Gaydar and Grindr, have relied on users developing static profiles within the parameters set by drop-down menu categories regarding users' physical descriptions and the like, Instagram profiles present user updates as an aggregated self-portrait. This simple, but significant, feature instantly conveys greater authenticity upon Instagram profiles than those on services such as Gaydar or Grindr, given the level of complexity that would be involved in repeatedly fabricating identity on a dynamic profile compared to doing so on a one-off basis on a static one. Equally importantly, Instagram's dynamic profiles allow users the freedom to change and evolve and to be contradictory in a way that is not possible on Gaydar or Grindr. That is, as no one image stands alone on Instagram, but simply represents a moment in time, the possibility exists for a user to post content related to gay male life (even stereotypically so), but to not be defined by it, as such. While there is a more general shift towards dynamic profiles occurring across social media for this reason (Ellison & boyd, 2013), given the participants in this study railed against stereotypes of gay male identity and consistently repeated that they tried to construct their Gaydar and Grindr profiles using everyday 'lifestyle' images, it makes sense that Instagram would be particularly well received by this demographic.

Further encouraging this positive reception, of course, is the fact that Instagram is not a platform purpose built for pursuing romantic/sexual relationships. One of the key concerns of the young men seen in this study regarding Gaydar and Grindr was that they perpetuated ideas about gay male identity being deeply tied up with casual sex. Instagram's terms of service, however, state that users "may not post nude, partially nude...pornographic or sexually suggestive photos or other content via the Service" (Instagram, 2013, np). While Grindr also has a set of user terms and conditions that explicitly prohibits the posting of such content (Grindr, 2015) it is nonetheless a service targeted exclusively at gay male audiences with marketing material that directly addresses using Grindr in the pursuit of romantic/sexual encounters. Instagram's terms and conditions regarding sexual content, combined with its much broader range of users and uses, however, can be read as encouraging modes of participation that more closely align with the kind of post-gay sensibilities (see Ghaziani, 2011, p. 102) expressed by the cohort studied here, who desired to be defined by more than their sexualities and to live (work, socialise, reside and so on) amongst sexually mixed company. It is not surprising in this sense, that localised gay Instagram communities (such as #gaybrisbane) are sometimes also used as places to directly demonstrate users' antipathy towards services such as Grindr, and towards the sexually driven culture perceived to define them through, for example, the reposting of Grindr profiles and exchanges that call out what users see as inappropriate or undesirable Grindr behaviour – in a similar fashion to posts seen at www.doucebagsofgrindr.com.

This is not to say that sexually explicit or suggestive posts, comments and other behaviours are absent from gay community networks within Instagram. These certainly exist, and in some cases (e.g., at hashtags such as #gaymuscle)[2] are more prominent than other kinds of content. However, for the most part, sexually explicit or suggestive material is simply part of a much broader flow of everything else that finds its way onto Instagram. Content posted to the #gaybrisbane hashtag, for example, includes everything from the kinds of underwear shots, bare bottoms and torsos that have been part of the erotic coding of gay men's bodies for decades (see Mowlabocus, 2010) to everyday images of food, travel, sport, partners, friends and family members, homes and offices, landscapes/cityscapes, pets/animals, advertising, popular memes and more. Hence, these hashtagged community networks – and the individual profiles connected to them – are much more diverse in content than the profiles and community-oriented spaces of niche networking services such as Gaydar and Grindr.

In terms of direct user engagement occurring via Instagram, from the sexually suggestive to the banal, hashtagged images get repurposed as sites for engagement with other gay men through Instagram's comments feature and direct messaging capabilities. In addition to compliments ("that's hot!") and direct propositions ("please post a full frontal shot"), commenters often leave invitations on users' posts to direct message them ("DM me!"), follow their account ("follow me") or exchange usernames for the ephemeral social messaging service, Snapchat ("snap: @ readyforyou", "what's your snap?"). In fact, Snapchat is a key part of this culture and requests for Snapchat usernames occur with such frequency that many users who post to hashtags oriented towards gay men signal their intentions to engage with others through the pre-emptive inclusion of Snapchat usernames in their Instagram biographies, or as text overlays on a particular (often sexually suggestive) image.

Snapchat is a key part of gay men's Instagram culture on account of two things. First, as with the use of MSN to augment Gaydar's limited messaging capabilities in the 1990s and early 2000s, Snapchat has greater capacity than Instagram to sustain user conversation through back-and-forth real-time messaging. Instagram's focus on the consumption of image and video content and its clunky sidebar commenting feature (designed this way to keep images front and centre) makes it less convenient in this regard. Secondly, the ephemeral nature of Snapchat messages (or 'snaps') and its much more relaxed terms of service concerning nudity and the sending of sexually suggestive material (see Snap

Inc., 2014) means that Snapchat has, since its very inception, been perceived as an ideal tool for private flirtatious communication and 'sexting' (see Dickey, 2012).

This paired use of localised Instagram hashtags and Snapchat to facilitate real-time conversation and face-to-face interaction is similar to arrangements that existed in previous iterations of gay men's digital culture where, for example, Gaydar was used in conjunction with MSN, and later Facebook. It is distinctive from these earlier arrangements, however, in the sense that neither Instagram nor Snapchat has been designed especially for gay male users. While some – generally older – men clearly set up accounts on these services designed specifically for seeking out sexual relationships with other gay men (by, e.g., not posting identifying images to pseudonymous Instagram accounts and creating suggestive Snapchat usernames such as @readyforyou), for the most part, users engaging in these spaces in are doing so through accounts that link to identifiable representations of their everyday lives. Indeed, considering the thoughts of participants in this study regarding gay male identity, this deep integration of gay men's digital culture with users' everyday digital selves, would appear to be a large part of the appeal of using Instagram and Snapchat together for the demographic of participants studied here, who tended towards a post-gay sensibility. This is because using Instagram and Snapchat in tandem in this way creates an environment amenable to constructing the kinds of non-metropolitan gay male identities that participants related to in this study, but felt unable to present in highly sexualised spaces such as Gaydar and Grindr. And moreover, because Instagram and Snapchat create broad possibilities for gay male identity expression while simultaneously delivering users an almost equivalent capacity to visualise proximate gay male communities as existing niche social spaces for gay men, as well as the ability to engage in unlimited real-time dialogue with each other.

The capacity of geolocative social applications primarily targeted at heterosexual users, such as Tinder, to deliver similar outcomes, plus the convenience of doing so all within the one application, has also seen a recent rise in the use of these services amongst gay men as an alternative to niche tools, such as Grindr. Some social commentators have in fact gone so far as to declare Tinder the service that might come to "the salvation of gay dating" (Hilton, 2014). In its bid to attract demographics, such a heterosexual women, that have traditionally seen online dating as a high-risk endeavour for the 'desperate' (Anderson, 2005) Tinder was developed with features that address common deterrents to online dating, such as concerns around personal safety and user misrepresentation (Gibbs, Ellison & Lai, 2011). One of these key features, for example, is the linking of Tinder profiles to users' broader social networks, through an automated connection process that draws Tinder profile data from users' existing Facebook accounts. This automated integration process is a mechanism through which users can better establish the authenticity of other users' profiles, in terms of the expression of a consistent identity. The drawing of Tinder profile data from Facebook means that users are identified by real names (albeit first names only) and that users are aware of any mutual friends or overlaps in their respective social networks. As gay entertainment commentator Danny Hilton (2014) has put it, "these details make the people on the other end of the screen real". For gay male users he says, these features mean "you'll see 'Alan' or 'Danny' or 'Vladimir.' Not 'Discreet Top' or 'Up4itnow'", as can be the case in services like Grindr.

The nature of the Tinder environment is also vastly different from Grindr on account of Tinder's 'swipe' feature. This prevents users from contacting each other without mutual willingness to do so, as indicated via corresponding right swipes on each other's profiles. In safeguarding users from receiving uninvited communication, Tinder's swipe feature makes defensive pre-emptive dismissals of other users and the kind of anticipatory identity territorialism (Payne, 2007) that has been common within spaces such as Grindr, and Gaydar before it, unnecessary. Combined with the fact that Tinder offers gay men the possibility to seek out other gay men without framing homosexuality as a particular kind of identity – by simply allowing for male users to indicate they are also 'looking for' other men – this makes Tinder an attractive alternative to the more sexual identity focused spaces of Grindr and Gaydar, where users have effective free reign in terms of approaching each other and where taking protective measures against uninvited correspondence (such as blocking individual users) are more onerous. Indeed, confirming the growing popularity of Tinder for all of these reasons, an 18-year-old man I recently interviewed for an upcoming project listed the applications he used for engaging with the gay male community as Tinder, Instagram, Snapchat, and Grindr. And he was quick to follow up with the clarification that he had listed them in his order of preference, saying he actually rarely used Grindr, since it was "mostly for older guys these days".

For gay men cautious about revealing their sexuality, however, Tinder's automated connection with users' Facebook profiles has raised concerns about potential privacy breaches. Users postings to the sub-Reddit 'AskGayBros', for example, answering the question "How does Tinder work for gay dudes? Will my straight friends see me?", debated this point in 2014, with several users advising the original enquirer that Tinder could not be counted on to be as safe or anonymous as other applications (AskGayBros, 2014). A similar point was made on the GayBros sub-Reddit (GayBros, 2015) where posters noted that Tinder would not capture anybody without a Facebook profile and that it is therefore wise, for privacy reasons, to create a fake/hollow Facebook account in order to use Tinder. Hence, while Tinder use has certainly grown amongst the gay male population in recent times (see MacKee, 2016, p. 3), it still does not have the same critical mass of users as applications such as Grindr, particularly in rural areas and smaller cities like Brisbane. While undertaking a month-long test-run of popular dating apps and chronicling their various pros and cons for meeting gay men, journalist JP Mangalindin (2015) noted, for example, that even in a city like San Francisco with a substantial gay male population, Tinder ran out of nearby matches for him in less than 25 minutes. This aligns with 2015 figures from Globalwebindex which show that only 1 per cent of internet users globally are using Tinder on a monthly basis (see McGrath, 2015).

In fact, there are very few services of this kind with the numbers of gay male users that Grindr has, having been the first geolocative social media product on the market for this demographic. Gay dating applications, Scruff and Hornet, with eight and six million users, respectively (Rukkle, 2015), come closest. Hence, while Grindr faces growing competition from these services, as well as from more mainstream applications such as Instagram, Snapchat and Tinder, it continues to be the most widely used single application in the Western world for gay men seeking to engage with their peers (Rukkle, 2015). However, while it might be more convenient technologically than a paired platform arrangement, like that between Instagram and Snapchat, and more private and densely populated than Tinder, in failing to provide the kind of environment that these alternate services offer users in terms of presenting non-traditional gay male identities, Grindr continues to operate amidst a culture of participatory reluctance. Moreover, I would argue that the culture of participatory reluctance on Grindr may now be more acute than it was on Gaydar previously. And not just because Grindr initially sold itself as something that would be entirely different from Gaydar.[3] Since Grindr's arrival, society has continued to become more attuned to post-gay sensibilities through the ongoing global fight for marriage equality and its focus on highlighting the normality of same-sex lives and love. Users of social media, particularly in younger demographics, are also much more accustomed to presenting the details of their everyday lives in online spaces to be consumed by others, due to the trend towards dynamic, ongoing narratives in social media (Ellison & boyd, 2013; Robards, 2012). And a greater volume of social media is now available overall, giving users more services (both niche and mainstream), and more individual features of services, to compare Grindr against than Gaydar could ever be compared to during the early-to-mid, and even, late, 2000s. Moreover, the convergence of mainstream media with creative content and interpersonal communication on social media (Burgess & Banks, 2014) has given rise to phenomena such as Douchebags of Grindr (www.douchebagsofgrindr.com and @grindrdouches), which works across several platforms to legitimise and amplify the discontent of Grindr users.

Summary of Findings

I have argued here that a culture of participatory reluctance – where large numbers of users engage with a digital platform in a state of discontent – has been a key feature of gay men's digital spaces in recent years and an important factor helping to forge the development of a much more diverse and complex style of contemporary gay men's digital culture. Or, more precisely, that the shift from Gaydar to a Gaydar/Facebook symbiosis in the early 2000s, to a broad ecology of applications, including, for example, Grindr, Instagram, Snapchat, Tinder and others in the early to mid-2010s has been largely underpinned, particularly amongst younger demographics, by identity-driven participatory reluctance within traditional sites of gay men's digital activity. In addition to identifying the existence of a culture of participatory reluctance within key popular online spaces of gay male activity, however, this study has also provided in depth qualitative data about the ways that identity and the negotiation of privacy inform young gay men's use of social media.

As we saw in Chapter 3, through an examination of Gaydar, presentation of identity within gay men's digital spaces has often needed to occur within sites embedded with features that seek to emphasise and eroticise physical attributes and to foreground sexual desire. This situation is also intensified in Gaydar's case by the fact that the site promotes what Nakamura (2002) calls 'menu-driven identities', restricting people's abilities to control their own identity performance through the heavy use of drop-down menus and tick-box categories in its profile template. As Light (2007) has also noted, aesthetically and ideologically, this constructs Gaydar in such a way as to limit the range of masculinities on offer to its users. These features, combined with a lack of genuine alternatives to the site (see Mowlabocus, 2010) during its period of dominance in the 2000s, when it had little economic imperatives to change, worked to generate a culture of participatory reluctance within Gaydar amongst the group of users studied here.[4] This culture manifested, for example, in the large numbers of profiles belonging to men in the 18–28 year old bracket where users employed the free-text areas of the profile template to fervently dissociate themselves from the site and the imagined community contained therein, engaging in what Payne (2007, p. 532) calls 'identity territorialism'.

As I have shown in the current chapter, many of the key properties of Gaydar that were initially resisted by Grindr's developers were later added to the updated version of the Grindr app in 2013 (e.g., via the addition of Grindr Tribes), and the culture of participatory reluctance seen on Gaydar has carried over to Grindr as well. As the comments made by participants in this chapter regarding their tendency to respond disparagingly to all communication received from unknown Grindr users indicates, so too did the 'identity territorialism' (Payne, 2007).

As with Gaydar, this identity territorialism was typically displayed by users engaging in a form of identity management underpinned by hostile rhetoric denigrating the kinds of gay male identity encapsulated in Sinfield's (1998) metropolitan model of homosexuality – and the imagined audience of Grindr users they believed fit within this model.

This research also suggests that the identity territorialism apparent within Gaydar and Grindr can increase users' sense of isolation – both from other users of the site and, by extension, the broader gay male community. In trying to establish their own difference from Gaydar and Grindr's imagined audience of stereotypical gay men (which the digital infrastructure of these services are complicit in constructing), for example, we saw young gay men convincing themselves that they are, so to speak, "the only gay in the village" – or more accurately, the only users of these services who do not fit within existing stereotypes about gay men. This is particularly significant given that the men in this study noted that they had originally joined services such as Gaydar as teenagers looking to find other gay men to help them reduce their sense of isolation while living in country towns, staying at boarding schools and residing in other circumstances where they generally had limited access to the world of GLBT-friendly venues and events.

Despite their greater diversity of GLBT representations, the arrival of mainstream social media platforms has not so much corrected this situation as it has complicated it. In Chapter 4, for example, I discussed the expansion of gay men's networks into Facebook and introduced the idea that when Facebook began achieving popularity in Australia it was initially touted amongst some in the gay community as 'the new Gaydar'. However, while the specifics of Facebook's cultural and mechanical make-up (e.g., its real name policy, more mainstream user base, and collapsed contexts) clearly prevented the site from functioning as a wholesale alternative to Gaydar, the ways that Facebook had been taken up and embraced by the 18–28 year old men at the centre of this study to extend, verify, connect with, and navigate, gay men's social networks are nonetheless significant. The ways that participants in this study used Facebook to these ends can teach us much about what it is young gay men want from gay-oriented SNSs going forward. I noted in this chapter, for example, that one of the key reasons Facebook was embraced by the young gay men in this study was because – by comparison with Gaydar – it provides a digital framework in which a much wider range of GLBT identities can be expressed in a fashion that makes homosexuality, ostensibly, banal. Seeing how Instagram has been taken up by gay men more recently to present everyday contemporary homosexual identities only further reinforces this point.

Taking Chapters 3 and 4 together, then, it is clear that the kinds of social networking experience that many young gay men are currently seeking is one where meeting and interacting with other gay men in a relatively private online context does not necessitate identifying or engaging with the forms of masculinity associated with Sinfield's (1998) metropolitan model of homosexuality. It was because neither Gaydar nor Facebook alone could provide this sort of experience that participants in this study developed patterns of use around these sites that deeply entwined the two services; thereby demonstrating the ways in which Facebook has been an important facet of gay men's digital culture in recent times.

We saw in Chapter 5, however, how the reliance on Facebook to provide (in conjunction with Gaydar) a social networking environment more amenable to the wants and needs of these young gay men created a catch-22 style situation in that the extension of gay men's networks into Facebook generated additional privacy and safety concerns for both users and non-users of the site, and compounded safety and privacy concerns associated with Gaydar use. Comparing the affordances with regards to privacy of both Gaydar and Facebook as they stood at the time of the study's focus groups, it was established that Gaydar operated using a simple and stable set of privacy controls which allowed participants to balance the pros and cons of potentially being recognised from the site by other users in such a way that limited their concerns regarding privacy and safety. Indeed, the most significant concerns of the participants in this study with regard to their own privacy while using Gaydar related to protecting their reputations as a particular kind of gay man amongst other gay men. Nobody who partook in this study, for example, wanted to provide personal information about himself within Gaydar that could lead to others reading him as the sort of gay man who fits the stereotypes that have traditionally been associated with urban gay men's culture. And the worst experiences reported by participants as a result of using Gaydar were described as "awkward" interactions with other Gaydar users in "non-gay" environments where those interactions could not be openly acknowledged.

By comparison, Facebook's privacy and safety controls were identified as complex and unstable – particularly because they are frequently reset by the company in a bid to establish greater openness and transparency in online contexts. The resulting inability of participants to operate these controls and their failure to understand all of the ways that their information could be made accessible to various parties lead to the implementation of ad-hoc, ineffective privacy measures (such as 'lagging') across the board. And thus, across the board there were also considerable privacy breaches reported as a result of using Facebook: the most serious of these incidents included three cases where participants were directly outed via the site, and several more where participants were stalked and/or bullied (both online and off). In the final section of Chapter 5 the ways that Facebook also increased the safety concerns associated with Gaydar when these two services were routinely used together was discussed. I noted, for example, how the system of recognition that Young (2004) also established exists around Gaydar – and urban gay male communities more generally – was fundamentally changed by the fact that Facebook introduced real names into the mix. In this way, Facebook's existence heightened the dangers associated with using Gaydar by increasing the possibilities for pseudonymous Gaydar profiles to be linked with identifiable ones on Facebook. There was also discussion of the implications that Facebook's increasing importance in gay male communities had for the extent that commercial gay spaces could be considered safe zones for young gay men, as venturing into such spaces in their physical sense since Facebook's arrival also means potentially appearing in photographs on the Facebook pages associated with these venues.

Because of the benefits that participants in this study noted they experienced as a result of Facebook's tendency to allow them access to information about other gay men which helped them to navigate various aspects of their social lives more easily – by, for example, helping them make more informed decisions about who to engage with on Gaydar and in other social contexts offline – nobody who directly participated in this study had experienced a breach of privacy which prompted them to completely stop using Facebook. Nevertheless, there was much evidence to suggest that the job of balancing these benefits with the costs of reduced privacy that Facebook generates, was a difficult one. For example, even those who very openly self-identified as gay men found difficulty in preserving a balance between privacy protection and social media engagement within the context of Gaydar and Facebook's sociotechnical convergence – highlighting one of the core reasons for continued use of Gaydar even amongst men with strong ideological opposition to the site.

As this concluding chapter has shown however, Grindr, Tinder and the paired use of Instagram and Snapchat present similar challenges. While Grindr and Tinder offer users the capacity to visualise a proximate gay community, both present challenges associated with privacy. For Grindr this is on account of geolocation features, which participants indicated they made significant use of, but were not always comfortable with, due to the potential for such features to compromise their safety and security. For Tinder, which has equivalent geolocative capacity, privacy concerns also included issues around potential context collapse due to the sourcing of data from Facebook that is imposed on users by the service. While Instagram and Snapchat are less afflicted by privacy concerns (although not completely devoid of them), the labour involved in effectively using this arrangement to facilitate engagement with other gay men could be more onerous than that required in a single application setting.

Implications and Emerging Questions

Findings from this study indicate that many young gay men are craving a digital space where social networking with their peers can occur in an environment that does not focus on the sexual or railroad them into identifying with what they see as outmoded models of gay masculinity. These men would also prefer such a space to have easily useable functions for private chatting and to seamlessly integrate into the rest of their online activities. As we saw in Chapter 5, it was these desires that prompted the practice of shifting interactions from Gaydar to Facebook to occur – and more recently, for interactions emerging from Instagram to shift to Snapchat. This turn towards more mainstream social media use within gay male networks, and the culture of participatory reluctance within niche spaces of gay men's digital activity that underlies it, adds additional layers of complexity to the kinds of identity-based issues young GLBT people already face. As social media are key sites of identity formation and development for the present generation of youth (James et al., 2008, p. 15), both GLBT and otherwise, extrapolating from this data to productively consider recent movements in contemporary sites of gay men's digital culture raises a number of issues to consider in future for researchers in this area and for community organisations alike.

Firstly, if two of the most successful social networking applications developed for gay men (Gaydar and Grindr, respectively) have been afflicted by participatory reluctance, how might platform designers do a better job of creating (and monetizing) the kind of niche spaces wanted by gay men? This study has provided in depth qualitative data about the key reasons a particular group of young gay men patronise SNSs specific to the gay male community (Chapter 3) and about the kinds of features they do and do not use in these spaces, along with detailed justifications for these preferences. While this provides valuable information for designers of social networking environments aimed at this demographic, with focus group participants asking (in Chapter 5), "[w]hy can't you have a gay-based friendship meeting site like Facebook [in Gaydar's stead]"? there is clearly more to be done in this regard.

Of course, in the wake of Grindr's success, in the period after focus groups for this study were carried out, several all-male, location-based social networking services that have profile templates similarly non-taxonomising of sexualities as Facebook, have been developed to compete with Grindr. And there is now a whole new wave of social networking apps (both gay oriented and otherwise) available, which also offer the geolocative services (see, e.g., Salerno, 2012) Grindr initially introduced to gay men's digital cultures. 'Hornet' (www.gethornet.com), for example, boasts that it is the "app that Grindr should have been!" on the basis that it allows users to have a 'virtual location'. However, at the same time, Hornet emphasises sex and the erotic by including functions that advertise users' HIV status and the date of their last sexual health check.

While Mowlabocus' (2010) work suggests that gay men's digital culture is defined by the principle of cybercarnality, and that, therefore, sexually oriented spaces such as Gaydar, Grindr and Hornet will continue to dominate gay men's social media, the arrival of mainstream social networking spaces alongside the coming of age of a generation of men for whom the history of gay men's culture is experienced differently (i.e., via GLBT rights movements based around gay marriage rather than around the legalization of homosexuality itself), does seem to indicate that there is now additional room for greater experimentation. Social media researchers and application designers asking this demographic what the 'gay Facebook' environment participants here notionally argued would be a better alternative to sites like Gaydar might actually look like, would be a prudent place to start.

Secondly, and perhaps more importantly, given that GLBT youth in Australia are still more likely to experience anxiety and depression than their non-GLBT contemporaries (Leonard et al., 2012), and more likely to attempt suicide or have suicidal thoughts (National LGBTI Health Alliance, 2010a; Suicide Prevention Australia, 2009, p. 20), in highlighting some of the reasons for young gay men's increased take-up of mainstream social media for gay men's networking purposes, this study draws attention to a potential need for GLBT organisations to better update community support guidelines to account for the era of social media. It also points to a need for the emphasis in research on GLBT-oriented networking platforms to shift from concerns about sexual health issues (as has traditionally been the case with studies on gay men's use of SNSs) to mental health ones. To date, for instance, attention on mental health issues faced by GLBT youth has been placed most heavily on combating isolation and depression linked to issues such as homophobia and heteronormativity. The Australian National LGBTI Health Alliance (2010b) in their 'Submission to beyondblue on the draft Clinical Practice Guidelines: Depression in Adolescents and Young Adults', for example, focuses on issues such as discrimination, fear of homophobic abuse, and diminished feelings of connection to the broader community as risk factors for young GLBT people with regards to the experience of depression. This document also lists 'belonging to or participation in' the GLBT community as a protective factor against such experiences. In mapping the ways that young gay men in Brisbane managed their identities within gay-oriented SNSs and how they responded to various features of these sites, this project provides insight into the sorts of identity-based concerns presently felt by young gay men in these contexts. It highlights that, for the group of men studied here, identity-based concerns playing out within social media arenas are oftentimes also focused around experiencing feelings of isolation, not from the broader community, but from *within* the GLBT community itself.

For organisations that operate support programmes aimed at GLBT youth, or which otherwise provide information and assistance to this population, already trying to cope with and ameliorate the raised levels of anxiety and depression that young GLBT people tend to feel in comparison to their non/GLBT peers (e.g., Beyondblue, OpenDoors,

Coming Out Australia), the arrival and popular take up of SNSs and the extension of gay men's networks into mainstream social networking services clearly adds an additional layer of complexity. Accordingly, there is a need for such organizations to reconsider the nature of advice provided in these contexts to account for the arrival of social media. At the time of writing, for example, Coming Out Australia incorporates a list of suggestions about coming out as a gay person on its website[5] that includes advice in relation to choice of timing; choice of audience; clarity in relation to one's own feelings; and the need to gather support in advance. Placing one's identity in the hands of the network, as is the case in many mainstream social networking services, such as Facebook, however, a person's ability to adhere to these suggestions and comfortably manage the coming-out process is made significantly more difficult. This points towards the possible emergence of a situation where young gay men might be pressured into coming out to the broader community before they would otherwise feel ready to do so – either to prevent the occasion being forced upon them unexpectedly via Facebook, or Tinder, or simply in order to allow themselves to operate within spaces such as Gaydar, and even gay men's hashtag networks on Instagram, more successfully. Alternatively, the prevalence of practices such as shifting interactions from Gaydar to Facebook and the rise of gay men's hashtag networks on Instagram might put young gay men in a position where (instead of feeling pressured to be out in all aspects of their lives) they feel the need (on account of the additional layers of digital labour involved in maintaining distinct social contexts through social media) to choose between having access to gay men's networks or having access to the cultural and social capital embedded in more mainstream networks. Indications that these kinds of pressures are very real could be seen in this study in Chapter 5.

For social media researchers, these findings problematise longstanding ideas regarding the place of the internet as an avenue to greater inclusion and participation for minority groups (Rheingold, 1993), and for identity demarginalisation amongst GLBT populations (McKenna & Bargh, 1998). Namely, this is because findings from this study draw attention to the ways that some social media platforms designed for gay men at present, appear to extend, and in certain cases, help generate, feelings of marginalization amongst their users (see Chapter 3). This suggests that the emphasis on sexual health issues that prevails in studies of gay men's use of SNSs at present ought to be matched more evenly in future by work considering the mental health concerns associated with these environments. Individual issues that immediately arise from this project as seeming worthy of examination, include, for example, the nature and levels of anxiety related to social media use experienced by this demographic; if/how feelings of disconnection and difference from others in the gay male community differ when users engage with gay men's digital networks exclusively via niche social networking services versus mainstream social networking services, or a combination of the two; and how to update community guidelines about coming out processes for the era of social media.

The final key implication/emerging question from this study is the need for further research into gay men's digital cultures in more diverse social and cultural contexts. In her book, *A private sphere: Democracy in a digital age*, Zizzi Papacharissi (2010a) argues that, in commercializing personal information, internet-based platforms, such as social networking sites, have turned privacy into a luxury commodity. What renders privacy a luxury commodity, she says, is that "obtaining it implies a level of computer literacy that is inaccessible to most, and typically associated with higher income and education levels, and certain ethnic groups, in ways that mirror dominant socio-demographic inequalities". In this way, she argues, digital literacy has become a social stratifier, dividing people into classes of have and have-nots, and bringing about the emergence of a growing "privacy divide".

The present study demonstrates how the convergence of technologies, practices and spaces associated with gay men's digital culture can swiftly impose the affects of this divide onto young gay men. Hence, it also demonstrates that being on the socially disadvantaged side of the emerging privacy divide is not always a case of being more or less digitally literate than others – or even a case of coming from a disadvantaged socioeconomic or demographic background. While there was an approximately 50/50 breakdown between numbers of focus groups participants in this study who were and were not university educated, the three men who found themselves outed via Facebook and the two men whose circumstances saw them engaging in stressful daily censoring routines were all from the university-educated group. They were also all from middle or upper-middle class backgrounds, had been using SNSs since their early teens, and four out of five of these men were white. Of course, all of these men were also gay, and therefore part of a minority group. But in the increasingly accepting environment that now exists in many Western countries, being gay does not in itself suggest that a person will feel socially disadvantaged or need or want to take greater measures to protect their privacy than any other person. Indeed, there were men in this study for whom not being able to keep up with Facebook's changing privacy provisions was not a concern, as they were comfortable with the information on their Facebook profile becoming publicly visible (including those items which clearly indicated their sexuality). What this indicates is that identifying those groups of people who could potentially be most affected by the emerging privacy divide created in social networking environments is almost impossible, as the factors which will impact upon the extent to which one's access to sociality/need for privacy in these spaces will likely be comprised of a range of life circumstances specific to each individual – e.g.,

What industry do they work in? Are they out to their family? What is the religious background of their friends? How do the cultures and affordances of all the different services they use converge?

Therefore, educating ourselves about the ways that various SNSs work and about the ways that convergence of the technologies, practices and environments surrounding these services impacts not just upon our own uses of them, but upon others' as well, is key. As user experiences in this and the previous chapter demonstrates, the expansion of gay men's digital culture across a broader ecology of niche and mainstream service types brings with it increased privacy concerns that impact some users more than others, even in contemporary Western cities, like Brisbane, where relative freedom around homosexuality can now be enjoyed. Accordingly, it might also be said that the diversification of gay men's digital culture and the trend towards alternate mainstream spaces is being driven primarily by those with greater freedom to express non-normative sexual identities within the context of their everyday lives, as research findings shown in earlier chapters of this book demonstrates. Indeed, the fact that a majority 60 per cent stake in Grindr was sold to the Beijing Kunlun Tech Company in January 2016 (Price, 2016), indicates that Grindr executives are aware the application may have already reached its peak in Western markets and may need to rely on users in areas less advanced with regards to GLBT visibility to continue thriving in the years ahead in what is becoming an increasingly crowded market. Hence, how social media users negotiate issues of identity management in the spaces of gay men's digital culture in places such as China – which, despite strict regulations around the publication of homosexual imagery, is now home to the biggest social networking application for gay men anywhere in the world[6] – will be an important area of future research in this field.

Coda

In 1998, looking toward the new millennium, Alan Sinfield wrote that "les/bi/gay people" may be "growing out of 'gay'" and entering "the period of the post-gay – a period when it will not seem so necessary to define, and hence to limit, our sexualities". "Suddenly, improbably," he said, "we are in a position to envisage a new refocusing of sexual dissidence for the next millennium. It is a point at which to reassess our situation and the cultural resources through which we comprehend it" (pp. 1–14). For the generation of same-sex-attracted men who have come of age since the turn of that new millennium in Australia, and indeed in most Western countries, Sinfield's (1998) notion of the period of the 'post-gay' is apt. His "Millenial visions" (Sinfield, 1998, p. 1) depict almost perfectly the positions of the young men described in this study, who fervently proclaimed, for instance, that they do not define themselves by their sexuality and that they are looking for relationships not in any way different from those available to their heterosexual peers (see Chapter 3). These men need not have "grow[n] out of 'gay'", as such, they simply came of age, in the mid-2000s, at a time when what Sinfield describes as being 'post-gay' was already normalised – at least amongst their contemporaries. In 2012, for example, launching the magazine *Hello Mr.*, its 20-something creater, Ryan Fitzgibbon, was pitching squarely to this audience when he described his new publication in the following way:

> *Hello Mr.* is a magazine about men who date men. It's the overdue response to the unending cliché's that surround current gay lifestyle publications...it's about relevant material for a misrepresented generation with an evolved range of interests. A chronicle of everyday life, and the narratives which define it...It's the start of a conversation that extends beyond the images that come to mind when you think of the way gay men are portrayed in the media today. It's a chance to expose our vulnerabilities and redefine our identities. What you won't find here are articles tagged with recycled stock imagery of multicoloured flags...or idolized midsections of seemingly flawless men. If that's your thing, there is a sea of glossy mags filled with those images readily available at your local newsstand. We believe that Hello Mr. can address the need, felt by the modern majority, to rebrand 'gay' and move beyond any unrepresentative depictions defined by our past.
>
> (Fitzgibbon, 2012)

Most notable here is the rejection of the highly sexualised identities that have typically been associated with male homosexuality, as well as the very clear notion of generational change and the failure of modern media to move beyond "unrepresentative depictions of our past". There are references to men who "date" men, rather than, for example, 'men who have sex with men'.[7] And there is the reference to "an evolved range of interests". This aligns very clearly with the dominant positions of those men who repeatedly noted in this book that they are not defined by their sexuality, that their lives do not revolve around the gay 'scene', and that they are looking for long-term monogamous relationships developed out of dating scenarios, rather than sex or 'hook-ups', from other men. These are the same people Fitzgibbon (2012) refers to above as "the modern majority". The kind of homosexuals that Sinfield (1998) envisioned would inhabit the not-too-distant future in 1998.

The existence of participatory reluctance within gay men's social networking services observed in this study, and my young participants' reasons for leaning ever more heavily towards using mainstream social media platforms in their place, can be traced to these same frustrations. Indeed the participatory reluctance seen within platforms such as Gaydar and Grindr here demonstrates that, at least in Western cities like Brisbane, Sinfield's (1998) visions with regards to dominant models of gay male identity have now largely come to pass. What remains to be seen, as yet, even as a plethora of new niche applications emerge trying to capitalise on these users' resentment/frustrations is whether services designed specifically for gay male users will be able to keep pace with the rapid social- and identity-based shifts occurring within and around this community and continue to flourish alongside more mainstream social networking services – or be entirely subsumed them. Either way, as I have shown here, the culture of participatory reluctance that emerged in flagship services, such as Gaydar and Grindr, will have been a driving force in the process.

Notes

1 At the time of writing, for example, the hashtag #brisbears had just 432 posts, while #beardedhomosaustralia had 11,604 and the aggregator account @beardedhomosaustralia had close to 50,000 followers.
2 At the time of writing, for example, all recent posts to #gaymuscle had been hidden by Instagram because they had been reported as having not met Instagram's community guidelines.
3 See quote earlier from Grindr's initial release regarding it being better than existing dating sites.
4 It is worth pointing out here, once more, that 'participatory reluctance' is not necessarily limited to young users of Gaydar. However, there is evidence that the reasons for participatory reluctance amongst users older than the demographic studied here are different.
5 See www.comingout.com.au/coming-out/.
6 In 2016 the Chinese built social application for gay men, Blued, announced that it had become the largest application designed specifically for this demographic anywhere in the world, with an estimated value larger than Grindr (Woodley, 2016).
7 The term 'men who have sex with men' (typically abbreviated to MSM) has been used in recent decades to identify those men who are homosexually inclined but who do not identify themselves either as 'gay' or 'homosexual' as such (see Young & Meyer, 2005). Its replacement here with 'date' is a significant shift.

Bibliography

Agomuoh, F. (2012, October 11). National coming out day celebrates 12 celebrities who came out as gay in 2012. *International Business Times*. Retrieved November 2, 2012 from www.ibtimes.com/national-coming-out-day-celebrates-12-celebrities-who-came-out-gay-2012-845039

Akrich, M. (1992). The de-scription of technical objects. In W. Bijker & J. Law (Eds.) *Shaping technology/building society: Studies in sociotechnical change* (pp. 205–224). Cambridge, MA: MIT Press.

Albrechtslund, A. (2008). Online social networking as participatory surveillance. *First Monday*, *13*(3). doi:10.5210/fm.v13i3.2142.

Alexander, J. (2002). Introduction to the special issue: Queer webs: Representations of LGBT people and communities on the World Wide Web. *International Journal of Sexuality and Gender Studies*, 7(2/3), 77–84.

Altman, I., & Taylor, D. (1973). *Social penetration: The development of interpersonal relationships*. New York, NY: Holt.

Anders, A. (Director). (1999). La Douleur Exquise! [Television series episode – Season 2, Episode 12]. In D. Star (Writer), *Sex and the City*. New York, NY: HBO.

Anderson, B. (1991). *Imagined communities: Reflections on the origin and spread of nationalism*. London, UK: Verso.

Anderson, T. L. (2005). Relationships among Internet attitudes, Internet use, romantic beliefs, and perceptions of online romantic relationships. *Cyberpsychology & Behaviour*, *8*(6), 521–531.

Anon. (2008, April 20). Goodbye 80s homo. *Sydney Star Observer*. Retrieved November 24, 2011 from www.starobserver.com.au/news/local-news/new-south-wales-news/2008/04/20/goodbye-80s-homo/11843

Anon. (2012, May 10). Evolved' Obama supports gay marriage. *Sydney Morning Herald*. Retrieved May 10, 2012 from www.smh.com.au/world/evolved-obama-backs-gay-marriage-20120510-1ydsj.html

AskGayBros. (2014, September 5). How does Tinder work for gay dudes? Will my straight friends see me? *Reddit* [Subreddit]. Retrieved March 9, 2016 from www.reddit.com/r/askgaybros/comments/2fl8lv/how_does_tinder_work_for_gay_dudes_will_my/

Aussies turn to MySpace, Facebook to reunite with friends. (2007, December 30). *Sunday Territorian*, p. 39.

Australian Bureau of Statistics. (2014). *Regional population growth, Australia, 2012–2013*, cat. no. 3218.0. Canberra, ACT: ABS. Retrieved October 27, 2014 from www.abs.gov.au/ausstats/abs@.nsf/Products/3218.0~2012-13~Main+Features~Queensland?OpenDocument#PARALINK4

Australian Communication Council. (2012). *Best practice guide: Social media code of conduct.* Retrieved November 23, 2012 from www.communicationscouncil.org.au/downloads_tcc/2012/CC_Social%20Media%20Code%20of%20Conduct_FINAL.pdf

Australian Marriage Equality. (2012). *Public opinion: Nationally.* Retrieved December 9, 2012 from www.australianmarriageequality.com/wp/who-supports-equality/a-majority-of-australians-support-marriage-equality/

Avert. (2010a). *History of HIV and AIDS in the United States of America.* Retrieved March 27, 2012 from www.avert.org/aids-history-america.htm#

Avert. (2010b). *History of HIV and AIDS in the UK 1996 onwards.* Retrieved March 27, 2012 from www.avert.org/ukaids.htm

Ayers, T. (2000). Sexual identity and cultural identity: A crash course. *Journal of Australian Studies, 24*(65), 159–163.

Bakardjieva, M. (2005). *Internet society – The Internet in everyday life.* London, UK: Sage.

Balsamo, B. A. (2000). The virtual body in cyberspace. In D. Bell & B. M. Kennedy (Eds.), *The cybercultures reader* (pp. 489–503). London, UK: Routledge.

Barnes, S. (2006). A privacy paradox: Social networking in the United States. *First Monday, 11*(9). doi:10.5210/fm.v11i9.1394.

Barnett, E. (2010, January 11). Facebook's Mark Zuckerberg says privacy is no longer a 'social norm'. *The Telegraph.* Retrieved February 21, 2010 from www.telegraph.co.uk/technology/facebook/6966628/Facebooks-Mark-Zuckerberg-says-privacy-is-no-longer-a-social-norm.html

Bauman, Z. (2000). *Liquid modernity.* Cambridge, UK: Polity.

Baym, N. (2000). *Tune in, log on: Soaps, fandom, and online community.* Thousand Oaks, CA: Sage.

Baym, N. (2007). The new shape of online community: The example of Swedish independent music fandom. *First Monday, 12*(8). doi:10.5210/fm.v12i8.1978

Baym, N. (2010). *Personal connections in the digital age.* Malden, MA: Polity.

Baym, N. (2011). Social networks 2.0. In M. Consalvo & C. Ess (Eds.), *The handbook of Internet studies* (pp. 384–405). Hoboken, NJ: Wiley-Blackwell.

Baym, N., & Markham, A. (Eds.). (2009). *Internet inquiry: Conversations about method.* New York, NY: Sage.

BBC Sport. (2009). Ex-Lion Gareth Thomas reveals he is gay. *BBC News.* Retrieved November 2, 2012 from http://news.bbc.co.uk/sport2/hi/rugby_union/welsh/8421956.stm

Bell, D., & Kennedy, B. M. (Eds.). (2000). *The cybercultures reader.* London, UK: Routledge.

Beninger, J. R. (1987). Personalization of mass media and the growth of pseudo-community. *Communication Research, 14*, 352–371.

Benkler, Y. (2006). *The wealth of networks: How social production transforms markets and freedom.* New Haven, CT: Yale University Press.

Berry, C., Martin, F., & Yue, A. (2003). *Mobile cultures: New media in queer Asia.* Durham, NC: Duke University Press.

Biernacki, P., & Waldorf, D. (1981). Snowball sampling: Problem and techniques of chain referral sampling. *Sociological Methods and Research, 10*(2), 141–163.

Bird, D., Ling, M., & Haynes, K. (2012). Flooding Facebook – The use of social media during the Queensland and Victorian floods. *The Australian Journal of Emergency Management, 27*(1), 27–33.

Blackwell, C., Birnholtz, J., & Abbott, C. (2015). Seeing and being seen: Co-situation and impression formation using Grindr, a location-aware gay dating app. *New Media & Society*, *17*(7), 1117–1136.

Bodker, M., & Christensen, M. (2003). *Trust in the network society*. Paper presented at the Research 4.0: Broadening the Band, Association of Internet Researchers 4th Annual Conference, Toronto.

Boswell, J. (1994). *Same-sex unions in pre-modern Europe*. Oxford, UK: Villard Books.

boyd, d. (2001). *Sexing the Internet: Reflections on the role of identification in online communities*. Paper presented at 'Sexualities, Medias, Technologies', University of Surrey, 21–22 June, 2001. Retrieved March 21, 2008 from www.danah.org/papers/SexingTheInternet.conference.pdf

boyd, d. (2002). *Faceted id/entity: Managing representation in a digital world*. Cambridge, MA: MIT Master's Thesis. Retrieved April 4, 2008 from www.danah.org/papers/Thesis.FacetedIdentity.pdf

boyd, d. (2004). Friendster and publicly articulated social networks. In *Proceedings of ACM Conference on Human Factors in Computing Systems* (pp. 1279–1282). New York, NY: ACM Press.

boyd, d. (2006). Friends, Friendsters, and MySpace Top 8: Writing community into being on social network sites. *First Monday*, *11*(12). doi:10.5210/fm.v11i12.1418.

boyd, d. (2008a). Facebook's privacy Trainwreck: Exposure, invasion, and social convergence. *Convergence*, *14*(1), 13–21.

boyd, d. (2008b). Why youth (heart) social network sites: The role of networked publics in teenage social life. In D. Buckingham (Ed.), *MacArthur foundation series on digital learning – Youth, identity, and digital media volume*. Cambridge, MA: MIT Press.

boyd, d. (2008c). None of this is real: Identity and participation in Friendster. In J. Karaganis (Ed.), *Structures of participation in digital culture* (pp. 132–157). New York, NY: SSRC Books.

boyd, d. (2011). Social network sites as networked publics: Affordances, dynamics, and implications. In Z. Papacharissi (Ed.), *A networked self: Identity, community, and culture on social network sites* (pp. 39–58). New York, NY: Routledge.

boyd, d., & Ellison, N. B. (2007). Social network sites: Definition, history, and scholarship. *Journal of Computer-Mediated Communication*, *13*(1), article 11. Retrieved April 20, 2008 from http://jcmc.indiana.edu/vol13/issue1/boyd.ellison.html

boyd, d., & Hargittai, E. (2010). Facebook privacy settings: Who cares? *First Monday*, *15*(8). doi:10.5210/fm.v15i8.3086.

boyd, d., & Heer, J. (2006). Profiles as conversation: Networked identity performance on Friendster. In *Proceedings of the Thirty-Ninth Hawai'i International Conference on System Sciences*. Los Alamitos, CA: IEEE Press. Retrieved March 5, 2008 from www.danah.org/papers/HICSS2006.pdf

boyd, d., & Marwick, A. (2011). *Social privacy in networked publics: Teens' attitudes, practices, and strategies*. Paper presented at the Oxford Internet Institute Decade in Internet Time Symposium, September 22. Retrieved March 5, 2012 from www.danah.org/papers/2011/SocialPrivacyPLSC-Draft.pdf

Branwyn, G. (2000). Compu-sex: Erotica for cybernauts. In D. Bell & B. M. Kennedy (Eds.), *The cybercultures reader* (pp. 396–402). London, UK: Routledge.

Brightest Young Gays. (n.d). *Facebook* [Group page]. Retrieved March 9, 2012 from www.facebook.com/BYGays

Bronski, M. (1984). *Culture clash: The making of gay sensibility.* Cambridge, MA: South End Press.

Bronski, M. (2000). *The pleasure principle: Sex, backlash, and the struggle for gay freedom.* New York, NY: St. Martin's Press.

Bronski, M. (2011). *A Queer history of the United States.* Boston, MA: Beacon Press.

Brown, M. (2014). Gender and sexuality II: There goes the gayborhood? *Progress in Human Geography, 38*(3), 457–465.

Brown, G., Maycock, B., & Burns, S. (2005). Your picture is your bait: Use and meaning of cyberspace among gay men. *Journal of Sexual Research, 42*(1), 63–73.

Brubaker, J. R., Ananny, M., & Crawford, K. (2016). Departing glances: A sociotechnical account of "leaving" Grindr. *New Media & Society, 18*(3), 373–390.

Bruns, A. (2008). *Blogs, Wikipedia, Second life and beyond: From production to produsage.* New York, NY: Peter Lang.

Bruns, A., & Burgess, J. (2015). Twitter hashtags from ad hoc to calculated publics. In N. Rambukkana (Ed.), *Hashtag publics: The power and politics of discursive networks* (pp. 13–28). New York, NY: Peter Lang.

Bruns, A., & Jacobs, J. (2006). Introduction. In A. Bruns & J. Jacobs (Eds.), *Uses of blogs* (pp. 1–11). New York, NY: Peter Lang.

Buckingham, D. (2008). Introducing identity. In *Youth, identity, and digital media* (pp. 1–24). Cambridge, MA: The MIT Press.

Bull, M., Pinto, S., & Wilson, P. (1991, January). Homosexual law reform in Australia (Report No. 29). *Australian institute of criminology – Trends and issues in crime and criminal justice.* Canberra: Australian Institute of Criminology. Retrieved March 17, 2008 from http://aic.gov.au/documents/F/2/E/%7BF2ED9BD3-0314-4EAA-AD03-410635E620DE%7Dti29.pdf

Burgess, J., & Banks, J. (2014). Social media. In S. Cunningham & S. Turnbull (Eds.) *The media and communications in Australia* (4th ed.) (pp. 285–290). Sydney, NSW: Allen & Unwin.

Butler, J. (1990). *Gender trouble: Feminism and the subversion of identity.* New York, NY: Routledge.

Byrne, D. N. (2007a). Public discourse, community concerns, and civic engagement: Exploring black social networking traditions on BlackPlanet.com. *Journal of Computer-Mediated Communication, 13*(1), article 16. Retrieved April 20, 2008 from http://jcmc.indiana.edu/vol13/issue1/byrne.html

Byrne, D. N. (2007b). The future of (the) 'race': Identity, discourse and the rise of computer-mediated public spheres. In A. Everett (Ed.), *MacArthur foundation book series on digital learning: Race and ethnicity volume* (pp. 15–38). Cambridge, MA: MIT Press.

Campbell, J. E. (2004). *Getting it on online: Cyberspace, gay male sexuality, and embodied identity.* New York, NY: Harrington Park Press.

Carter, D. (2004). *Stonewall: The riots that sparked the gay revolution.* New York, NY: St. Martin's Press.

Castells, M. (1983). *The city and the grassroots.* Los Angeles: University of California Press.

Castells, M. (2001). Virtual communities or network society? In *The Internet galaxy: Reflections on the Internet, business, and society* (pp. 116–136). Oxford: Oxford University Press.

Chan, D. K. S., & Cheng, G. H. L. (2004). A comparison of offline and online friendship qualities at different stages of relationship development. *Journal of Personal and Social Relationships*, *21*(3), 305–320.

Chang, J., Rosenn, I., Backstrom, L., & Marlow, C. (2010). ePluribus: Ethnicity in social networks. In *Proceedings of the Fourth International AAAI Conference on Weblogs and Social Media*. Retrieved August 8, 2012 from http://aaai.org/ocs/index.php/ICWSM/ICWSM10/paper/view/1534/1828

Chasin, A. (2000). *Selling out: The gay and lesbian movement goes to market*. New York, NY: Palgrave.

Chauncey, G. (1995). *Gay New York: Gender, urban culture, and the making of the gay male world, 1890–1940*. New York, NY: Basic Books.

Chauncey, G. (2005). *Why marriage? The history shaping today's debate over gay equality*. New York, NY: Basic Books.

Chauncey, G. (2009). *Why marriage? The history shaping today's debate over gay equality – With a new preface*. New York, NY: Basic Books.

Cherny, L., & Weise, E. R. (Eds.). (1996). *Wired women: Gender and new realities in cyberspace*. Berkeley, CA: Seal Press.

Choi, J. H. (2006). Living in cyworld: Contextualising cy-ties in South Korea. In A. Bruns & J. Jacobs (Eds.), *Uses of blogs* (pp. 173–186). New York, NY: Peter Lang.

Citron, D. (2009). Cyber civil rights. *Boston University Law Review*, *89*, 61–125.

Clark, C. (1991). Pornography without power? In M. Kimmel (Ed.) *Men Confront Pornography* (pp. 281–284). New York, NY: Meridian.

Cohen, J. (2011, January 21). Return of gay teen suicide over Facebook taunts? *AllFacebook: The unofficial Facebook blog*. Retrieved January 29, 2011 from http://allfacebook.com/return-of-gay-teen-suicide-over-facebook-taunts_b30051

Cohen, R., & Lipman, D. (Producers). (2000–2005). *Queer as Folk* [Television Series]. New York, NY: Showtime.

Collins, D., & Metzler, D. (Producers). (2003–2007). *Queer Eye for the Straight Guy* [Television Series]. New York, NY: Bravo.

Cooper, M., & Dzara, K. (2010). The Facebook revolution: LGBT identity and activism. In C. Pullen & M. Cooper (Eds.) *LGBT identity and online new media* (pp. 100–112). New York, NY: Routledge.

CPC Connect. (2013). Our future. *About Us*. Retrieved June 19, 2013 from www.cpcconnect.co.uk/?page_id=128

D'Emilio, J. (1983). *Sexual politics, sexual communities: The making of a homosexual minority in the United States, 1940–1970*. Chicago, IL: University of Chicago Press.

D'Emilio, J. (1992). *Making trouble: Essays on gay history, politics and the university*. New York, NY: Routledge.

D'Emilio, J., & Freedman, E. B. (1988). *Intimate matters: A history of sexuality in America*. Chicago, IL: University of Chicago Press.

Danet, B., Ruedenberg-Wright, L., & Rosenbaum-Tamari, Y. (1997). "Hmmm... Where's that smoke coming from?" Writing, play and performance on Internet Relay Chat. *Journal of Computer-Mediated Communication*, 2(4). doi:10.1111/j.1083-6101.1997.tb00195.x

DaveyWavey. (2011, August 18). *What I Look for in a Guy!* [Video File]. Retrieved February 18, 2012 from www.youtube.com/watch?v=dI3yq5t4JWI

Davies, R. T. (Producer). (1999–2000). *Queer as Folk* [Television Series]. London, UK: Channel 4.

Davison, W. (1983). The third-person effect in communication. *Public Opinion Quarterly*, *47*(1), 1–15.

DeGeneres, E. (Producer). (2003–). *The Ellen DeGeneres Show* [Television Series]. Burbank, CA: Warner Bros. Television Distribution.

Dickey, M. (2012, December 1). Let's be real: Snapchat is totally used for sexting. *Business Insider.* Retrieved June 19, 2013 from www.businessinsider.com.au/snapchat-growth-sexting-2012-11

di Gennaro, C., & Dutton, W. H. (2007). Reconfiguring friendships: Social relationships and the Internet. *Information, Communication and Society*, *10*(5), 591–618.

Di Maggio, P., Hargittai, E., Neuman, W. R., & Robinson, J. P. (2001). Social implications of the Internet. *Annual Review of Sociology*, *27*, 307–336.

Doherty, B. (2007, September 5). 'Kevvy' keeps a lid on it as high-schoolers mob new kid in class. *The Age*, p. 8.

Donath, J. (2007). Signals in social supernets. *Journal of Computer-Mediate Communication*, *13*(1), 231–251.

Donath, J., & boyd, d. (2004). Public displays of connection. *BT Technology Journal*, *22*(4), 71–82.

Drushel, B. (2010). Virtually supportive: Self-disclosure of minority sexualities through online social networking sites. In C. Pullen & M. Cooper (Eds.), *LGBT identity and online new media* (pp. 62–74). New York, NY: Routledge.

Duberman, M. (1994). *Stonewall.* New York, NY: Plume.

Dugdale, K. (2007). *Cool brands: An insight into some of Britain's coolest brands, 2007–2008*. London, UK: TransAtlantic Publications.

Duguay, S. (2016, April–June). Lesbian, gay, bisexual, trans and queer visibility through selfies: Comparing platform mediators across Ruby Rose's Instagram and Vine presence. *Social Media + Society*, 1–12. doi:10.1177/2056305116641975.

Dwyer, C. (2007). Digital relationships in the "MySpace" generation: Results from a qualitative study. In *Proceedings of the Fortieth Hawaii International Conference on System Sciences* (p. 19). Los Alamitos, CA: IEEE Press.

Dyer, R. (1989). A conversation about pornography. In S. Shepherd & M. Wallis (Eds.) *Coming on strong: Gay politics and culture* (pp. 198–212). London, UK: Unwin Hyman.

E. (2007, December 19). Is Facebook the new Gaydar. *Awkward sex in the city.* Retrieved March 21, 2008 from http://awkwardsexinthecity.blogspot.com.au/2007/12/is-facebook-is-new-gaydar.html

Ellison, N., & boyd, d. (2013). Sociality through social network sites. In W. H. Dutton (Ed.), *The oxford handbook of Internet studies* (pp. 151–172). Oxford, UK: Oxford University Press.

Ellison, N., Heino, R., & Gibbs, J. (2006). Managing impressions online: Self-presentation processes in the online dating environment. *Journal of Computer-Mediated Communication*, *11*(2), article 2. Retrieved March 18, 2008 from http://jcmc.indiana.edu/vol11/issue2/ellison.html

Ellison, N., Lampe, C., Steinfield, C., & Vitak, J. (2011). With a little help from my friends: How social network sites affect social capital processes. In Z. Papacharissi (Ed.), *A networked self: Identity, community and culture on social network sites* (pp. 124–145). London, UK: Routledge.

Ellison, N., Steinfield, C., & Lampe, C. (2007). The benefits of Facebook "friends:" Social capital and college students' use of online social network sites. *Journal of Computer-Mediated Communication*, *12*(4), 1143–1168.

Elm, M. S. (2009). How do various notions of privacy influence decisions in qualitative internet research? In N. Baym & A. Markham, (Eds.), *Internet inquiry: Conversations about method* (pp. 127–171). New York, NY: Sage.

Enochsson, A. B. (2007). Tweens on the Internet: Communication in virtual guest books. *Seminar.net – International Journal of Media, Technology and Lifelong Learning*, *3*(2), 1–14.

Erickson, B. (1996). Culture, class, and connections. *American Journal of Sociology 102*, 217–251.

Erickson, B. (2003). Social networks: The value of variety. *Contexts*, 2, 25–31.

Facebook. (2010, October 19). *Facebook's network of support*. Retrieved November 30, 2010 from www.facebook.com/note.php?note_id=161164070571050

Facebook. (2015). Registration and account security. *Statement of Rights and Responsibilities*. Retrieved March 10, 2015 from www.facebook.com/legal/terms.

Facebook. (2016). *Company info*. Retrieved January 17, 2016 from http://newsroom.fb.com/Key-Facts

Facebook Help Centre. (2010). *How do I help an LGBT person who has posted suicidal content on Facebook?* Retrieved 23 November, 2012 from www.facebook.com/help/151072898296969

Fincher, D. (Director). (2010). *The Social Network* [Motion picture]. Culver City, CA: Columbia Pictures.

Fiske, S., & Taylor, S. (1984). *Social cognition*. Boston, MA: Addison-Wesley.

Fitch, J. H., & 'Out' Magazine Editors. (1997). *Gay and lesbian World Wide Web directory (Australia/New Zealand Ed)*. Emeryville, CA: Lycos Press.

Fitzgibbon, R. (2012). About the magazine. *HelloMr*. Retrieved December 8, 2012 from http://hellomrmag.com

Fletcher, G., & Light, B. (2007). Going offline: An exploratory cultural artifact analysis of an Internet dating site's development trajectories. *International Journal of Information Management*, 27(6), 422–431.

Flew, T. (2014). *New media* (4th ed.). Sydney, NSW: Oxford University Press.

Flood, M., & Hamilton, C. (2005, July 1). Mapping homophobia in Australia. *Australia Institute Web Paper*. Retrieved March 17, 2008 from www.tai.org.au/index.php?q=node%2F19&pubid=350&act=display

Florida, R. (2002). *The rise of the creative class: And how it's transforming work, leisure, community and everyday life*. New York, NY: Basic Books.

Fluffy. (n.d). *Facebook* [Fan page]. Retrieved March 9, 2012 from www.facebook.com/ILoveFluffy

Fono, D., & Raynes-Goldie, K. (2006). Hyperfriendship and beyond: Friends and social norms on LiveJournal. In M. Consalvo & C. Haythornthwaite (Eds.), *Internet research annual volume 4: Selected papers from the AOIR conference* (pp. 91–103). New York, NY: Peter Lang.

Fontana, A., & Frey, J. H. (2003). The interview: From structured questions to negotiated text. In N. K. Denzin & Y. S. Lincoln (Eds.), *Collecting and interpreting qualitative materials* (2nd ed.) (pp. 61–106). London, UK: Sage.

Ford, T. (Director). (2009). *A Single Man* [Motion picture]. New York, NY: The Weinstein Company.

Foster, T. (Ed.). (2007). *Long before stonewall.* New York: New York University Press.

Foth, M. (2003). If you build it they won't necessarily come: The need for online communication research into communities of place. *Communications research forum 2003*, 1–2 October 2003, Canberra, Australia.

Foucault, M. (1978). *The history of sexuality: Volume 1 – An introduction* (R. Hurley, Trans.). New York, NY: Pantheon Books. (Original work published 1976).

Foucault, M. (1980). Truth, power and sexuality. In C. Gordon (Ed.), *Power/knowledge: Selected interviews and other writings 1972–77* (pp. 89–96). Brighton, UK: Harvester Press.

Fowler, G. (2012, October 13). When the most personal secrets get outed on Facebook. *Wall Street Journal.* Retrieved, October 14, 2012 from http://online.wsj.com/article_email/SB10000872396390444165804578008740578200224-lMyQjAxMTAyMDEwMjAxODI3Wj.html

Gajjala, R. (2007). Shifting frames: Race, ethnicity, and intercultural communication in online social networking and virtual work. In M. B. Hinner (Ed.), *The role of communication in business transactions and relationships* (pp. 257–276). New York, NY: Peter Lang.

Gay Australia Connect. (n.d). *Facebook* [Group page]. Retrieved March 9, 2012 from www.facebook.com/gayaustralia.connect

Gay Boys with Beards. (n.d). *Facebook* [Group page]. Retrieved March 9, 2012 from www.facebook.com/pages/Gay-Boys-with-Beards/220697574339

Gay Doctors. (n.d). *Facebook* [Group page]. Retrieved March 9, 2012 from www.facebook.com/gaydoctors

Gay Equality in Schools. (n.d). *Facebook* [Fan page]. Retrieved March 9, 2012 from www.facebook.com/EqualSchools

Gay Geeks. (n.d). *Facebook* [Group page]. Retrieved March 9, 2012 from www.facebook.com/groups/gaygeeks1/

Gay Marriage Rights in Australia. (n.d). *Facebook* [Fan page]. Retrieved March 9, 2012 from www.facebook.com/GMRA1

Gay Men's Opera Club. (n.d). *Facebook* [Group page]. Retrieved March 9, 2012 from www.facebook.com/groups/108130465950864/

Gay Somerset. (n.d). *Facebook* [Group page]. Retrieved March 9, 2012 from www.facebook.com/gay.somersetlbgt

Gay Sports. (n.d). *Facebook* [Group page]. Retrieved March 9, 2012 from www.facebook.com/pages/Gay-Sports/232215623494361

Gay Thailand. (n.d). *Facebook* [Group page]. Retrieved March 9, 2012 from www.facebook.com/GayThailandClub

GayBros. (2015, September 2). What's a good app/site for gay dating nowdays? *Reddit* [Subreddit]. Retrieved March 9, 2016 from www.reddit.com/r/gaybros/comments/3jb44i/whats_a_good_appsite_for_gay_dating_nowadays/

Gaydar. (2010). *Site tour.* Accessed September 28, 2010 at www.gaydar.com.au/#

Gaydar. (2012). *Gaydar privacy policy.* Retrieved January 30, 2012 from www.gaydar.com.au/info/privacy.asp

Gaydar. (2013, February 19). *Behind the Scenes at Gaydar* [Video File]. Retrieved February 21, 2013 from www.youtube.com/watch?v=8Zg-Hr9aScc&list=FL2jxxzoz2cFOa4kOytFzPhA&index=1

Geidner, N. W., Flook, C. A., & Bell, M. W. (2007, April). *Masculinity and online social networks: Male self-identification on Facebook.com.* Paper presented at the Eastern Communication Association 98th Annual Meeting, Providence, RI.

Ghaziani, A. (2011). Post-gay collective identity construction. *Social Problems, 58*(1), 99–125.

Ghaziani, A. (2014). *There goes the gayborhood?* Princeton, NJ: Princeton University Press.

Gibbs, J., Ellison, N., & Lai, C. (2011). First comes love, then comes Google: An investigation of uncertainty reduction strategies and self-disclosure in online dating. *Communication Research, 38*(1), 70–100.

Giddens, A. (1991). *Modernity and self-identity: Self and society in the late modern age.* Stanford, CA: Stanford University Press.

Giffen, M., 2008. Online privacy. *Current Health, 34*(7), 8–11.

Gilbert, E., Karahalios, K., & Sandvig, C. (2008). *The network in the garden: An empirical analysis of social media in rural life.* Paper presented at the ACM CHI 2008. Retrieved 11 July 2008, from http://social.cs.uiuc.edu/people/gilbert/papers/chi08-rural-gilbert.pdf

Ginger, J. (2008). *The Facebook project: Performance and construction of digital identity.* Unpublished Masters, University of Illinois at Urbana-Champaign.

GLAAD. (2016). *27th annual GLAAD media awards.* Retrieved from www.glaad.org/mediaawards

GLBT Historical Society. (n.d). *Facebook* [Group page]. Retrieved March 9, 2012 from www.facebook.com/GLBTHistory

GLOE: GLBT Outreach and Engagement. (n.d). *Facebook* [Group page]. Retrieved March 9, 2012 from www.facebook.com/DCJCC.GLOE

Goad, R., & Mooney, T. (2007). The impact of social networking in the UK. *Hitwise Experian.* Retrieved April 20, 2008 from http://melcarson.com/wp-content/uploads/2008/01/hitwise-social-networking-report-2008.pdf

Goedel, W., Halkitis, P., Greene, R., Hickson, D., & Duncan, D. (2016). HIV risk behaviors, perceptions, and testing and preexposure prophylaxis (prep) awareness/use in Grindr-using men who have sex with men in Atlanta, Georgia. *Journal of the Association of Nurses in AIDS Care*, 27(2), 133–142.

Goffman, E. (1959). *The presentation of self in everyday life.* Carden City, NY: Doubleday Anchor.

Goffman, E. (1963a). *Behaviour in public places: Notes on the social organization of gatherings.* New York, NY: Free Press.

Goffmam, E. (1963b). *Stigma: Notes of the management of spoiled identity.* New York, NY: Simon and Schuster.

Golder, S. A., Wilkinson, D., & Huberman, B. A. (2007, June). Rhythms of social interaction: Messaging within a massive online network. In C. Steinfield, B. Pentland, M. Ackerman, & N. Contractor (Eds.), *Proceedings of the Third International Conference on Communities and Technologies* (pp. 41–66). London, UK: Springer.

Gordon-Logan, L. (Producer). (2011, January 6). *The Facebook Obsession* [Television Broadcast]. New York, NY: CNBC.

Gosine, A. (2007). Brown to blonde at Gay.com: Passing white in queer cyberspace. In K. O'Riordan & D. J. Phillips (Eds.), *Queer online: Media, technology & sexuality* (pp. 139–154). New York, NY: Peter Lang.

Granovetter, M. S. (1973). The strength of weak ties. *The American Journal of Sociology, 78*(6), 1360–1380.

Gray, M. (2009). *Out in the country: Youth, media, and queer visibility in rural America* (Intersections: Transdisciplinary Perspectives on Genders and Sexualities Series). New York, NY: New York University Press.

Gregg, M. (2011). *Work's intimacy.* Cambridge, UK: Polity.

Grindr. (2012). *0 feet away: Our mission for you.* Retrieved August 8, 2012 from http://grindr.com/learn-more

Grindr. (2013, October 1). New Grindr. New useful tips. *The Grindr blog.* Retrieved January 12, 2014 from www.grindr.com/blog/new-grindr-new-useful-tips/

Grindr. (2015). *Grindr profile guidelines.* Retrieved January 19, 2015 from www.grindr.com/profile-guidelines/

Gross, L. (2003). The gay global village in cyberspace. In N. Couldry & J. Curran (Eds.), *Contesting media power: Alternative media in a networked world* (pp. 259–272). New York, NY: Rowman and Littlefield.

Gross, L. (2007). Foreword. In K. O'Riordan & D. J. Phillips (Eds.), *Queer online: Media, technology and sexuality* (pp. vii–x). New York, NY: Peter Lang.

Gross, R., & Acquisti, A. (2005). Information revelation and privacy in online social networks (The Facebook Case). In *Proceedings of the 2005 Workshop on Privacy in the Electronic Society (WPES'05)* (pp. 71–80). Alexandria, VA: ACM.

Gudelunas, D. (2012). There's an app for that: The uses and gratifications of online social networks for gay men. *Sexuality & Culture, 16*(4), 347–365.

Hakken, D. (1999). *Cyborgs@cyberspace? An ethnographer looks to the future.* New York, NY: Routledge.

Halloran, J. (2008, May 24). Out, proud and ready for gold. *Sydney Morning Herald.* Retrieved November 2, 2012 from www.smh.com.au/articles/2008/05/23/1211183107597.html

Hammersley, M., & Atkinson, P. (1995). *Ethnography: Principles in practice* (2nd ed.). London, UK: Routledge.

Hansen, D., Ackerman, M., Resnick, P., & Munson, S. (2007). Virtual community maintenance with a repository. In *Proceedings of the American Society for Information Science and Technology Annual Meeting* (ASIS&T '07). Milwaukee, WI. Retrieved March 2, 2012 from http://presnick.people.si.umich.edu/papers/asist07/hansen.pdf

Hargittai, E. (2012, July 17). *Social implications of digital media.* Seminar conducted from The University of Queensland, Brisbane.

Hargittai, E., & Hsieh, Y. P. (2011). From dabblers to omnivores: A typology of social network site usage. In Z. Papacharissi (Ed.), *A networked self: Identity, community and culture on social network sites* (pp. 146–168). London, UK: Routledge.

Hart, K. (2008, January 7). Niche networks attract advertisers. *Canberra Times*, p. 13.

Haythornthwaite, C. (2005). Social networks and Internet connectivity effects. *Information, Communication and Society*, *8*(2), 125–147.

Heath, R. (2006). *Please just F* off it's our turn now: Holding baby boomers to account*. Melbourne, VIC: Pluto Press.

Heer, J., & boyd, d. (2005). Vizster: Visualizing online social networks. In *Proceedings of Symposium on Information Visualization* (pp. 33–40). Minneapolis, MN: IEEE Press. Retrieved March 4, 2008 from www.danah.org/papers/InfoViz2005.pdf

Henderson, S., & Gilding, M. (2004). I've never clicked this much with anyone in my life: Trust and hyperpersonal communication in online friendships. *New Media and Society*, *6*(4), 487–506.

Henry-Waring, M., & Barraket, J. (2008). Dating and intimacy in the 21st century: The use of online dating sites in Australia. *International Journal of Emerging Technologies and Society*, *6*(1), 14–33.

Hern, A. (2012, July 4). Facebook introduces icons for same-sex marriage. *NewStatesman*. Retrieved July 7, 2012 from www.newstatesman.com/blogs/sci-tech/2012/07/facebook-introduces-icons-same-sex-marriage

Hewitt, A., & Forte, A. (2006, November 4). *Crossing boundaries: Identity management and student/faculty relationships on the Facebook*. Paper presented at the 2006 Computer Supported Cooperative Work Conference (CSCW), Banff. Retrieved February 28, 2008 from www-static.cc.gatech.edu/~aforte/HewittForteCSCWPoster2006.pdf

Highfield, T. (2016). *Social media and everyday politics*. Cambridge, UK: Polity.

Hildebrand, J. (2008, 3 March). How net predators lure kids. *Daily Telegraph*, p. 9.

Hillier, L., & Harrison, L. (2007). Building realities less limited than their own: Young people practising same sex attraction on the Internet. *Sexualities: Studies in Culture and Society*, *10*(1), 82–100.

Hillier, L., Kurdas, C., & Horsley, P. (2001). *"It's just easier": the Internet as a safety-net for same sex attracted young people*. Melbourne, VIC: Australian Research Centre in Sex Health and Society, La Trobe University. Retrieved March 18, 2009 from http://apo.org.au/node/15390

Hilton, D. (2014, February 27). Why tinder might be the salvation of gay dating. *Huffington Post Tech UK*. Retrieved February 28, 2014 from www.huffingtonpost.co.uk/danny-hilton/gay-dating-tinder_b_4860405.html

Hinduja, S., & Patchin, J. W. (2008). Personal information of adolescents on the Internet: A quantitative content analysis of MySpace. *Journal of Adolescence*, *31*(1), 125–146.

Hine, C. (2000). *Virtual ethnography*. London, UK: Sage.

Hjorth, L. (2007). Home and away: A case study of Cyworld minihompy by Korean students studying in Australia. *Asian Studies Review*, *31*, 397–407.

Hogan, B. (2010). The presentation of self in the age of social media: Distinguishing performances and exhibitions online. *Bulletin of Science, Technology and Society*, *30*(6), 377–386

Hogan, B. (2011, August 8). *Real name sites are necessarily inadequate for free speech*. Message posted to http://people.oii.ox.ac.uk/hogan/

Hogan, B. (2012). Pseudonyms and the rise of the real-name web. In J. Hartley, J. Burgess, & A. Bruns (Eds.), *A companion to new media dynamics* (pp. 290–308). Chichester, UK: Blackwell.

Hogan, S., & Hudson, L. (1998). *Completely Queer: The gay and lesbian encyclopedia.* New York, NY: Henry Holt and Company.

Hoofnagle, C., King, J., Li, S., & Turow, J. (2010). *How different are young adults from older adults when it comes to information privacy attitudes and policies?* Berkeley: University of California. Retrieved March 6, 2012 from http://papers.ssrn.com/sol3/papers.cfm?abstract_id=1589864

Horrigan, J. B., Raine, L., & Fox, S. (2001). *Online communities: Networks that nurture long-distance relationships and local ties.* Washington, DC: Pew Internet and American Life Project. Retrieved March 5, 2008 from www.pewinternet.org

Horta, S., & Hayek, S. (Producers). (2006–2010). *Ugly Betty* [Television Series]. New York: ABC.

Huntley, R. (2006). *The world according to Y: Inside the new adult generation.* Crows Nest, NSW: Allen and Unwin.

Instagram. (2013, January 19). Terms of use. *Instagram Help Centre.* Retrieved June 4, 2016 from https://help.instagram.com/478745558852511

Ito, M., Baumer, S., Bittanti, M., boyd, d., Cody, R., Herr-Stephenson, B., ... Tripp, L. (2010). *Hanging out, messing around, geeking out: Kids living and learning with new media.* Cambridge, UK: MIT Press.

Ito, M., Horst, H. A., Bittanti, M., boyd, d., Herr-Stephenson, B., Lange, P. G., ... Robinson, L. (2008). *Living and learning with new media: Summary of findings from the digital youth project.* Chicago, IL: John D. and Catherine T. MacArthur Foundation. Retrieved December 12, 2008 from www.macfound.org/learning/research/

Jackson, E. (2012, April 30). Here's why google and Facebook might completely disappear in the next 5 years. *Forbes.* Retrieved May 6, 2012 from www.forbes.com/sites/ericjackson/2012/04/30/heres-why-google-and-facebook-might-completely-disappear-in-the-next-5-years/

Jagatic, T., Johnson, N., Jakobsson, M., & Menczer, F. (2007). Social phishing. *Communications of the ACM, 5*(10), 94–100.

James, C. (with Davis, K., Flores, A., Francis, J. M., Pettingill, L., Rundle, M., & Gardner, H.). (2008). Young people, ethics, and the new digital media: A synthesis from the good play project. *GoodWork® Project Report Series, Number 54.* Boston, MA: Harvard Graduate School of Education, Harvard University. Retrieved February 7, 2011 from www.pz.harvard.edu/library.php

Jenkins, H. (1992). *Textual poachers: Television fans and participatory culture.* New York, NY: Routledge.

Jenkins, H. (2006). *Convergence culture: When old and new media collide.* New York: New York University Press.

JockBoy26. (2010). *The big book of Gaydar (Uncut!).* Brighton, UK: The Book Guild.

Johnson, C. (2009, September 20). Project 'Gaydar': An MIT experiment raises new questions about online privacy. *Boston Globe.* Retrieved September 28, 2009 from www.boston.com/bostonglobe/ideas/articles/2009/09/20/project_gaydar_an_mit_experiment_raises_new_questions_about_online_privacy/

Jones, S. G. (Ed.). (1999). *Doing Internet research: Critical issues and methods for examining the net.* Thousand Oaks, CA: Sage.

Karppi, T. (2014). Disconnect.Me: User engagement and Facebook. PhD Thesis, University of Turku, Turku.

Kellner, D. (2003). Cultural studies, multiculturalism, and media culture. In G. Dines & J. M. Humez (Eds.), *Gender, race, and class in media: A text-reader* (2nd ed.) (pp. 9–19). Thousand Oaks, CA: Sage.

Kendall, L. (2002). *Hanging out in the virtual pub: Masculinities and relationships online*. Berkeley: University of California Press.

Kiesler, S., Siegel, J., & McGuire, T. W. (1984). Social psychological aspects of computer-mediated communication. *American Psychologist, 39*(10), 1123–1134.

Kirby, I. (2012, June 3). Twice as nice! Neil Patrick Harris and partner David Burtka enjoy a sunny New York stroll with their twins. *Mail Online*. Retrieved November 2, 2012 from www.dailymail.co.uk/tvshowbiz/article-2153935/Neil-Patrick-Harris-partner-David-Burtka-enjoy-sunny-New-York-stroll-twins.html

Kirkpatrick, D. (2010). *The Facebook effect: The inside story of the company that is connecting the world*. New York, NY: Simon and Schuster.

Kohan, D., & Mutchnick, M. (Producers). (1998–2006). *Will and Grace* [Television Series]. New York, NY: CBS.

Kumar, R., Novak, J., & Tomkins, A. (2006). Structure and evolution of online social networks. In *Proceedings of 12th International Conference on Knowledge Discovery in Data Mining* (pp. 611–617). New York, NY: ACM Press.

Kuntsman, A. (2007). Belonging through violence: Flaming, erasure, and performativity in queer migrant culture. In K. O'Riordan & D. J. Phillips (Eds.), *Queer online: Media technology and sexuality* (pp. 101–120). New York, NY: Peter Lang.

Lake, A. (2008, March 26). Interview: How the internet changed gay society. *Pink News*. Retrieved March 30, 2008 from www.pinknews.co.uk/2008/03/26/interview-how-the-internet-changed-gay-society/

Lally, E. (2002). *At home with computers*. New York, NY: Berg.

Lambe, S. (2012, August 2). Matt Bomer steps out with his partner and kids. *Buzzfeed*. Retrieved November 2, 2012 from www.buzzfeed.com/stacylambe/matt-bomer-steps-out-with-his-partner-and-kids

Lampe, C., Ellison, N., & Steinfield, C. (2006). A Face(book) in the crowd: Social searching vs. social browsing. In *Proceedings of CSCW-2006* (pp. 167–170). New York, NY: ACM Press.

Lampe, C., Ellison, N., & Steinfield, C. (2007). A familiar Face(book): Profile elements as signals in an online social network. In *Proceedings of Conference on Human Factors in Computing Systems* (pp. 435–444). New York, NY: ACM Press.

Lampinen, A., Lehtinen, V., Lehmuskallio, A., & Tamminen, S. (2011). We're in it together: Interpersonal management of disclosure in social network services. In *Proceedings of the SIGCHI Conference on Human Factors in Computing Systems* (pp. 3217–3226). New York: ACM Press.

Lampinen, A., Tamminen, S., & Oulasvirta, A. (2009). All my people right here, right now: Management of group co-presence on a social networking site. In *GROUP 09: Proceedings of the ACM 2009 International Conference on Supporting Group Work* (pp. 281–290). New York, NY: ACM Press.

Langer Research Associates. (2012, November 14). *Majority supports path to citizenship; greater division on other social issues*. Retrieved November 16, 2012 from www.langerresearch.com/uploads/1144a1SocialIssues.pdf

Larsen, M. C. (2007). *Understanding social networking: On young people's construction and co-construction of identity online*. Paper presented at

Internet Research 8.0: Let's Play, Association of Internet Researchers 8th Annual Conference, Vancouver.

Latour, B. (1997). *Aramis, or the love of technology*. London, UK: Routledge.

Lea, M., & Spears, R. (1991). Computer-mediated communication, de-individuation and group decision-making. *International Journal of Man Machine Studies*, *34*, 283–301.

Lee, A. (Director). (2005). *Brokeback Mountain* [Motion picture]. Universal City, CA: Focus Features.

Lee, S. (2012). Get off the Internet: A challenge to reconnect with yourself. *Hongkiat: Design, Inspiration, Technology*. Retrieved August 8, 2012 from www.hongkiat.com/blog/challenge-to-disconnect/

Lenhart, A., & Madden, M., (2007). *Teens, privacy and online social networks*. Washington, DC: Pew Internet and American Life Project, Pew Research Center. Retrieved May 2, 2008 from www.pewInternet.org/Reports/2007/Teens-Privacy-and-Online-Social-Networks.aspx

Leo, J. (2012a, December 4). Employers, beware online staff hunting. *The Advertiser*. Retrieved December 4, 2012 from www.news.com.au/business/worklife/employers-beware-online-staff-hunting/story-e6frfm9r-1226530040905

Leo, J. (2012b, September 16). Online checks catch out job-seekers. *Adelaidenow*. Retrieved December 4, 2012 from www.news.com.au/business/worklife/online-checks-catch-out-job-seekers/story-e6frfm9r-1226475206458

Leonard, W., Pitts, M., Mitchell, A., Lyons, A., Smith, A., Patel, S., ... Barrett, A. (2012). *Private Lives 2: The second national survey of the health and wellbeing of gay, lesbian, bisexual and transgender (GLBT) Australians*. Monograph Series Number 86. Melbourne, VIC: The Australian Research Centre in Sex, Health and Society, La Trobe University. Retrieved April 26, 2012 from www.glhv.org.au/files/PrivateLives2Report.pdf

Lessig, L. (1999). *Code and other laws of cyberspace*. New York, NY: Basic Books.

Levit, A. (2009, May 2–3). Go on, aquire a brand in order to sell yourself. Weekend Professional Education. *The Weekend Australian* (Reprinted from *The Wall Street Journal*).

Levitan, S., & Lloyd, C. (Producers). (2009–). *Modern Family* [Television Series]. Los Angeles, CA: 20th Century Fox Television.

Lewis, G. H. (1990). Community through exclusion and illusion: The creation of social worlds in an American shopping mall. *Journal of Popular Culture*, *24*, 121–136.

Liben-Nowell, D., Novak, J., Kumar, R., Raghavan, P., & Tomkins, A. (2005). Geographic routing in social networks. *Proceedings of National Academy of Sciences*, *102*(33), 11623–11628.

Licoppe, C., Riviere, C. A., & Morel, J. (2016). Grindr casual hook-ups as interactional achievements. *New Media & Society*, *18*(11), 2540–2558.

Light, B. (2007). Introducing masculinity studies to information systems research: the case of Gaydar. *European Journal of Information Systems*, *16*, 658–665.

Light, B. (2014). *Disconnecting with social networking sites*. London, UK: Palgrave Macmillan.

Light, B., & Cassidy, E. (2014). Strategies for the suspension and prevention of disconnection: Rendering disconnection as socioeconomic lubricant with Facebook. *New Media and Society*, *16*(7), 1169–1184.

Light, B., Fletcher, G., & Adam, A. (2008). Gay men, Gaydar and the commodification of difference. *Information Technology and People*, *21*(3), 300–314.

Limkin, R. (2008, January 7). Friends offer more than a link. *Courier-Mail*, p. 18.

Lin, D. (2006). Sissies online: Taiwanese male queers performing sissinesses in cyberspaces. *Inter-Asia Cultural Studies*, 7(2), 270–288.

Liu, H. (2007). Social network profiles as taste performances. *Journal of Computer-Mediated Communication*, *13*(1), article 13. Retrieved April 20, 2008 from http://jcmc.indiana.edu/vol13/issue1/liu.html

Liu, H., Maes, P., & Davenport, G. (2006). Unraveling the taste fabric of social networks. *International Journal on Semantic Web and Information Systems*, *2*(1), 42–71.

Livingstone, S. M. (2002). *Young people and new media*. London, UK: Sage.

Livingstone, S. M. (2008). Taking risky opportunities in youthful content creation: teenagers' use of social networking sites for intimacy, privacy and self-expression. *New Media and Society*, *10*(3), 393–411.

Livingstone, S., & Bovill, M. (Ed.). (2001). *Children and their changing media environment: A European comparative study*. Hillsdale, NJ: Lawrence Erlbaum Associates.

Longhurt, T. (2012, December 14). Top 10 things gay men fear (but shouldn't). *QNews*, *314*, 21.

Lyons, D. (2012, November 1). Yes, we're a tech site. Yes, we're suggesting you spend less time online. *ReadWrite*. Retrieved November 4, 2012 from http://readwrite.com/2012/11/01/dont-read-this-article

Maaß, W. (2011). The elderly and the Internet: How senior citizens deal with online privacy. In S. Trepte & L. Reinecke (Eds.), *Perspectives on privacy and self-disclosure in the social web* (pp. 235–249). Berlin: Springer.

Mackay, H. (1997). *Generations: Baby boomers, their parents, and their children*. Sydney, NSW: Pan Macmillan.

MacKee, F. (2016, July-September). Social media in gay London: Tinder as an alternative to hook-up apps. *Social Media + Society*, 1–10. doi:10.1177/2056305116662186

Madden, M., & Smith, A. (2010). *Reputation management and social media: How people monitor their identity and search for others online*. Washington, DC: Pew Internet and American Life Project, Pew Research Center. Retrieved January 11, 2012 from www.pewinternet.org

Magnuson, M. J., & Dundes, L. (2008). Gender differences in "social portraits" reflected in MySpace profiles. *CyberPsychology and Behavior*, *11*(2), 239–241.

Malinowski, B. (1922). *Argonauts of the western pacific: An account of native enterprise and adventure in the archipelagoes of Melanesian New Guinea*. London, UK: Routledge.

Mallan, K., & Singh, P. (2006). *ARC discovery – Growing up in networked spaces: Tech-savvy youth constructing identities and forming social relations in online and offline worlds*. Brisbane: Queensland University of Technology.

Manago, A. M., Graham, M. B., Greenfield, P. M., & Salimkhan, G. (2008). Self-presentation and gender on MySpace. *Journal of Applied Developmental Psychology*, *29*, 446–458.

Mangalindin, J. P. (2015). 13 apps, 17 dates, 30 days: I tried 13 dating apps in 30 days in search of love. *Mashable*. Retrieved February 12, 2016 from http://mashable.com/2015/09/13/13-dating-apps-in-30-days/

Markham, A. (1998). *Life online: Researching real experience in virtual space.* Walnut Creek, CA: AltaMira Press.

Marwick, A. (2005, October). *"I'm a lot more interesting than a Friendster profile:" Identity presentation, authenticity, and power in social networking services.* Paper presented at Internet Research 6.0: Internet Generations, Association of Internet Researchers 6th Annual Conference, Chicago, IL.

Marwick, A., & boyd, d. (2011). I tweet honestly, I tweet passionately: Twitter users, context collapse, and the imagined audience. *New Media and Society, 13*, 96–113.

Massoud, J. (2007, August 10). Football's cyber secrets – Blogging with the stars on internet. *Daily Telegraph*, p. 56.

Mazzarella, S. (Ed.). (2005). *Girl wide web: Girls, the Internet, and the negotiation of identity.* New York, NY: Peter Lang.

Mazzuca, J. (2004, October 12). Gay rights: U.S. more conservative than Britain, Canada. *Gallup.* Retrieved October 7, 2012 from www.gallup.com/poll/13561/gay-rights-us-more-conservative-than-britain-canada.aspx

McDonald, H. (2015, May 24). Ireland becomes first country to legalise gay marriage by popular vote. *The Guardian.* Retrieved 30 May 2015 from www.theguardian.com/world/2015/may/23/gay-marriage-ireland-yes-vote

McGrath, F. (2015, April 24). What to know about tinder in 5 charts. *Globalwebindex.* Retrieved April 24, 2015 from www.globalwebindex.net/blog/what-to-know-about-tinder-in-5-charts

McIntosh, W., & Harwood, P. (2002). The Internet and America's changing sense of community. *The Good Society, 11*(3), 25–28. Retrieved March 4, 2012 from http://muse.jhu.edu/journals/good_society/toc/gso11.3.html

McKee, A. (2001). A policy argument for Federal Government subsidies for the production of Australian gay pornographic videos. In K. Atkinson & J. Richards (Eds.), *Queer in the 21st century: The body, queer and politic* (pp. 119–138). Fortitude Valley, QLD: Gay and Lesbian Welfare Association. Retrieved February 2, 2012 from http://eprints.qut.edu.au/view/person/McKee,_Alan.html

McKee, A. (2005). *The public sphere: An introduction.* Cambridge, UK: Cambridge University Press.

McKenna, K. Y. A., & Bargh, J. A. (1998). Coming out in the age of the Internet: Identity 'demarginalization' through virtual group participation. *Journal of Personality and Social Psychology, 75*, 681–694.

McLelland, M. (2002). Virtual ethnography: Using the Internet to study gay culture in Japan. *Sexualities, 5*(4), 387–406.

McNair, B. (1996). *Mediated sex: Pornography and postmodern culture.* London, UK: Arnold.

Mendelson, A., & Papacharissi, Z. (2011). Look at us: Collective narcissism in college student facebook photo galleries. In Z. Papacharissi (Ed.), *The networked self: Identity, community and culture on social network sites* (pp. 251–273). London, UK: Routledge.

Miller, D., & Slater, D. (2000). *The Internet: An ethnographic approach.* New York, NY: Berg Press.

Mills, M. (Director). (2010). *Beginners* [Motion picture]. Universal City, CA: Focus Features.

Molluzzo, J., Lawler, J., & Doshi, V. (2012). An expanded study of net generation perceptions on privacy and security on social networking sites (SNS). *Information Systems Education Journal, 10*(1), 21–36. Retrieved March 19, 2012 from http://isedj.org/2012-10/N1/ISEDJv10n1p21.pdf

Moore. C. (2001). *Sunshine and rainbows: The development of gay and lesbian culture in Queensland.* St. Lucia: The University of Queensland Press.

Morahan-Martin, J. (1999). The relationship between loneliness and Internet use and abuse. *Cyber Psychology and Behavior*, 2, 431–440.

Morgan, D. L. (1988). *Focus groups as qualitative research.* London, UK: Sage.

Moses, A. (2008, February 12). Women flock to social networking sites. *Sydney Morning Herald.* Retrieved March 4, 2012 from www.smh.com.au/articles/2008/02/12/1202760259343.html

Mowlabocus, S. (2004). *Being seen to be gay: User profiles and the construction of gay male identity in cyberspace.* Paper presented at Internet Research 5.0: Ubiquity? Association of Internet Researchers 5th Annual Conference, University of Sussex, Brighton, UK.

Mowlabocus, S. (2008). Revisiting old haunts through new technologies: Public (homo)sexual cultures in cyberspace. *International Journal of Cultural Studies, 11*(4), 419–439.

Mowlabocus, S. (2010). *Gaydar culture: Gay men, technology and embodiment in the digital age.* Surrey, UK: Ashgate.

Munt, S. R., & Medhurst, A. (Eds.). (1997). *The lesbian and gay studies reader: A critical introduction.* London. UK: Cassell.

Murphy, R., & Adler, A. (Producers). (2012–2013). *The New Normal* [Television Series]. Los Angeles, CA: NBC.

Murphy, R., Falchuk, B., Di Loreto, D., & Brennan, I. (Producers). (2009–2015). *Glee* [Television Series]. Los Angeles, CA: 20th Century Fox Television.

Murphy, D., Rawstorne, P., Holt, M., & Ryan, D. (2004). *Cruising and connecting online: The use of internet chat sites by gay men in Sydney and Melbourne.* Sydney: National Centre in HIV Social Research, University of New South Wales.

Mybig Gaywedding. (n.d). *Facebook* [Group page]. Retrieved March 9, 2012 from www.facebook.com/Biggaywedding

Nakamura, L. (2002). Menu-driven identities: Making race happen online. In *A review of cybertypes: Race, ethnicity, and identity on the internet* (pp. 101–136). New York, NY: Routledge.

Nash, C. (2006). Toronto's gay village (1969–1982): Plotting the politics of gay identity. *The Canadian Geographer, 50*(1), 1–16.

Nash, C., & Gorman-Murray, A. (2014). LGBT neighbourhoods and 'new mobilities': Towards understanding transformations in sexual and gendered urban landscapes. *International Journal of Urban and Regional Research, 38*(3), 756–772.

National LGBTI Health Alliance. (2010a, November). *Suicide and LGBTI people (information sheet).* Retrieved February 19, 2012 from www.lgbthealth.org.au/briefingpapers

National LGBTI Health Alliance. (2010b, May). *Submission to beyondblue on the draft clinical practice guidelines: Depression in adolescents and young adults.* Retrieved February 19, 2012 from www.lgbthealth.org.au/submissions

National LGBTI Health Alliance. (2012). *Researching LGBTI health.* Retrieved February 19, 2012 from www.lgbthealth.org.au/research

Nonnecke, B., & Preece, J. (1999). Shedding light on lurkers in online communities. In K. Buckner (Ed.), *Proceedings of the ethnographic studies in real and virtual environments: Inhabited information spaces and connected communities conference*, Edinburgh, 24–26 January, pp. 123–128.

Notley, T. (2008). *The role of online networks in supporting young people's digital inclusion.* Unpublished Doctoral Thesis, Queensland University of Technology, Brisbane.

Nyland, R., & Near, C. (2007, February). *Jesus is my friend: Religiosity as a mediating factor in Internet social networking use.* Paper presented at the AEJMC Midwinter Conference, Reno, NV.

O'Riordan, K. (2005). From usenet to Gaydar: A comment on queer online community. *ACM SIGGROUP Bulletin (Special issue on virtual communities), 25*(2), 28–32.

O'Riordan, K., & Phillips, D. J. (Eds.). (2007). *Queer online: Media technology and sexuality.* New York, NY: Peter Lang.

Opsahl, K. (2010, April 28). Facebook's eroding privacy policy: A timeline. *Electronic Frontier Foundation.* Retrieved March 9, 2012 from www.eff.org/deeplinks/2010/04/facebook-timeline

Page, X., Kobsa, A., & Knijnenburg, B. (2012). Don't disturb my circles! Boundary preservation is at the center of location-sharing concerns. In *Proceedings of the 2012 AAI Conference on Weblogs and Social Media.* Retrieved August 8, 2012 from www.aaai.org/Library/ICWSM/icwsm12contents.php

Palfrey, J. G., & Gasser, U. (2008). *Born digital: Understanding the first generation of digital natives.* New York, NY: Basic Books.

Paolillo, J., & Wright, E. (2005). Social network analysis on the semantic web: Techniques and challenges for visualizing FOAF. In V. Geroimenko & C. Chen (Eds.), *Visualizing the semantic web* (pp. 229–242). Berlin: Springer.

Papacharissi, Z. (2010a). *A private sphere: Democracy in a digital age.* Cambridge, UK: Polity.

Papacharissi, Z. (2010b, August 2). Privacy as a luxury commodity. *First Monday, 15*(8). doi:10.5210/fm.v15i8.3075

Papacharissi, Z. (2011). Conclusion: The networked self. In *A networked self: Identity, community and culture on social network sites* (pp. 304–318). London, UK: Routledge.

Parks, M. R., & Floyd, K. (1996). Making friends in cyberspace. *Journal of Computer-Mediated Communication, 1*(4). Retrieved March 4, 2012 from http://jcmc.indiana.edu/vol1/issue4/parks.html

Patton, M. Q. (1990). *Qualitative evaluation and research methods* (2nd ed.). Newbury Park, CA: Sage.

Payne, R. (2007). "Str8acting". *Social Semiotics, 17*(4), 525–538.

Pearson, E. (2007). Digital gifts: Participation and gift exchange in Livejournal communities. *First Monday, 12*(5). doi:10.5210/fm.v12i5.1835

Pew Research Centre for The People and The Press. (2010, October 6). *Gay marriage gains more acceptance.* Retrieved February 4, 2012 from www.pewresearch.org/2010/10/06/gay-marriage-gains-more-acceptance/

Pike, L. (2007, November 22). City slams cyber gates on staff. *Geelong Advertiser*, p. 3.

Poh, M. (2012). Social lives online versus offline: Finding the right balance. *Hongkiat: Design, Inspiration, Technology*. Retrieved August 8, 2012 from www.hongkiat.com/blog/online-vs-offline-social-life/

Power, L. (1995). *No bath but plenty of bubbles: An oral history of the gay liberation front 1970–7*. London, UK: Cassell.

Price, R. (2016, January 12). Gay hookup app Grindr sold a majority stake to a Chinese gaming company. *Business Insider Australia*. Retrieved January 12, 2016 from www.businessinsider.com.au/grindr-sells-60-stake-to-beijing-kunlun-tech-company-2016-1?r=UK&IR=T

Prensky, M. (2001). Digital natives, digital immigrants. *On the Horizon, 9*(5). Retrieved April 2, 2012 from www.marcprensky.com/writing/

Prost, A., Ariès, P., & Vincent, G. (1991). *A history of private life: Riddles of identity in modern times*. Cambridge, MA: Harvard University Press.

Pryor, L. (2007, November 17). At work, at play, it's all the same thing to the new white-collar intelligentsia. *Sydney Morning Herald*, p. 35.

Pullen, C. (2010). Introduction. In C. Pullen & M. Cooper (Eds.), *LGBT identity and online new media* (pp. 1–16). New York, NY: Routledge.

Pullen, C., & Cooper, M. (Eds.). (2010). *LGBT identity and online new media*. New York, NY: Routledge.

QSoft Consulting. (2010). *Gaydar media pack 2010*. London, UK: Author. Retrieved March 6, 2012 from www.qsoft.co.uk/pdf/GaydarMediaPack.pdf

Queensland Association for Healthy Communities. (n.d). *Facebook* [Group page]. Retrieved March 9, 2012 from www.facebook.com/qahc.qld

QueerMeUp. (2014, 25 March). Grindr Turns Five! *QueerMeUp*. Retrieved 27 March 2014 from http://queermeup.com/lgbt-community-2/grindr-turns-five%E2%80%8F/

Quercia, D., Las Casas, D., Pesce, J., Stillwell, D., Kosinski, M., Almeida, V., & Crowcroft, J. (2012). Facebook and privacy: The balancing act of personality, gender and relationship currency. In *Proceeding of the Sixth International AAAI Conference on Weblogs and Social Media*. Retrieved August 8, 2012 from http://aaai.org/ocs/index.php/ICWSM/ICWSM12/paper/view/4613

Quiroz, P.(2013). From finding the perfect love online to satellite dating and "Loving-the-one-you"re near: A look at Grindr, Skout, Plenty of Fish, Meet Moi, Zoosk and assisted serendipity. *Humanity & Society, 37*(2), 181–185.

Race, K. (2010). Click here for HIV status: Shifting templates of sexual negotiation. *Emotion, Space and Society, 3*, 7–14.

Race, K. (2014). Speculative pragmatism and intimate arrangements: Online hook-up devices in gay life. *Culture, Health & Sexuality, 17*(4), 37–41.

Raun, T. (2014). Video blogging as a vehicle of transformation: Exploring the intersection between trans identity and information technology. *International Journal of Cultural Studies, 18*(3), 365–378.

Ravetz, J. R., & Sardar, Z. (Eds.). (1996). *Cyberfutures: Culture and politics on the information superhighway*. New York, NY: New York University Press.

Read, B., 2006. Think before you share. *The Chronicle of Higher Education, 52*(20), A38–A41.

Real Gay Bears. (n.d). *Facebook* [Group page]. Retrieved March 9, 2012 from www.facebook.com/pages/Real-Gay-Bears/135872426487123

Reilly, A., & Saethre, E. (2014). The hankie code revisited: From function to fashion. *Critical Studies in Men's Fashion, 1*(1), 69–78.

Reynolds, R. (2008). Imagining gay life in the Internet age or why I don't Internet date. *International Journal of Emerging Technologies and Society*, *6*(1), 2–13.

Rheingold, H. (1993). *The virtual community: Homesteading on the electronic frontier.* New York, NY: Harper Perennial.

Rice, R. E. (2002). Primary issues in Internet use: Access, civic and community involvement, and social interaction and expression. In L. A. Lievrouw and S. M. Livingstone (Eds.), *Handbook of new media: Social shaping and consequences of ICTs* (pp. 105–129). London, UK: Sage.

Ridinger, R. B. (1996). *The gay and lesbian movement: References and resources.* New York, NY: G.K. Hall.

Rifkin, E. (2012, November 30). Good gay netiquette. *QNews*, *313*, 20.

Robards, B. (2012). Leaving MySpace, joining Facebook: 'Growing up' on social network sites. *Continuum: Journal of Media and Cultural Studies*, *26*(3), 385–398.

Robinson, S. (2007). Queensland's queer press. *Queensland Review*, *14*(2), 59–78.

Roth, Y. (2015). "No overly suggestive photos of any kind": Content management and the policing of self in gay digital communities. *Communication, Culture & Critique*, *8*(3), 414–432.

Rukkle. (2015). The ten best gay dating apps for iphone and android. *Ruckle.com.* Retrieved February 12, 2016 from http://rukkle.com/features/best-gay-dating-apps-2014/

Rutter, J., & Smith, G. (1999). *Presenting the offline self in an everyday, online environment.* Paper presented at Identities in Action, University of Wales. Retrieved January 11, 2012 from www.cric.ac.uk/cric/staff/Jason_Rutter/papers/Self.pdf

Salerno, R. (2012, May 17). Life beyond Grindr: Can any other app compare? *Xtra: Canada's Gay and Lesbian News.* Retrieved May 20, 2012 from www.xtra.ca/public/National/Life_beyond_Grindr-11999.aspx

Same-sex Marriage. (2012). *Wikipedia.* Retrieved December 4, 2012 from http://en.wikipedia.org/wiki/Same-sex_marriage

Schäfer, M. T. (2011). *Bastard culture! How user participation transforms cultural production.* Amsterdam: Amsterdam University Press.

Schiappa, E., Gregg, P. B., & Hewes D. E. (2006). Can one TV show make a difference? Will & Grace and the parasocial contact hypothesis. *Journal of Homosexuality*, *51*(4), 15–37.

Schlenker, B. (1980). *Impression management: The self-concept, social identity, and interpersonal relations.* Monterey, CA: Brooks/Cole.

Schmidt, K. (2011, January 19). Gay "dating" online: A user's guide. *Popingay.* Retrieved February 27, 2011 from http://popingay.com/post/2818824999/gay-dating-online-a-users-guide

Schwabel, D. (2011, February 21). 5 reasons why your online presence will replace your resume in 10 years. *Forbes.* Retrieved December 4, 2012 from www.forbes.com/sites/danschawbel/2011/02/21/5-reasons-why-your-online-presence-will-replace-your-resume-in-10-years/

Sender, K. (Producer). (2006). *Further off the straight and narrow: New gay visibility on television, 1998–2006* [Documentary]. Northampton, MA: Media Education Foundation.

Senft, T. (2008). *Camgirls: Celebrity and community in the age of social networks.* New York, NY: Peter Lang.

Shields, R. (Ed.). (1996). *Cultures of the Internet: Virtual spaces, real histories, living bodies.* London, UK: Sage.

Simkhai, J. (2013, October 1). The new Grindr is here. A word from Grinr CEO and Founder Joel Simkhai. *The Grindr Blog.* Retrieved January 12, 2014 from www.grindr.com/blog/the-new-grindr-is-here-a-word-from-grindr-ceo-and-found-joel-simkhai/

Simons, N. (2013, July 17). Gay marriage is now legal in England and Wales after 'Historic' bill gets royal assent. *Huffingtonpost UK.* Retrieved 11 March, 2014 from www.huffingtonpost.co.uk/2013/07/17/gay-marriage-is-now-legal-in-the-uk_n_3610453.html

Simon, L., & Daneback, K. (2013). Adolescents' use of the Internet for sex education: A thematic and critical review of the literature. *International Journal of Sexual Health, 24*(4), 305-319.

Sinfield, A. (1998). *Gay and after.* London, UK: Serpent's Tail.

Skog, D. (2005). Social interaction in virtual communities: The significance of technology. *International Journal of Web Based Communities, 1*(4), 464–474.

Smaal, Y., & McKay, B. (Eds.). (2007). Campaign against moral persecution (CAMP): Cynthia Mcride, as told to Jude Abbs. *Queensland Review, 14*(2), 55.

Smith, A. (2007). Teens and online stranger contact. *Pew Internet and American Life Project Memo.* Retrieved March 5 from www.pewinternet.org/PPF/r/223/report_display.asp

Snap Inc. (2014). *Snap Inc. terms of service.* Retrieved December 18, 2014 from www.snap.com/en-US/terms/

Snyder, J., Carpenter, D., & Slauson, G. J. (2006). MySpace.com: A social networking site and social contract theory. *Proceedings of ISECON 2006.* Retrieved February 9, 2012 from http://proc.isecon.org/2006/3333/ISECON.2006.Snyder.pdf

Solove, D. (2011). *Nothing to hide: The false tradeoff between privacy and security.* New Haven, CT: Yale University Press.

Spertus, E., Sahami, M., & Buyukkokten, O. (2005). *Evaluating similarity measures: A large-scale study in the Orkut social network.* Paper presented at the 11th International Conference on Knowledge Discovery in Data Mining (KDD-2005).

Springhall, J. (1998). *Youth, popular culture and moral panics: Penny gaffs to gangsta-rap, 1830–1996.* Basingstoke, UK: Macmillan.

Stefanone, M., Kwon, K., & Lackaff, D. (2011). The value of online friends: Networked resources via social network sites. *First Monday, 16*(2). doi:10.5210/fm.v16i2.3314.

Stein, L., & Sinha, N. (2002). New global media and communication policy: The role of the state in twenty-first century. In L. Lievrouw & S. Livingstone (Eds.), *Handbook of new media: Social shaping and consequences of ICTs* (pp. 410–431). London, UK: Sage.

Stempfhuber, M., & Liegl, M. (2016). Intimacy mobilized: Hook-up practices in the location-based social network Grindr. *Österreich Z Soziol, 41*(1), 51–70.

Stephens, T. (Director). (2006). *Another Gay Movie* [Motion picture]. Berkeley, CA: Luna Pictures.

Stonewall. (2012). *Living together: British attitudes to lesbian, gay and bisexual people in 2012*. London, UK: Author. Retrieved December 10, 2012 from www.stonewall.org.uk/documents/living_together_2012.pdf

Strossen, N. (1995). *Defending pornography: Free speech, sex and the fight for women's rights*. New York, NY: Scribner.

Str8 Acting Gay Guys. (n.d). *Facebook* [Group page]. Retrieved March 9, 2012 from www.facebook.com/SAGG4LIFE

Stutzman, F. (2006). An evaluation of identity-sharing behavior in social network communities. *Journal of the International Digital Media and Arts Association, 3*(1), 10–18.

Subrahmanyam, K., Greenfield, P. M., & Tynes, B. (2004). Constructing sexuality and identity in an online teen chatroom. *Journal of Applied Developmental Psychology, 25*, 651–666.

Suicide Prevention Australia. (2009). *SPA position statement: Suicide and self-harm among gay, lesbian, bisexual and transgender communities*. Retrieved December 3, 2010 from www.suicidepreventionaust.org/PositionStatements.aspx

Sultana Lubna, A., MacKrell, D., & Rizvi, S. (2012). Crowdsourcing travel experience: A case study of user participation on the Tourism Australia Facebook page. In *MCIS 2012 Proceedings*, Paper 32. Retrieved November 2, 2012 from http://aisel.aisnet.org/mcis2012/32

Sunden, J. (2003). *Material virtualities*. New York, NY: Lang.

Sunden, J., & Sveningsson, M. (2012). *Gender and sexuality in online game cultures: Passionate play*. New York, NY: Routledge.

Support Gay Adoption and Gay Parents. (n.d). *Facebook* [Fan page]. Retrieved March 9, 2012 from www.facebook.com/pages/Support-Gay-Adoption-and-Gay-Parents/199985536724405

Tapscott, D. (1996). *The digital economy: Promise and peril in the age of networked intelligence*. New York, NY: McGraw-Hill.

Tapscott, D., & Williams, A. (2006). *Wikinomics: How mass collaboration changes everything*. New York, NY: Portfolio.

Teutsch, D. (2007, 12 August). Girls warned of cyber stalkers. *Sun Herald*, p. 42.

The Beat Megaclub. (n.d). *Facebook* [Fan page]. Retrieved March 9, 2012 from www.facebook.com/pages/The-Beat-Megaclub/62391371631

The Wickham Hotel. (n.d). *Facebook* [Fan page]. Retrieved March 9, 2012 from www.facebook.com/TheWickhamHotel

Thelwall, M. (2008a). Fk yea I swear: Cursing and gender in a corpus of My Space pages. *Corpora, 3*(1). Retrieved November 29, 2008 from www.scit.wlv.ac.uk/~cm1993/papers/MySpaceSwearing_online.doc

Thelwall, M. (2008b). Social networks, gender and friending: An analysis of MySpace member profiles. *Journal of the American Society for Information Science and Technology, 59*(8), 1321–1330.

Thornham, H., & McFarlane, A. (2011). Discourses of the digital native. *Information, Communication and Society, 14*(2), 258–279.

Thornton, S. (1996). *Club cultures: Music, media, and subcultural capital*. Hanover: University Press of New England.

Tong, S. T., Van Der Heide, B., Langwell, L., & Walther, J. B. (2008). Too much of a good thing? The relationship between number of friends and interpersonal impressions on Facebook. *Journal of Computer-Mediated Communication, 13*(3), 531–549. Retrieved March 14, 2012 from www.msu.edu/~jwalther/vita/vita.htm

Top the Chef: Gay Cooking Club. (n.d). *Facebook* [Group page]. Retrieved March 9, 2012 from www.facebook.com/groups/140451482710800/

Trepte, S., & Reinecke, L. (Eds.). (2011). *Perspectives on privacy and self-disclosure in the social web.* Berlin: Springer.

Tsang, D. (2000). Notes on queer 'n' Asian virtual sex. In D. Bell & B. M. Kennedy (Eds.), *The cybercultures reader* (pp. 432–438). London, UK: Routledge.

Tufekci, Z. (2012). Facebook, youth and privacy in networked publics. In *Proceeding of the Sixth International AAAI Conference on Weblogs and Social Media* (pp. 338–334). Retrieved September 29, 2012 from www.aaai.org/Library/ICWSM/icwsm12contents.php

Turkle, S. (1995). *Life on the screen: Identity in the age of the Internet.* New York: Touchstone.

Tyler, T. R. (2002). Is the Internet changing social life? It seems the more things change, the more they stay the same. *Journal of Social Issues, 58*(1), 195–205.

University of Sydney. (2012). *Social media guidelines for staff.* Retrieved November 23, 2012 from http://sydney.edu.au/staff/marketing_communications/web/social_media.shtml#tips

Van Amsterdam, N. (2007). Gaywaves. *Queensland Review, 14*(2), 57–59.

Van Sant, G. (Director). (2008). *Milk* [Motion picture]. Universal City, CA: Focus Features.

Vivienne, S., & Burgess, J. (2012). The digital storyteller's stage: Queer everyday activists negotiating privacy and publicness. *Journal of Broadcasting and Electronic Media, 56*(3), 362–377.

Wakeford, N. (1997). Cyberqueer. In S. R. Munt & A. Medhurst (Eds.), *The lesbian and gay studies reader: A critical introduction* (pp. 20–38). London, UK: Cassell.

Walliams, D., & Lucas, M. (Producers). (2003–2007). *Little Britain* [Television Series]. London, UK: BBC.

Walther, J. B., Van Der Heide, B., Kim, S. Y., Westerman, D., & Tom Tong, S. (2008). The role of friends' appearance and behaviour on evaluations of individuals on Facebook: Are we known by the company we keep? *Human Communication Research, 34*(1), 28–49.

Ward, K. (2005). Internet consumption in Ireland – Towards a 'Connected' domestic life. In R. Silverstone (Ed.), *Media, technology and everyday life in Europe* (pp. 130–136). Aldershot, UK: Ashgate.

Warren, P. N. (2000). *Chasing rainbows: GLBT identity and the Internet.* Retrieved 14 February, 2008 from www.cybersocket.com

Waugh, T. (1996). *Hard to imagine: Gay male eroticism in photography and film from their beginnings to stonewall.* New York, NY: Columbia University Press.

Waugh, T. (Ed.). (2002). *Out/lines: Gay underground erotic graphics from before stonewall.* Vancouver, BC: Arsenal Pulp.

Weerakkody, N. (2009). *Research methods for media and communication.* Melbourne, VIC: Oxford University Press.

Weitzner, M. (Producer). (2010). *The Facebook Obsession* [Documentary]. Englewood Cliffs, NJ: CNBC.

Wellman, B. (2001). Physical place and cyberplace: The rise of personalized networking. *International Journal of Urban and Regional Research*, *25*(2), 227–252.

Wellman, B., & Haythornthwaite, C. A. (Eds.). (2002). *The Internet in everyday life*. Oxford, UK: Blackwell.

Wenger, E., McDermott, R. A., & Snyder, W. (2002). *Cultivating communities of practice: A guide to managing knowledge*. Boston, MA: Harvard Business School Press.

Weston, K. (1991). *Families we choose: Lesbians, gays, kinship*. New York, NY: Columbia University Press.

Weston, K. (1995). Get thee to a big city: Sexual imaginary and the great gay migration. *GLQ: A Journal of Lesbian and Gay Studies*, 2(3), 253–277. Retrieved February 17, 2012 from http://glq.dukejournals.org/content/2/3/253.full.pdf+html

White, R. (2012, November 9). Elton John baby No2: Rocket Man is 'over the moon'. *The Sun*. Retrieved November 9, 2012 from www.thesun.co.uk/sol/homepage/showbiz/4637042/elton-john-baby.html

Whitty, M., & Gavin, J. (2001). Age/sex/location: Uncovering the social cues in the development of online relationships. *Cyberpsychology and Behavior*, *4*, 623–630.

Wilken, R. (2013). An exploratory comparative analysis of the use of metaphors in writing on the Internet and mobile phones. *Social Semiotics*, *23*(5), 632–647.

Williams, L. (1992). Pornography on/scene or diff'rent strokes for diff'rent folks. In L. Segal & M. McIntosh (Eds.), *Sex exposed: Sexuality and the pornography debate* (pp. 233–265). London: Virago.

Williams, J. P. (2006). Authentic identities. Straightedge subculture, music, and the Internet. *Journal of Contemporary Ethnography*, *35*(2), 173–200.

Williams, A. L., & Merten, M. J. (2008). A review of online social networking profiles by adolescents: Implications for future research and intervention. *Adolescence*, *43*(170), 253–274.

Wilson, L. (2007, 14 September). Web stalkers targeted. *Australian*, p. 2.

Winetrobe, H., Rice, E., Bauermeister, J., Petering, R., & Holloway, I. (2014). Associations of unprotected anal intercourse with Grindr-met partners among Grindr-using young men who have sex with men in Los Angeles. *AIDS Care: Psychological and Socio-medical Aspects of AIDS/HIV*, *26*(10), 1303–1308.

Woodley, E. (2016, June 7). Blued claims it is now bigger than Grindr after closing latest series C funding. *Globaldatinginsights News*. Retrieved 7 June 2016 from https://globaldatinginsights.com/2016/06/07/blued-claims-its-now-bigger-than-grindr-after-closing-latest-series-c-funding/

Wright, G. (2007, December 21). You will never be alone. *Sydney Morning Herald*, p. 23.

Wuest, B. (2014). Stories like mine: Coming out videos and queer identities on YouTube. In C. Pullen (Ed.), *LGBT youth and media cultures* (pp. 19–33). New York, NY: Palgrave.

Ybarra, M. L., & Mitchell, K. J. (2008). How risky are social networking sites? A comparison of places online where youth sexual solicitation and harassment occurs. *Pediatrics*, *121*(2), E350–E357.

Yep, G. A., Lovaas, K., & Elia, J. P. (Eds.). (2004). *Queer theory and communication: From disciplining queers to queering the disciplines*. Binghampton, NY: Harrington Park Press.

Young, G. (2004). From broadcasting to narrowcasting to 'Mycasting': A newfound celebrity in queer Internet communities. *Continuum: Journal of Media and Cultural Studies*, *18*(1), 43–62.

Young, R., & Meyer, I. (2005). The trouble with "MSM" and "WSW": Erasure of the sexual-minority person in public health discourse. *American Journal of Public Health*, *95*(7), 1144–1149. Retrieved November 3, 2012 from www.ncbi.nlm.nih.gov/pmc/articles/PMC1449332/

Zuckerberg, M. (2008, August 26). Our first 100 million. *The Facebook Blog*. Retrieved May 19, 2012 from http://blog.facebook.com/blog.php?post=28111272130

Zuckerberg, M. (2009, December 1). An open letter from Facebook founder Mark Zuckerberg. *The Facebook Blog*. Retrieved March 9, 2012 from http://blog.facebook.com/blog.php?post=190423927130

Appendix

FACILITATOR: Alright guys, I don't actually have any other questions. We've covered all the questions I've got, but if you've got any interesting things you want to add or anything like that, I would love to have any other opinions, ideas, experiences or examples of things you can give, even if you want to go back to something we started talking about earlier. Anything else at all you can think of.

PARTICIPANT 1: I pretty much think that the Gaydar sites and even Manhunt and all them, they're probably a good starter for people who are coming out because it makes them comfortable in the community. But I think you can link that on with Facebook too. You can take some bits from there, even people too, into Facebook.

PARTICIPANT 2: I think it's a bad thing for people that are starting coming out.

FACILITATOR: Which is, Gaydar?

PARTICIPANT 2: Yeah, just because of the sexualness of it, like with your penis size and stuff like that. If someone's coming out to [look for friends], and there's the majority of people, I think it's fair to say, are on there for sex. It's designed for them to hook up and I think that it's going to put a lot of younger people into situations that they probably aren't ready for, just because there's going to be people hunting that down and looking for that.

Young people like 18-year-olds are naive enough to think that they would be going over somewhere just to watch a movie or just to hang out with a friend. It's not just set up as like a social networking site. It puts all your sexual statuses and your sexual preferences and your positions and your interests and stuff like that. I don't know – I would imagine that going on there, they don't have the information about having safe sex on there.

I would imagine that they don't try and inform younger people that this is what you have to do and if you're meeting up with people up there, I think that they shouldn't be investing money into advertising. They should be investing money into educating younger people about – like I hate when you see people out on the beat handing out Manhunt stickers. It would be like, you should be handing out condoms. It pisses me off.

PARTICIPANT 1: No, I agree with that but I disagree a little bit with what you're saying because you can screen different things out. Like I used it I think a lot for that, just to be comfortable, because when I first used it I wasn't really out in the community. It didn't make me more or less comfortable, comfortable just to go out, but it makes you more comfortable familiar with the community or the scene.

But I think because you can screen different things out and you can make your profile private. Like obviously you have to pay for things like that, but if you want to really protect yourself obviously you're going to use those sort of tools. But I disagree. I think it definitely makes people more comfortable. People can actually see the difference – everyone knows it's the Gaydar website, so they know there's going to be some sort of sexual explicit nature.

PARTICIPANT 2: But why? That's what pisses me off about it, is that because it's gay that it must be sex. It's that friggin' negative stereotype that [enforces], that makes people think that it's okay to be promiscuous because it's encouraging because, oh it's gay, it must be a sex site. Why can't you have a gay-based, friendship-meeting site like Facebook?

PARTICIPANT 1: That's the reason people use it is because there isn't one of those. That's why you have such an eclectic group of people on that website.

PARTICIPANT 2: But it encourages people to think that gay people are promiscuous.

PARTICIPANT 1: I don't think it encourages...

PARTICIPANT 2: Because you said that, it's a gay site so people are there for sex which is just frustrating.

PARTICIPANT 1: It possibly encourages people outside the circle, but I don't think it encourages people inside, but I think you're either going to be promiscuous or you're not. I used it for the sense of getting familiar with the scene and I'm not promiscuous in that sense.

Index